Songs of the Caged, Songs of the Free

SONGS OF THE CAGED,

SONGS OF THE FREE

Music and the Vietnamese Refugee Experience

ADELAIDA REYES

 Temple University Press   Philadelphia

Temple University Press, Philadelphia 19122

Copyright © 1999 by Temple University.

All rights reserved

Published 1999

Printed in the United States of America

Library of Congress Cataloging in Publication Data

Reyes, Adelaida.

    Songs of the caged, songs of the free : music and the Vietnamese

refugee experience / Adelaida Reyes.

      p. cm.

    Includes bibliographical references (p.) and index.

    ISBN 1-56639-685-9 (alk. paper). — ISBN 1-56639-686-7

(pbk. : alk. paper)

    1. Vietnamese Americans—Music.   2. Political refugees—United

States. I. Title.

ML3560.V5R49   1999

780′.89′9592073—dc21   98-54778

To my parents

To Mia, Steve, and Sallie

To Kate

CONTENTS

LIST OF ILLUSTRATIONS

Tables

PREFACE

In 1979, thirteen colleagues and I, supported by Jersey City State College and a Title IX Ethnic Heritage grant, undertook a brief field research project among migrant groups in central New Jersey.[1] We represented ten academic departments and fields of study and brought to our work different perspectives, foci, and approaches to subject matter. Aware of the impact that immigrants' pasts have on their handling of the present, we paid close attention to the different cultural histories that the groups we studied brought to bear on contemporary life—the transformations, accommodations, and adaptations they made in response to new contexts. But we failed to fully consider the degree to which we had adopted what Paul Friedrich called a debilitating premise, one that is "part of the intellectual history of a field of knowledge . . . carry-overs from an earlier stage where they were necessary or at least significant." Once that stage is past, what had been "wisely accepted" becomes "basically wrong" (although that may not be immediately evident), and its continued use leads scholars "to avoid the exploration and description of facts and causes" (Friedrich 1979:2), relying instead on "expectations of the model" (Gould 1989:132). What in the early stage were springboards to discovery thus become conceptual barriers. Precisely because we had taken it as premise, we had not subjected to critical scrutiny the assumption that migrant adaptation can be accounted for using the prevailing model—one based on the experience of voluntary migrants.

Members of our research group studied Cubans, Iranians, Soviet Jews, and Vietnamese, most if not all of them refugees or asylum seekers.[2] But we approached these much as we did the other groups—Indians (from the subcontinent), Portuguese, Italians, Puerto Ricans, and other Hispanics—who had come of their own volition and in accord with standard U.S. immigration procedures. We failed to consider a crucial difference between these two sets of migrants. We failed to count forced migration as a significant variable.

It was not until after we had each gone our separate ways that some of the implications of our data hit me with sufficient force to motivate action.

Barbara Rubin's study, which she called a "failed ethnography," could not have been judged a failure (even with the qualifying quotation marks) had it been placed within the framework of forced migration (see Rubin 1980). In the middle of fieldwork during which she had established remarkable rapport with her Iranian informants, the Ayatollah Khomeini came into power in Iran, and Americans were taken hostage. Suddenly, many Iranians became migrants who could not return to Iran at will for political and ideological reasons. In Jersey City, they were buffeted by the anger and hostility of Americans reacting to the hostage situation. Rubin's informants became self-protective—isolating themselves, often absent from classes, and distancing themselves even from fellow Iranians and from Rubin herself. Held captive by our debilitating premise, my colleagues and I failed to assign full value to something being enacted right before our eyes, to the social dynamic being born as events unfolded continents away. Voluntary migrants had been transformed almost overnight into forced migrants. The same individuals, Rubin's informants, were radically changed—or behaved as though they were—by the turbulence from Iran that was wracking Washington and disrupting lives on campus. Rubin, with great insight, had documented the developments on a variety of levels—the international, the national, the local, and the individual—both as subject for study and as researcher. But she called her ethnography "failed" despite the richness of human experience that it captured, because the data she had hoped to collect became inaccessible when her informants withdrew. The real flaw, I think, lay in our collective inability to find the explanatory key, a more incisive theoretical framework that lay concealed beneath our debilitating premise.

Two years would pass before I could act on some of the implications of our joint efforts, specifically, on the taxonomic one that distinguished forced from voluntary migrants. I had begun to understand the historical grounds for the persistence of that debilitating premise and for its consequence: the theoretically and methodologically insignificant role assigned to forced migration in studies of migrant adaptation in the United States.

In a country where "pluralism was built into the system" (Greenfield 1992:482); where for the first one hundred years of its existence, there were no entry restrictions (Glazer 1985:4); where those who came displaced by religious, political, or ethnic upheavals were not customarily distinguished from other migrants (Zolberg, Suhrke, and Aguayo 1989:17); the absence of forced migrants from the national consciousness was almost to be expected. It was easy for Americans to believe that everyone came willingly, attracted by the prospect of belonging to a country that took pride in being a nation of immigrants. The image of the voluntary migrant stood for all migrants and was "wisely accepted." Migrants comprised an undifferentiated universe—undifferentiated as to circumstances of their departure from homeland, their reception in the United States, and the travails attendant upon their statelessness in between.

Until the first half of the twentieth century, American faith in the homogenizing effects of the melting pot and the fact that the majority of refugees admitted into the United States until the early 1960s were of Caucasian stock reinforced this nondifferentiating view.[3] It persisted despite the serious questions raised after World War I, when the League of Nations began to legitimize the status of the refugee. In the grip of a premise that had become debilitating, the United States "refused during the interwar period to make special provisions for refugees" (Zolberg, Suhrke, and Aguayo 1989: 26; see also Glazer 1985). Refugees, it was believed, were a temporary demographic category; both the refugees and the category would disappear when the wars that were thought to have created them ended, and refugees either returned home or had their legal status adjusted to some form of permanent residence in the host country. It was not until 1965 that the United States for the first time allocated part of its quota for migrant admissions to refugees, and not until 1980 that a refugee act was passed "which gave a real-life commitment to America's symbolic support of refugee protection" (Conover 1993:75).[4]

Gradually, the rising numbers of refugees in different parts of the world, despite the end of World War II and the cold war, and direct contact with refugees at home gave a new dimension to what the literature on and by forced migrants had already made clear. The effects of life experiences, particularly when they are traumatic, life threatening, and intensely disorienting, do not evaporate when the legal designation *refugee* is replaced with *immigrant* or with some form of hyphenated American label. It is a serious mistake to confuse the legal with life-historical realities or to assume that adjustments in legal status homogenize migrant experiences. This mistake becomes embedded in the taken-for-granted that ignores the distinction between forced and voluntary migration.

Apart from a colleague whose interest was in theater but who did not study a refugee population, I was the only one in our research group who belonged to a discipline to which expressive culture was central. As coordinator of the project and supervisor of the field research, however, I could not put my interests ahead of others'. But once the project was behind me, I felt free to wonder about music in the context of forced migration. If the proposition is true that circumstances of departure from homeland play an important role in migrant resettlement, how would it be reflected in the music of migrants? How would the ethnomusicological tenet that music is human behavior that must be placed in its social, cultural, and historical context become manifest in the context of forced migration?

Music is integral to life even under the most difficult circumstances. Much is communicated through song, instrumental music, and dance that may not find expression through other means. In the context of forced migration, which often inhibits speech and induces guardedness in migrants in the face of danger and as a result of trauma, would music as an activity more readily shared with others have particular advantages as point of entry to other areas of life? What might be learned from treating forced migration as a significant variable in the study of a music?

Of the refugee groups to which our research project had given me exposure, the Vietnamese seemed to offer the most instructive possibilities. Their exodus was an unprecedented, highly visible mass movement with fairly clear temporal boundaries: it began in 1975 with the fall of Saigon (and would end officially in 1995 with the normalization of diplomatic relations between Vietnam and the United States). In 1975, there was no established Vietnamese community in the States to facilitate adjustment to U.S. society. The vast majority of Vietnamese now in the United States were or are legally identified as refugees. They are among the best- if not the best-documented refugee population in the country. Their plight has influenced legislation and policies—national and international (through the United Nations)—governing refugees worldwide. They come from a culture that can be readily distinguished from U.S.

culture in general. These features reduce the number of variables that have complicated studies of other migrant populations. And finally, the Vietnamese offer an important opportunity for comparative studies through their resettlement in other Western countries within approximately the same time period under similar conditions.

Because the full story of the Vietnamese exodus is extremely complicated, involving huge numbers of people and many different paths to resettlement, and because critical differences between forced and voluntary migrants become crystallized in the interim period between departure and resettlement, I chose to trace the Vietnamese journey along a trajectory that begins from a camp of first asylum, proceeds to a refugee processing camp, and ends with resettlement in the United States. The data were collected intermittently as my teaching schedule, funds, and permission from camp authorities would allow, over a period of more than ten years (1983–93). Visits to Hong Kong and Manila to interview officials of the United Nations High Commissioner for Refugees (UNHCR) and local voluntary agencies, and to Ho Chi Minh City and Hanoi, as well as three terms as visiting research fellow at Oxford University's Refugee Studies Programme (Michaelmas 1990, Trinity 1993, and Michaelmas 1996) supplemented the materials gathered through fieldwork. I have remained in contact with people I met in those places by mail, phone, and e-mail.

I would be the first to deplore the inadequacy of the fieldwork for this project. The resources deployed could not meet the heavy demands of the subject under study. An interdisciplinary team would have been better able to cover the geographic spread and respond to the difficult schedules and the multiplicity of perspectives that the project required. It would have been infinitely better if I had a command of the Vietnamese language instead of having to rely on interpreters.[5]

But all these would have required far more time and funding than I had access to, given the fledgling nature of the enterprise and the lack of ethnomusicological precedent that would have helped attest to the feasibility of the project. The expediency that made me proceed despite the limitations was the relative invisibility of forced migration in the *methods* of ethnomusicology, even when it was becoming increasingly visible in the data. Veit Erlmann, for example, notes the importance of expressive culture in the adaptive strategy of South African labor migrants for whom, as for refugees, "migration is no longer a matter of choice but . . . a bitter and absolute necessity for survival" (1990:200). This is one of the few, though elliptical, admissions in the ethnomusicological literature of the growing presence of forced migration. It needs an explicit and systematic statement of its methodological consequences.

This book aspires to take a step in that direction. I hope that others will be provoked to rectify its flaws and build on its premises.

ACKNOWLEDGMENTS

Over the years, I have accumulated a mountain of debt as I proceeded with what, in the beginning, seemed like a quixotic tilting at windmills. I could not have foreseen how dependent I would be on the kindness of so many people—strangers, friends, colleagues, family members. Now, looking back, I see the magnitude of that kindness, and it is humbling.

The thoughtful work of colleagues from Jersey City State College provided the trigger for this project when they shared their findings and their thoughts on the research we undertook together.

In 1990, when I was overcome with doubt about the feasibility and usefulness of what I was trying to do and seriously entertaining giving it up altogether, Barbara Harrell-Bond, then director of the University of Oxford's Refugee Studies Programme, gave me a much needed shot in the arm by making me feel that I was engaged in something commonsensical. Colleagues and friends have kept me going with their moral and intellectual support, an occasional bop on the head, an occasional wake-up call, and lots of rejuvenating laughter and encouragement. Among these I count (alphabetically) Ingrid Monson, Phong Tuyet Nguyen, Kay K. Shelemay, Tuyen Tonnu, Vu Thanh Vinh, and Su Zheng. Phong T. Nguyen and Tuyen Tonnu in particular were extremely helpful on a number of fronts— in Vietnam and in the States, psychologically and technically.*

It would have been impossible to make sense of my experiences in the camps and subsequently in California without the friendship and

---

*Vietnamese in the United States frequently omit diacritics in their personal proper names, particularly in contexts where the usage must take into consideration a large number of non-Vietnamese readers. This practice is observed throughout the text, although Vietnamese diacritics have been retained in the Appendix.

help of Hoang Bich Thu, who was confidante, companion, translator, and instructor. With her family, she welcomed me to Orange County, helped me get settled and find my way, and gave me wonderful infusions of her mother's cooking and her parents' wisdom. Bui Minh Duong, whom I had met in Bataan and found again in Orange County, was the source of important insights on the life he had left in Vietnam and on the life he, his family, and his conationals are rebuilding in the States. I have benefited from other Vietnamese whom I had originally met in the camps—Ly Thi Nga, Le Thi Ngoc Lan, Nguyen Xuan Dan, and others, too numerous to mention, but who must be acknowledged with thanks.

Some I originally met in an official capacity later became friends: Tony Carpio, and his wife, Bernardita, who steered me in the right direction when I was floundering in my efforts to gain access to the Philippine camps; Cita Fernandez, whose generous hospitality made my stay in camp a pleasure; Dorothy Lee, who introduced me to the work of Caritas (a voluntary agency) in Hong Kong, admitted me into the Jubilee camp in that city, and has since been a source of great wisdom; Lanh Ngoc Pham and his wife, Ninh, who helped make my Vietnam visit a memorable experience; Herman Tiu Laurel and his staff both in Manila and in the camps; William Applegate of the Joint Voluntary Agency and Janvier de Riedmatten of the UNHCR office in Manila, who allowed me the exploratory visits in the camps; Dolores B. Lasan of the UNHCR office in Hong Kong, who was a fount of information—all of these facilitated fieldwork for me.

Without funding, none of this would have been possible. I therefore acknowledge my debt to Jersey City State College, which twice gave me funds from the Separately Budgeted Research program; the Asian Cultural Council, which funded my first fieldwork in Orange County; the National Endowment for the Humanities Fellowship for College Teachers Grants # FB-29300-92 and FB-22122-83, and Summer Stipend FT-34468-90; and the Rockefeller Foundation for a residency in Bellagio, Italy.

Sometimes I wonder if editors are granted special gifts of patience; I am a grateful beneficiary of Doris Braendel's, Bobbe Needham's, Debby Stuart's, and Joan Saidel's.

My greatest debt is to the refugees as a group, who taught me some of the most valuable lessons in my life; to the refugees as individuals, who at a very difficult point in their lives took the time and made the effort to help me; and to those who, in resettlement, continued to instruct me through their artistry, both in life and in music. Some of these I have already mentioned. Others include Pham Duy, Viet Hung, Hoang Oanh, Kim Tuyen, Tam Tri, Nam Tran, Minh Duc Hoai Trinh, Thu Nguyen and his family, Chau Nguyen, and Dang T. Nguyen and his family. To all of them I give my sincerest thanks.

Beyond anything I can possibly express in words is the gratitude I feel toward my parents and my children, Mia, Steve, and Sallie, for their forbearance and inspiration, and toward Kate, who introduced me to a new and lovely world.

Introduction

Birds in cages sing badly. . . . let the birds fly free and sing their
best songs. —*Nguyen Quang Sang*

The logical is "that which it is necessary to admit in order to render the universe intelligible." —*Charles Sanders Peirce*

Refugees barely cast a shadow on the ethnomusicological landscape. They
make music and they use music, but their refugeeness—the wounds, the
scars, the epiphanies, and revelations of human strength and ingenuity
that inform historians and memoirists and inspire novelists, filmmakers,
and other artists—seems to leave the lightest, most ephemeral of marks
on studies of their music.

Approximately 14,500,000 people now conform to the United Nations
definition of refugee.[1] Many more who satisfy all the requirements of this
definition except that of crossing geopolitical boundaries are notoriously
difficult to count because they are inaccessible to outside monitors. A
conservative estimate of the so-called internally displaced persons (IDPs)
is 20 million.[2] One would think that a human group of this size, with a
history that dates back to the nation-state, or, from another perspective,
to the expulsion of Adam and Eve from Eden, a group that undoubtedly
makes music not just because it wants to but because it must, would have
a place in the ethnomusicological consciousness. It does not.

The reasons are many and complex. Refugees evoke images of flight,
the chaos of war, and other cataclysms. The air of crisis that surrounds
them and the intensity of the reactions they tend to provoke are exhaust-
ing. The term *compassion fatigue* is a feeble reflection of a tangled world
of feelings. What is devoutly wished reshapes reality. For the longest time,
people clung to the belief that refugee phenomena are no more than temporary disruptions. The signing of treaties and the official cessation of
hostilities were expected to bring those who had been forced out back to
their homes, where they will cease to be refugees and become citizens
once again. Order, presumably society's "normal" condition, will be restored.

But forced migration and its effects on the human psyche often outlast a lifetime and spill over generations. The literature on diasporas and the many films and debates that continue to probe such events as the Vietnam War testify to their enduring effects on the individual and the national psyche. "Never again" is a message passed on to all and for all time by victims of and witnesses to the Holocaust. Bruno Bettelheim is only one among many who have documented the long-term consequences of "living under extreme fear and terror."[3] He captures survivors' guilt and other feelings that, he tells us, "are irrational, but this does not reduce their power to dominate a life; in more ways than one, it is this irrationality which makes them so very difficult to cope with" (1979:27).[4]

Why Music?

The irrationality that Bettelheim refers to, the nonrationality of the intense emotions that the refugee experience ignites, and the rationality of keeping quiet to guard against saying the wrong things at the wrong time to the wrong people often make speech a difficult medium for expressing what forced migration has wrought. New U.S. laws that require asylum seekers to recount events demonstrating fear of persecution in order to legitimize their bid have created untold difficulties for "genuine victims [who] often can't face doing so" (Rosenberg 1997:32).[5] Traumatized by their experiences, refugees are often reduced to silence or incoherence. "Asylum-seekers," as Ted Conover notes, "most of them so alone in the world and so at risk, have many secrets" (1993:78). It takes time and a measure of detachment for them to sort out feelings and to give narrative order to their story.

Yet, the body of music called *la nueva cancion* flourished among Chilean refugees in California who were torn by "the torment of remembering and the fear of forgetting" (Eastmond 1992:304). Isadora Duncan could well have been referring to the peculiarities of verbal communication when she said, "If I could tell it to you, I would not have to dance it."[6] Psychotherapy has used the visual arts to get at what seems inaccessible to speech.[7] And David Conquergood found that refugee camps are replete with cultural performance—theatre, music, dance, and other forms of expressive culture—not only because refugees have time on their hands but because they must respond to psychological and cultural needs:

"Refugee camps are liminal zones where people displaced by trauma and crisis . . . must try to regroup and salvage what is left of their lives. They are in passage . . . not quite sure where they will end up or what their lives will become. Betwixt and between worlds, suspended between past and future, they fall back on the performance of their traditions as an empowering way of securing continuity and some semblance of stability. . . . There are good reasons why in the crucible of refugee crisis, performative behaviors intensify" (Conquergood 1988:180).

As part of expressive culture, music is a mirror that migration studies have yet to hold up to the refugee experience, and forced migration is a key that ethnomusicology has yet to turn to gain entry into another world that music inhabits.

Labels

Refugees come by many different names, and what those names stand for changes rather quickly as they respond to social and political developments. Not infrequently, new names are devised. Those of particular concern to this book are *asylum seekers, refugees, forced migrants,* and *internally displaced persons* (IDPs). Often these terms are taken to be synonymous. Technically, they differ. But the groups they designate all are "unsure whether any country would accept them and their families, powerless to control their future, afraid to return home" (Smyser 1987:xiv), and owe their absence from their habitual place of residence to "a well-founded fear of violence" (Zolberg, Suhrke, and Aguayo 1989:33), a rewording of the UN definition's principal criterion for refugee status, "fear of persecution."

The term *asylum-seeker* finds its meaning restricted variously by different agencies (see note 2 of the Preface). The term will be used here in the literal and most general sense to apply to those seeking protection. *Refugee* and *forced migrant,* for present purposes, are interchangeable terms. They differ, however, in one important respect. Having been officially defined by the United Nations and by receiving nations, *refugee* is a label with legal connotations. Zetter contends that the designation's purpose is managerial; host governments use it in part to grant or withhold entitlements. Zetter also points to its strong tendency to bureaucratize and stereotype (1991:49). The label therefore powerfully affects the identity and identification of refugees, whose powerlessness and dependence it underscores. It is not a self-ascribed label; refugees have had no part in its definition. Even those who accept it as a temporary necessity feel derogated by it. For these reasons, the issue of identity becomes an even more crucial one for those who have been refugees. This will become obvious as the narrative proceeds.

Forced migrant, in contrast, is a term that seeks to be objective and originates not from those who control the legality of migration but from those who describe and study the phenomenon of migration and its various forms. Forced migrants include both the so-called traditional, statutory, or Convention refugees (after the UN Convention of 1951 and the 1967 Protocol) and the IDPs who, because they remain within the boundaries of their nation-state, are excluded from the Convention definition.

Particularizing Vietnamese Refugees

Like any sizeable group, the Vietnamese in the United States are a heterogeneous population not only on the basis of age, socioeconomic status, educational background, religious affiliation, ethnicity, and so forth, but also on the basis of distinctions brought about by forced migration.

Before the fall of Saigon in 1975 and the Vietnamese mass exodus, few Vietnamese lived in the United States—only 603 in 1964, mostly students and diplomats (Takaki 1989:448). With the reunification of Vietnam under communist rule, most of them remained in the United States. They did not see themselves as a Vietnamese community, but they came to be perceived as a discrete group once the refugees, from whom many of the earlier Vietnamese distinguished and distanced themselves, began to arrive in large numbers.

Evacuees—those who left Vietnam shortly before, during, or shortly after the U.S. evacuation of Saigon—also differentiated themselves from refugees.[8] Evacuees who left Vietnam with the direct sponsorship or help of U.S. government entities or private organizations experienced neither the Southeast Asian refugee camps set up for "processing" asylum seekers nor life under a communist regime.

The bulk of the refugee population consisted of two major groups: (1) former asylum seekers who, upon leaving Vietnam, became stateless, often for long periods of time; and (2) the so-called ODPs—those who left Vietnam under the Orderly Departure Program, an understanding between Vietnam and Western receiving countries intended to eliminate the dangers of escape and to facilitate family reunification. With their property confiscated upon departure, and because many ODPs suffered the limbo of no job, no access to education during the two- to five-year wait for a visa, they were considered "members of a group for whom persecution should be presumed" (Refugee Reports, April 28, 1989, p. 6).

Only two of the three categories of ODPs receive refugee entitlements—(1)former employees of the U.S. government, U.S. foundations, and voluntary agencies; and (2) political prisoners, Amerasians, and former civil servants and military officials of the former South Vietnam. ODPs in the third category—family reunification cases—are the responsibility of the families who sponsor them.

These bases for differentiation—those that are intrinsic to most cultural groups and those that are largely the consequence of a legal system's management of forced migrants—overlap in their application to the Vietnamese population in the States. The categories and subcategories within each set are not mutually exclusive either. Most ODPs, for example, are considered refugees. The social and intellectual elite as well as farmers and fishermen are represented in all segments of the refugee population. But despite the lack of taxonomic neatness, the differences must be kept in mind so that the generalizations called for by the study do not obscure the diversity of the population and the extent to which, at some points, those generalizations apply more to one segment of the population than to others.

The segments of the Vietnamese population most easily isolated from the rest and therefore excluded from this study except as point of reference or contrast are: (1) the pre-1975 arrivals; (2) those who left Vietnam before 1975 and resettled elsewhere before coming to the United States after 1975; (3) the Amerasians (for reasons that will be discussed in Chapter 2); and (4) those born and raised in the States. The study, therefore, focuses on the so-called Convention refugees and the ODPs.

Statistically significant but peripheral to this study are the ethnic Chinese and what Ruben G. Rumbaut calls the "1.5 generation." There are two reasons for the marginality of the ethnic Chinese as a discrete group to this study. The first goes back to Vietnam, where Sino-Vietnamese were "least likely to have had any prior involvement with the Republic of

Vietnam . . . during the war" (Rumbaut 1991:70) and were "induced, encouraged and permitted by the SRVN's [Socialist Republic of Vietnam's] government to leave" at the outbreak of the border war between Vietnam and China in 1979 (Zolberg, Suhrke, and Aguayo 1989:165). The second reason derives from precedents set by other studies of resettled Vietnamese (e.g., Dorais, Pilon-Le, and Nguyen Huy 1987 and Bousquet 1991).[9] The exemption of the 1.5 generation, those "young people who were born in their countries of origin but who are being formed in the U.S. . . . in the interstices of two societies and cultures, between the 'first' and 'second' generations, between being refugees and being 'ethnics' or 'hyphenated Americans'" (Rumbaut 1989:168), comes out of what I feel is a lack of sufficient information about them.

The resulting picture of the Vietnamese refugees or forced migrants may seem amorphous, but it gains clarity through contrast with voluntary migrants. Zolberg, Suhrke, and Aguayo lay a useful foundation: "It has long been recognized that migration is governed by social and economic forces that themselves are somewhat regular and thus are amenable to theoretical analysis. By contrast, however, refugee flows are unruly in that they result from events such as civil strife, abrupt changes of regime, arbitrary governmental decisions, or international war, all of which are generally considered singular and unpredictable occurrences" (1989:v).

Other contrasts are frequently couched in terms of migrants' motivation, their psychosocial health as affected by contexts of exit from the home country and of reception in the host country, and their adaptation to the new environment.

One of the earliest formal statements of migrant motivation comes from Egon F. Kunz (1973), who differentiated between voluntary and involuntary migrants through what he called pull or push factors. Voluntary migrants respond to the pull or the perceived attractiveness of a country to which they eventually migrate. Involuntary migrants feel themselves pushed out by pressures from within their country to which they respond by fleeing.

Ruben G. Rumbaut (1989) notes, however, that migrant motivations for leaving are not reducible to simple push and pull factors, that motives are usually a complex mix of responses—a thesis that he illustrates through what he calls "PULLALL" and "PUSHALL" distinctions. These recognize a whole range of motives and different degrees of "motivational duress" among migrants, from socioeconomic pressures (e.g., poverty, loss of personal property) to fear for their lives. His extensive studies showed that "despite the diversity of motives in the refugees' decision to leave, by far more fear/force motives were reported overall than any of the other . . . motive types" (1991:67).

Approaching the issue of differentiation from the standpoint of mental health and resettlement, Rumbaut found that forced migrants moved from elation over having made good their escape, to depression when day-to-day realities set in. At this point, refugees in general "experience significantly greater psychological distress and dysfunction than other immigrants" (1989:166) before their recovery begins. Schematically, the progression roughly follows a U-shape. Voluntary migrants, on the other hand, follow a more-or-less straight ascending pattern from depression to recovery (Portes and Rumbaut 1990: 156–65). These findings lead Rumbaut to conclude that "the refugee [is] not merely another class of immigrant, but at least on psychosocial grounds [is] a qualitatively different social type" (1989:167).

To voluntary migrants, then, the home country is a place they left at will, one to which they believe they can freely return. The host country is a place they chose for reasons of their own and for a price—economic and emotional—they could carefully consider before deciding to pay. To forced migrants, in contrast, the home country is most frequently a place they did not wish to leave, especially since the possibility of return seemed at best problematic and at worst totally foreclosed. The personal costs of the move were incalculable and the outcome highly unpredictable. To the forced migrant, the host country can be a safe haven, but it can also be a place of exile—inescapable, at least for the foreseeable future. Inevitably, these contrasting perspectives affect the way migrants reconstruct their lives in the new environment.

Methodological Considerations

Music as Social Act

In the early days of fieldwork in Bataan, I heard two songs that seemed to share the same stylistic features; the same harmonic idiom (Western, with rare departures from the tonic, dominant, and subdominant) and form (strophic); and similar tempi, meter (duple), and texts (both were love songs).[10] Each was performed by a male singer, both of approximately the same age, each accompanied by a guitar. On the basis of their musical attributes, I was going to put the two songs under the same genre in the same corpus. My Vietnamese informants were indignant. They pronounced one of the songs unacceptable, and they argued against putting the two songs in the same class. I struggled to find the evidence that supported their argument: was there something I was not hearing in the music? Although they answered in the affirmative, they could not point to what it was. Finally, all their objections—at least those they could articulate—turned out to be nonmusical. The objectionable song was a Communist song, as could be inferred from the date of its composition: it was composed after 1975 when government authorities controlled what music was permitted or proscribed.

I had no way of verifying the date of composition outside of inquiring from the singer's cohorts in Bataan, but the refugees' perceptions were the significant issue. Perhaps the writer commenting on Michael Kammen's 1992 *Mystic Chords of Memory: The Transformation of Tradition in American Culture* was right. "What people believe to be true about their past is usually more important in determining their behavior and responses than truth itself" ("The Persistence of Dreams" 1992). It is an echo of Nietzsche's often cited dictum that anything is real that is real in its effects.

I discuss this event and the surrounding circumstances more fully in Chapter 2, but I mention it here because it was a strong reminder that what appear to be cognates in the realm of tangible form may hold different and even contradictory meanings. Along with several similar incidents, it reinforced my initial inclination to focus on people—on the way they lived their lives, the place they gave to music, and the meanings they assigned to it as it emerged from the life that was its context.[11] That incident was also a forceful reminder that what linguists call the expression system (the realm of sounds and physical, material elements) and the content system (the realm of meaning and the nonmaterial components of communication) do not always coincide and coincide even less under conditions of great social turbulence. The expression system, "whose units are sounds having no positive meaning of their own . . . and content, whose units have a positive meaning but no expression apart from the inherently meaningless sounds" (Shapiro 1991:12), are components of a symbolic system whose relations need to be established if each is to realize its function. Ernst Cassirer's view that "a symbol is a part of the *human* world of meaning" (1944:32; emphasis added) places people at the juncture where the expression and content systems meet: it is people who join them together by assigning and interpreting meanings. To paraphrase Jakobson, it is *we* who "seek to be heard in order to be understood" (1978:19).[12]

Music as Public Event

People's acts give meaning an external and observable form. I confine myself to public acts because "culture is public" (Daniel 1984:13; Geertz 1973:10), "cultural forms find articulation in social action," and "culture . . . is public because meaning is" (Geertz 1973:17, 12). Even more to the point, refugee movements are almost always mass movements open to public view.

These considerations make music (as acoustic phenomenon) not just a social act, but a cultural object as well, inseparable from the community whose musical language it uses. Music as tangible reality is a contingent one—shaped by the logic of its use and by the values assigned to it by the society out of which it emerges.

I recognize that music has an intra-aesthetic logic that lights up musical compositions or utterances from within through the coherence of its internal relations. By discovering those relations, one comes to possess the music's structural meaning and all the satisfactions, intellectual and emotional, that the listener draws from and associates with it. But "one can no more understand aesthetic objects as concatenations of pure form than one can understand speech as a parade of syntactic variations or myth as a set of structural transformations" (Geertz 1983:98). For music to illumine and be illumined by the refugee experience, we must accord priority to cultural meaning, which is a product of collective experience. And in light of the constant and inevitable alterations that accompany the music of those who are radically displaced, the role of collective experience is clarified by the words of Michael Shapiro: "innovations are produced by individuals, whereas change is social fact" (1991:8–9).

People as actors in the public domain also play an indispensable role in the contextuality of meaning. If music is polysemic by nature, then the principal task of analysis is to decipher, out of a range of possible meanings, the most plausible—one inaccessible through exploring prior formalisms alone. "The setting in which any message is emitted, transmitted, and admitted always decisively influences its interpretation and vice versa," and "context is often the crucial factor in resolving the significance of a message" (Sebeok 1991:29, 30). An object, be it a piece of music or an utterance, means "only when it means to someone, and this transaction often entails a somewhere and a sometime as well" (Daniel 1984:39).

All these, however, are components of an intellectual framework that has not yet captured the picture it is intended to contain. All these sources draw not on studies of social groups that were literally and metaphorically on the run, people violently dispersed, *spaesato, depaysé,* their sense of belonging challenged at every turn by the multiplicity of cultures into which they were thrust, and by the unpredictability of the locations where these encounters took place. I speculate that the concepts laid out here apply, but it has yet to be demonstrated that they do. For this reason, I lean heavily on two related ideas borrowed from Charles Sanders Peirce: musement and abduction.

Approach to the Study

Musement, which Peirce sometimes referred to as "Pure Play," he describes as a process that "begins passively" as an impression that "soon passes into attentive observation, observation into musing, musing into a lively give and take of communion between self and self" (Peirce 1935–66:6.459.[13] This "creative reverie" (Harrowitz 1988:195) is clearly outside the realm of scientific method. Only, Peirce continued, "if one's observations and reflections are allowed to specialize themselves too much [will] the Play . . . be converted into scientific study."

Abduction is the juncture at which scientific reasoning begins.[14] It partakes of musement in that it starts with a "surprising fact" (Peirce 1935–66:7.218) or an enigma (Carettini 1988:142), or perhaps an anomaly, in Kuhn's sense (1970), which, having arrested the attention, actively seeks an explanation. It is, in Peirce's own words, "nothing but guessing" (1935–66:7.219). But in guessing at an explanation, abduction parts company with musement in the activeness of its search and in requiring that the guess or hypothesis be subjected to the test of inquiry. Marcello Truzzi describes abduction pithily: it is "a conjecture about reality which needs to be validated through testing" (1988:70).

The conjectural, however, is not to be confused with the arbitrary. Peirce resolutely places abduction in the realm of method through his insistence that abduction is not an isolate; it initiates a guessing-testing-guessing chain that, when sustained, becomes the hallmark of excellent science (cf. Sebeok and Sebeok 1988:23). He places abduction within the framework of the canonical types of reasoning: "Deduction proves that something *must* be; Induction shows that something *actually is* operative; Abduction merely suggests that something *may be*" (Peirce 1935–66:5:171; emphasis in the original). Because it traffics in possibilities, abduction offers abundant opportunities for innovation. Because it presupposes apprehension of what Kuhn had called an anomaly as well as the freedom to guess, it is less beholden to a (debilitating) premise. It is perhaps the point at which Peirce and Geertz meet: "Cultural analysis is (or should be) guessing at meanings, assessing the guesses, and drawing explanatory conclusions from better guesses" (Geertz 1973:20).

> Abduction, then, bridges the domains of intuition and reason: When men have to guess, they find themselves guided by systematic and complex visions of reality, philosophical conceptions, of which they are more or less distinctly aware but which anyway shape their cast of mind, their deep habits which determine the bearings of judgment. These philosophies synthesize and organize, by processes of generalization, analogy and hierarchical ordering, the knowledge and cultural acquisitions deposited in the course of the centuries and derived from extensive social practices. So it is not to be wondered at that these philosophies possess (obviously in varying degrees) their force of truth, including the capacity to inspire new and valid scientific hypotheses. (Bonfantini and Proni 1988:134)

The events that led to this work conform to the descriptions of musement and abduction: from musing about the data from the 1979 project and the possible differences between the two sets of migrants my colleagues and I had studied, to the more active wondering about their implications for music and migration, to the still more active search for an explanation through fieldwork. Sustaining the guessing-testing-guessing chain to the point where it becomes what Sebeok and Sebeok (1988:23) called "excellent science" is an invitation this work offers to others.

Notes on Fieldwork and Data Gathering

Since the subject of this study imposes no predetermined boundaries, and since the effects of the refugee experience are not temporally bounded, being assumed in this study to extend beyond the expiration of legal refugee status, data collection did not follow the standard fieldwork pattern. Instead of moving fairly steadily from the apparent randomness of the cast-your-net-wide phase to increasingly more focused and more purposive collection, every change of site, every move to a different stage of the refugee journey felt, in many respects, as though I kept circling back to the point that Kuhn describes: "In the absence of a paradigm or some candidate for paradigm, all of the facts that could possibly pertain . . . are likely to seem equally relevant. As a result, early fact gathering is a far more nearly random activity than the one that subsequent scientific development makes familiar. Furthermore, in the absence of a reason for seeking some particular form of more recondite information, early fact gathering is usually restricted to the wealth of data that is ready to hand" (1970:15).

The logistics of entering the field were complex, involving several overlapping hierarchies whose jurisdictions were often unclear. Most of the camps that would have served the purposes of the study were under the supervision of the United Nations High Commissioner for Refugees (UNHCR), which could not exercise its mandate without careful regard to (1) issues pertaining to the sovereignty both of the countries within which the refugee camps were situated and of the receiving countries, and (2) the lines of authority governing the private organizations providing funds and services. To gain access to the refugee camps I needed the help of the offices of the UNHCR, the Joint Voluntary Agency, the local authorities directly and indirectly involved with the governance of the camps, and the different nongovernmental organizations (NGOs) that ran a variety of programs for the refugees. Changes in staff and personnel in these offices often meant delays as one started the process of seeking access all over again.

In November 1983, I was given permission by the Joint Voluntary Agency and the UNHCR office in Manila to pay exploratory visits of a few days each to the Philippine camps in Bataan and Palawan. Shortly thereafter, the counterparts of these offices in Hong Kong gave me access to the Jubilee camp in that city. I tried to include Thailand in this exploration. Its contiguity to Vietnam would have given me access not only to the largest camps in Southeast Asia but, more important, would have allowed me contact with the so-called land refugees—those who walk rather than take the sea route to escape. But difficult questions about its government's policies on refugees at that time made Thailand off limits to me.

Between September 1983 and May 1984, except when I was in the Philippines and Hong Kong, I did fieldwork among the Vietnamese in central New Jersey. It would take me another five years to get back to the Philippine camps. In 1988, I obtained permission to live in the Bataan camp for a month and in the Palawan camp for a week. In June and July 1990, I did fieldwork in Orange County, California, taking the opportunity to follow up on some of the refugees I had met in Bataan who were by then resettled in Orange County. I was back in Manila and the Philippine camps in July 1991 and returned to Orange County in October and November of 1992 and again in October 1995. In January 1993, I visited Ho Chi Minh City and Hanoi for a little over two weeks.

The weather presented formidable challenges, as monsoon rains pounding on tin roofs sometimes made recording and even conversation virtually impossible. In 1991, the eruption of Mt. Pinatubo rained lahar (a mudflow of volcanic debris and water) on the Bataan camp, damaging billets and in general claiming the attention of staff and refugees alike. Wearing masks against the volcanic dust was not conducive to singing. And the flooding caused by the eruption's having raised river beds sometimes made travel problematic. These events and conditions restricted time for fieldwork.

Data collection followed the course of my thinking on the subject, which happened to follow the Vietnamese exodus and resettlement in reverse chronological order. Musement was triggered by data from New Jersey. The guess that forced migration might be a significant factor in the adaptive strategies of migrants as they reconstructed their life, musical and social, led me backwards in the refugee chronology from resettlement in New Jersey to the Bataan processing camp and then to the camp of first asylum in Palawan, actually the first stop out of Vietnam.

I knew, however, that the New Jersey Vietnamese were still in the process of community building. Secondary migration—a move from where the refugees were initially assigned by voluntary agencies who had charge of resettling them—was still in progress in 1983 and 1984. The end of my journey would have to be an established community—hence, the choice of Orange County as fieldwork site. It is the oldest Vietnamese community in the United States and purportedly the largest outside Vietnam. It dates back to the earliest days of the mass exodus in 1975, when many evacuees were brought to Camp Pendleton in southern California, where many eventually resettled. Along with California's weather, this nucleus of Vietnamese attracted later arrivals who sought out relatives and friends. In 1983, when I asked refugees in Hong Kong where they would like to be resettled if they were given a choice, many did not name a country or a state. They answered, "Orange County."

The chapters follow the chronology of the Vietnamese exodus: from camp of first asylum to processing camp to resettlement in the United States; from flight to the transiency of camp existence to the relative permanence of resettlement. But the narrative resists linearity. Where Vietnamese escapees found asylum was often a matter of accident rather than design: it did not have to be Palawan. It might have been Hong Kong or Malaysia or Indonesia or China or any other country in the area. Where they are finally resettled is subject to the refugee policies of receiving countries.

This is therefore a case of the frame drawing its subject in two senses of the word *draw*: to pull in, and to produce a likeness of places and people in flux. Analytical commentary in each chapter provides a thread of continuity in a story riddled with discontinuities. To protect the privacy of individuals, only public figures and those who have given their permission are named in the narrative.

From a Broader Perspective

In the last decade, ethnomusicology has been confronting the modern and postmodern world's challenge to its space-bound view of subject matter; to its dichotomization of self and other, of insider and outsider; to its ambivalence toward Western influences and their effects on the orientalized others; to its use of hegemony, colonialism, and power relations in general as explanatory frame for musical phenomena—most, if not all, of which spring from the increased mobility of people, the music makers and users, responding to political, market, and natural forces that either disrupt lives or offer better alternatives to what they have. Where people go, music goes. They are inseparable.

For some time now and particularly in the last quarter of this century, ethnomusicology has availed itself of ideas offered by studies of migration. The early tentative steps that began with studies of the diffusion of musical ideas across cultural boundaries have snowballed into studies of migrant musics under such names as ethnic music, immigrant music, or world music. A few themes, however, undergird the rising flood of ethnomusicological research, among them: (1) musical identity and the role of tradition in the context of dislocation; and (2) the related issue of studying a musical culture in a contingent world where time and place are no longer the unequivocal anchors that they used to be.

Voluntary migration, either as a backdrop or an active ingredient, helps define the problems addressed by these studies or contributes to their explanation. Whether or not voluntariness is assumed, the relative orderliness and predictability of the circumstances surrounding migration are inherent in the description of subject matter. It is, however, reasonable to speculate—or guess, as this work does—that fresh insights might be gained into these issues by studying them under contrastive conditions: those of the disorderliness, unpredictability, and extreme pressures that forced migration brings to bear on musical life. Consider, for instance, that:

1. Forced migration not only removes people from country and culture of origin but cuts them off, often for long periods of time, and even alienates them, from those who share their roots. That such tragic dislocations, which all too often seem irreversible, nonetheless revive and nurture cultural traditions, albeit in a form different from those in the home country, should provide an effective conceptual tool not only for looking more closely at musical identity and the tradition it constantly invokes but, perhaps as important, for loosening the hold—sometimes still powerful, sometimes no more than vestigial—of the debilitating premise that cultural and geographic boundaries coincide. Perhaps there is still need for Geertz's reminder that "the locus of study is not the object of study" (1973:22)

2. The life of refugees, particularly in the interim between escape and resettlement, demonstrates an extreme case of decontextualization and recontextualization. Refugee flight is an act of deterritorialization, physical and jurisdictional. When responsibility for refugee protection and aid is assumed by international bodies like the UNHCR or by multinational agencies like the International Red Cross, locales such as refugee camps where sovereignty can be a contested issue become incubators for a host of ethnomusicological problems. One finds a layering of cultures inhabiting a space with criss-crossing lines of authority. Some emanate from within the refugee group, others from the local communities directly involved with camps, still others from individual nations, and from international bodies. In denseness and complexity, the resulting environment challenges any that the world has to offer.

3. Permeating the situations just described is that ubiquitous, amorphous, but unmistakable feature, heterogeneity—not that to which ethnomusicology has gotten accustomed in the last decade but an artificial and taxing heterogeneity. It is artificial because it is foisted upon a population by a status—refugee—assigned by foreign government bureaucracies that create new social categories or rearrange existing ones. It is taxing because it is not supported by those mechanisms that societies develop through time that allow its members to internalize criteria for differentiation and to respond or adapt to such differentiation in culturallly sanctioned ways. This heterogeneity collides violently with the European model of nation-state, which puts homogeneity—common language, culture, and race, until recently the hallmarks of ethnomusicology's subject populations—at the core of its structure.[15] Issues of social organization and identity—personal, cultural, musical—surface with a vengeance.

The old idea that the task of ethnomusicology is to strip away the "foreign" elements, the accretions from contact with "others" to arrive at a ur-form authentic and perceivable again in its native integrity has now been replaced by the realities of today's world and its nomadic citizens.[16] This is a world where a picture that Iain Chambers draws is no longer unusual: Yousou N'Dour from Dakar singing in Wolof in a tent in Naples just a few months after he sang in a New York club "in the context of the Japanese techno-pop/New Age sound of Ryuichi Sakamoto and No Wave New York guitarist Arto Lindsay" (1995:15). In this world, coherence is less an innate intactness than a piecing together of fragments collected as music-bearing migrants move through time and space. Forced migration exaggerates these processes through the relative speed and brashness with which they happen. Through such amplification and magnification, what may have escaped us before may now submit to closer examination.

PART I

THE JOURNEY

Prologue

Our century has sometimes been called the "Century of the Refugee." . . . never have so many remained so long in the kind of suspended animation that refugee status now all too often has come to mean. —*W.R. Smyser,* Refugees

And just beyond the frontier between "us" and the "outsiders" is the perilous territory of not-belonging.
—*Edward Said, "Reflections on Exile"*

No declaration of war marked the beginning of that chain of events known as the Vietnam War. Yet a historical moment marked the opening of the floodgates that brought to the United States a lasting consequence of that war: the country's first refugee influx as large, concentrated, and visible as the Indochinese.

The images of U.S. helicopters taking off from the roof of the American embassy in Saigon in April 1975 as Vietnamese tried to scramble on board appear frozen in time, etched onto the memory and replayed in written and stage accounts. If the significance of those images was somehow missed or denied, images of boat people soon followed to underscore the ubiquity of refugees on the modern international scene.

Two sets of accounts emerge from such scenes of human tragedy crammed into terms such as *refugee* and *forced migration.* One emanates from ground level, where the refugees stand. The other is pieced together from reports, memoranda, legislation, and other official documents from governments, international agencies, and the United Nations.

These accounts converge at certain points. Frequently, however, they diverge; constantly, there is tension between them. One is couched in the language of nonrefugee officialdom, dispassionate, and generalizing. The other throbs with the emotional nature of refugee phenomena, which are often matters of life and death. In this bifurcated view of people and events that make up the refugee scene lies great potential for distortion: those strong emotions excised or tempered in one are the defining elements of the other as a population is transformed from people who lived ordinary, everyday lives in a country they call home to forced migrants unable to claim, at a crucial period in their lives, the protection of citizenship.

The view from the ground begins with this: Refugee movements are triggered by cataclysmic events that result in an eruption of emotion-driven behavior. Particularly at its inception, the overwhelming impression that a refugee flow gives is one of chaos, of instinctual rather than premeditated or carefully considered action.

For the Vietnamese, beginning in 1975, flight was not a matter of a few miles but a long, perilous journey. For those who became "boat people," the distance was reckoned in terms of oceans and seas, and the chances of getting there, wherever "there" was, depended on the trust-worthiness of overcrowded boats and the skill of whoever piloted them. Many boats were piloted by people who had never been in international waters, did not know how to navigate in total darkness, and were not sure what destination they should aim for given the load they were carrying and their limited food, water, and fuel supplies. Much depended too on the cooperation of tides, and the mercy or the cruelty of pirates or of other ships at sea who were in a position to assist and of people on foreign beaches, who could either push escapees back to sea or give them asylum.

For those who chose to flee by land, success or failure depended on making it across geopolitical borders and mine fields—actual and metaphorical—on the bounty or treachery of jungles, and on unexpectedly encountered strangers.

Many who tried to flee died in the attempt. Family members were separated and lost track of each other permanently or for years.[1] The vast majority of escapees would end up in overcrowded camps run by local authorities in Southeast Asian countries, nongovernmental organizations

(NGOs), and United Nations personnel from other parts of the world. Many would arrive with nothing but the clothes on their backs, haunted by experiences of piracy, rape, and even cannibalism at sea or by guilt at having survived and having left others behind. And while the urgency and intensity of feelings tend to ebb as refugee movements mature, affect powerful enough to persist through years of rebuilding a life in resettlement plays a central role in refugee affairs.[2]

Regarding the view from outside the refugees' world, the scale of the Indochinese exodus triggered by the fall of Saigon in 1975, and the growing number of deaths among those attempting escape (about 60 percent, according to Hitchcox [1990:11]), brought the United Nations to Geneva in 1979 to see what could be done to ameliorate the situation. At that conference, a number of Southeast Asian nations agreed to grant temporary asylum to Indochinese refugees. They were to be housed in camps administered in partnership with the United Nations High Commissioner for Refugees. The camps were to have two principal objectives: the security and protection of those seeking asylum from Indochina, and their preparation for resettlement in third countries, mostly in the West.

Eventually, camps came to differ from each other in their emphasis: camps of first asylum sheltered both escapees and refugees, and processing camps received mainly those whose claim to refugee status had already been established. Most of the processing camp populations were bound for resettlement in the United States.

Other differences quickly surfaced. Host countries varied in the resources they could make available to camps. Domestic policies pertaining to migration and local attitudes toward hosting refugees differed from region to region. Partly, differences resulted from the pressure put on individual camps by the number of incoming refugees; some camps became severely overcrowded, their facilities strained beyond capacity. Other differences were created by the rate at which third countries resettled refugees. When proceeding apace, resettlement not only relieved the pressures of overcrowding and opened up spaces for new arrivals but, more important, reassured asylum countries that their role as host was indeed temporary and that refugees would not be a long-term responsibility. When resettlement slowed, as it did in the early 1980s, asylum countries responded with various policies of deterrence. To discourage escapees from coming, some countries tightened restrictions in camps, others converted open camps to closed camps, and still others pushed incoming boats back to sea. (Open camps allowed asylees to freely come and go and sometimes, as in Hong Kong, to work outside camp; closed camps confined asylees to camp grounds.)

Individual camps—their administration, their population, and hence, the flavors of camp life—changed over a relatively short period of time. In the course of a few months, for instance, an open camp run by Caritas (a voluntary agency) became a closed camp run by the Corrections Service, which in Hong Kong is part of the Prisons Department. Political changes in host countries might change administrative personnel in charge of camps, resulting in changes as basic as food suppliers and the quality of food distributed to refugees. The asylee and refugee populations themselves changed, in number as well as in nationality and general social composition. North and South Vietnamese in Hong Kong proved to be a volatile combination at one point and had to be segregated in separate camps. In the late 1980s, the Bataan camp population began to have an increasing proportion of Vietnamese whose refugee status came not from having fled the country but from having been permitted to leave in accordance with the Orderly Departure Program (ODP), set up by Vietnam and Western resettlement countries to help families reunite. In the late 1980s, an increase in the number of Amerasians changed the camp population to such a degree that the camp adjusted the number and nature of the programs it offered.

Flux and transiency are defining features of camp life. Data on camp life—qualitative as well as quantitative—can often seem erratic and inconsistent as a consequence. Populations are meant to come and go. What kinds of people come, the state they are in when they arrive, how long they stay, how well they will get along with each other and with camp personnel, and what kind of camp life different groups of actors will create are impossible to predict. The descriptions that follow are of people and events only in a small slice of time. The situation brings Heraclitus very much to mind: one does not step twice into the same river. The flux becomes identifiable only through contrast with the relatively stable phenomena around it.

Despite the difficulties, however, an attempt to describe the refugee experience at every stage is essential: for the great majority of Vietnamese refugees, camp life is part of the journey from their homeland. It is part of the string of contingencies that mark their lives in resettlement. Understanding camp life—or at least acknowledging its contextual role—makes forced migrants' lives more comprehensible.[3]

The two camps I describe are not representative of their respective designations (first asylum camp and processing camp). Rather, they exemplify an entry and an exit point into and out of that interim period between flight from Vietnam and resettlement specifically in the United States. The camp in Puerto Princesa in the Philippine island of Palawan is a camp of first asylum. For many Vietnamese, it was the first stop after flight from Vietnam. The camp in Bataan is a processing center. It was the last in a series of steps—locational and bureaucratic—beyond which lay resettlement. In both, one constant is the persistence of musical expression.

Incredibly, or perhaps not incredibly at all, asylees make music. They sing, they make new songs, they play instruments when they can find or make them. Music is everywhere. Morning, noon, and night its sounds come from billets, chapels, temples, and classrooms. There has been speculation about why people sing in the face of death, of terrible uncertainty, in times of extreme suffering. What do they sing? What does their music making mean in the rapidly changing contexts of their journey from flight to resettlement? These questions constitute the *cantus firmus* of this work.

First Asylum: The Camp in Palawan, Philippines

From the air, Palawan and the small surrounding islands look like a tropical paradise. The beaches, the vegetation, the mountains, the fishponds—one in the shape of a giant heart—present a breathtakingly beautiful picture. Once upon a time, I had been told, the remoteness of the island isolated two feared populations—lepers and criminals. Now the leper colony is gone, and although the penal colony remains, it is not what one remembers as the plane descends. In 1991 when I last visited, German tourists on the plane swore that in Palawan one finds the best scuba diving in the world. A Japanese restaurant owner from Tokyo talked about his weekly trips to Palawan, where he gets the best tuna available in this part of the world.

On the ground an army of "tricycles" congregated to await the daily flight from Manila. These bicycles, operated by boys and men of all ages, drew passenger conveyances that offered transport anywhere in and around Puerto Princesa, the provincial capital. Once, my "driver" was a grade school student taking time off during the 12:00 to 2:00 lunch break to earn a few pesos.

Palawan is the fifth largest of the Philippine Islands. It is about 4,550 square miles and is located north of Borneo between the Sulu Archipelago and the South China Sea at the same latitude as the southern part of Vietnam, a geographic circumstance of great significance to the character of the Palawan camp.[1] When engines failed and left boats to the mercy of tides, or when boats took advantage of monsoon winds between April and September, the likelihood of escapees ending up in Palawan was considerable. Thus, the asylee population in Palawan was not only all Vietnamese but almost all South Vietnamese.[2] This demographic feature gains importance in light of the country's bitter political and ideological division into North and South Vietnam from 1954 to 1975—a division that

The Vietnam Refugee Center in Puerto Princesa, Palawan, in the Philippines, 1987

echoed in Vietnamese social and interpersonal relations long after the country's reunification with the fall of Saigon.

The Vietnamese Refugee Center (VRC), a camp of first asylum, was about a mile from the Palawan airport. It sat on approximately 10 hectares of land (24.7 acres or .03 square mile) on a Sulu Sea shore that boasts spectacular sunsets.[3] Asylees swam when their schedules and the tides permitted, and many went out with their nets to fish. While a guardhouse at the gate was manned by members of the Philippine Western Command (WESCOM), a military unit, and the local implementing arm of the UNHCR, and while fences encompassed the camp on three sides (the fourth side is bordered by the sea), this was an open camp—refugees could come and go at will from 6:00 A.M. to 10:00 P.M. The physical environment therefore included the whole of Puerto Princesa itself, and asylees could achieve a measure of social integration through participation in the social and economic life of the city.

Refugee billets in the Vietnam Refugee Center, Palawan, 1987

Built in 1979, the camp was intended to accommodate 2,000. It had, however, held as many as 7,000. Renovated in 1983, the camp consisted of some 800 living units for asylees and communal barracks for staff. Asylee living units were divided into billets intended to accommodate eight that frequently housed more when the camp was filled to capacity. Asylees could also build simple living quarters which they could "sell" when they left camp. Units were grouped into zones for organizational purposes. There were six public water stations and six toilet blocks for refugee use. Camp structures were made primarily of local materials—wood, nipa palm for thatching, and bamboo for walls. Although there were no roads as such, the ground was hard and level enough to permit local traffic—jeeps or cars used by visitors and administrative personnel, and vehicles that brought in supplies. The small size of the camp put everything within easy walking distance.

There were houses of worship—Buddhist, Cao Dai, Catholic, Protestant—schools, libraries, and a restaurant; administrative offices for the UNHCR, WESCOM, the elected Vietnamese Refugee Council (VR Council), and various voluntary agencies (volags); and a detention center. Unaccompanied minors below the age of eighteen and unaccompanied sin-

Refugee billets in the Vietnam Refugee Center, Palawan, 1987

gle women lived in special homes. There were spaces for small businesses run by asylees: tailoring, noodle, and other cooked food stalls; manicuring; photo studios; and coffee shops. Asylees were allowed to raise pigs and poultry for their own consumption or to sell in or outside camp. Flower beds and vegetable gardens planted by the asylees for their pleasure or for commerce contributed splashes of color. There were monuments to the asylee presence and their literary and artistic impulses—short poems or aphorisms carved into rocks strewn along the seashore. To these testaments of human expressivity, nature added its own; sunsets, dramatic cloud formations against incredibly blue skies, and stars that seemed closer and bigger in the tropics made it possible to forget, from time to time, the drab physical appearance of the camp.

Administrative Structure

The partnership between the local government (represented in this case by WESCOM), the international community (represented by the UNHCR), and the voluntary agencies, local and international, is fairly standard for

Photograph taken in 1987 of one of many inscriptions carved by refugees on slabs of petrified wood that are scattered on the beach in Palawan. This one says: "If we try to observe and understand what we don't like, we can see things in a different light. For example, even if we don't like termites, we should admire their skill and patience. This is a way of learning." (Translated by Phong T. Nguyen.)

UNHCR-sponsored refugee camps all over the world. The differences lie in the ways that partnership is interpreted and funded from camp to camp and host country to host country.

The Palawan camp offered a wide range of activities—some compulsory, such as school attendance and work credit (fifteen hours a week of work at chores related to the maintenance of the camp and its facilities), but most optional. Of the 2,427 asylees in camp when I visited in 1983, 1,673 were enrolled in language and cultural orientation classes. Children attended schools, and gifted children were bused out of camp to Holy Trinity College in town, where they could be more academically challenged.

Because the VRC was an open camp, asylees could go to town to shop or to sell produce or fish. Schools organized outings, graduations, parties, and other cultural events. So did other groups like the Vietnamese Scouts, the Buddhist Youth Group, the Catholic Youth Group, the Martial Arts Group, the Veterans Association, and the Cao Daist Group, to say nothing of services and activities provided by nongovernmental organizations and voluntary agencies (Volags) such as the Red Cross, the Intergovernmental Committee on Migration, the British Voluntary Service Overseas, the Baptist World Allance, the Center for Assistance to Displaced Persons, the Mormon Christian Services, and the Sovereign Military Order of Malta. There were training courses for those interested in acquiring such skills as baking, typing, hotel management, cosmetology, sewing, vermiculture, and poultry raising. Services such as day care and elderly literacy classes were also available. These activities were intended to help the asylees both prepare for resettlement and cope with depression and stress by keeping busy. Camp figures showed that "about 40% of the camp population were involved in sports and cultural activities" (Reyes 1983:3).

But what was distinctive to Palawan was the Vietnamese Refugee Council, a Vietnamese governing body legitimized by WESCOM and given jurisdiction over the internal affairs of the Vietnamese asylee population. The council provided a form of governance that was understandable to the Vietnamese and that gave them the sense of purpose and cohesion they badly needed at that moment in their lives. It served a liaison function between the asylees and the local and international authorities and helped maintain a structure within which programs could be run effectively.

The idea and organization of the council came at the initiative of Sister Pascale, a Vietnamese nun, with Sister Delia, a Filipino nun, assisting in its implementation. Both belong to the order of the Daughters of Charity, which had charge of the Center for Assistance to Displaced Persons (CADP).

Headed by a president and vice-president, the council consisted of fourteen to sixteen members, each elected by residents of a camp zone.[4] To qualify for VR Council membership, a candidate had to be over thirty and an upstanding member of the camp community, which, among other things, meant no record of violating camp rules and no suspicion of Communist affiliation. Each council member headed a section, which had charge of specific services: food distribution, health care, mail services, currency exchange, sanitation, educational and cultural programs, and so on. The council therefore guaranteed a strong Vietnamese voice in the running of camp affairs.

The principal goal to which the council dedicated itself was the creation of a "small Vietnam," an effort symbolized by a ritual unique to this camp: the weekly flag ceremony at which the flag of the former Republic of South Vietnam was raised, the old national anthem was sung, and the chairman of the VR Council spoke to the gathered camp population to make announcements and to exhort the Vietnamese to uphold Vietnamese values. This ritual also reflected the strong presence of former members of the South Vietnamese military in camp. Most members of the VR Council came from this group.[5]

Further reinforcing the efforts to create a small Vietnam in Palawan was the VR Council's educational program, dedicated to ensuring that the young did not forget their language and were taught Vietnamese history, geography, and culture. Regular instruction in these subjects was intended to counterbalance the effects of cultural orientation classes that prepared refugees for entry into Western culture upon resettlement. This VR Council program also underscored what is often cited as an important reason for leaving Vietnam: to conserve a Vietnamese way of life that Communism has destroyed.

The Asylee Community

On the surface, the most striking feature of the VRC's asylee population was its homogeneity. This group spoke the same language, came from the same region of the same country, and presumably shared the same culture and the same ideological motivations to risk their lives and leave their homeland perhaps for good. Not too far below the surface, however, were fissures—some old and others that arose from the circumstances of escape and the camp environment. The fear that led citizens to escape cut a wide swath across the population in Vietnam. Internal diversity was intrinsic to the asylee population despite its broadly shared Vietnamese—and in this camp the strongly South Vietnamese—culture.[6] Asylees came from different social and economic strata, had different religious affiliations and varying levels of education, and were marked by rural or urban ways of life. As individuals arrived and departed, proportions changed, altering the character of the group. Sometimes there was a bigger representation from the military than at other times. A large influx of newcomers could have an impact on social life as people sized each other up: Who can be trusted?

Who comes from my part of the country and can bring me news of mutual acquaintances? How much social distance is warranted? By the time these issues were resolved, the asylees concerned might already have left.

The effects of differences were magnified by overcrowding and the lack of choice of one's billet mates. The protocols that governed social relations in Vietnam were thrown into question by the exigencies of escape and the new realities of camp life.[7] With the exception of the military and the clergy, who tended to retain their authority and whose authority the Vietnamese were accustomed to, social relations became confused.

These were the potentially disruptive differences that the VRC, the voluntary agencies, and the other camp personnel sought to ameliorate. The educational and social programs were initiated with those differences and needs in mind. Cultural events and celebrations were designed to serve similar purposes. According to Le Duc Ai, a former officer in the Army of the Republic of Vietnam (ARVN) who was vice-chairman of the VR Council in 1983, the Vietnamese in camp celebrated four major festivals: the midautumn festival, Christmas, Tet, and Buddha's birthday (fourth month of the lunar calendar). Tet was celebrated for three to six days (Reyes 1983; cf. Hitchcox 1990:242–44), during which time the asylees honored their ancestors, visited relatives and friends to exchange good wishes, played games, and made music.[8]

The sense of community and the solidarity of its Vietnamese members were further bolstered by a public address system run by Vietnamese that broadcast in Vietnamese from 6:00 A.M. to 6:00 P.M., an ever-present voice that provided asylees with information concerning events, news, activities, and other matters.

The significance of a sense of community in the Palawan context is hard to overestimate. It must be seen in the light of the recency of the break from homeland, the magnitude of that break, and the high cost it exacted—physically, financially, psychologically, and emotionally. Being a camp of first asylum, Palawan received escapees when psychic and somatic wounds were freshest and the shock of a new culture greatest. When everything seemed to have disintegrated, the order and security that a sense of community provided were essential if the asylees were to recover their equilibrium. Tenuous and imperfect though such a sense of community might be, it responded to urgent needs. Yet it was constantly under threat by the very conditions that made the camp necessary.

Camp life imposed another distinction with important social consequences, that between asylees who became refugees within a matter of months, and asylees who became long-stayers—those who stayed for two years to a decade or more. Compared to processing camps, where most of the population already had refugee status and could therefore expect to be on its way within approximately six months, the rate of departure from Palawan was much less predictable.[9]

Asylees became long-stayers for one or more of these reasons: they were judged as lacking in marketable skills, in poor health, or of questionable character, or they had been accused or found guilty of some infraction of the rules. Not infrequently, they were those who had been most traumatized during escape and, as a consequence, exhibited severe symptoms of physical and mental distress. They were therefore bypassed by Western resettlement agencies, a development that threw their prospects for resettlement further into limbo.[10]

A minority whose actual size was difficult to ascertain—the UNHCR field officer in 1988 placed it at approximately 3 percent of the total asylee population, although this varied as asylees came and went[11]—long-stayers nonetheless claimed a considerable share of attention from service providers, who were confronted with the difficult task of preparing for resettlement those whose ability to profit from such preparation was not at all clear, and of providing support to a population whose demoralization, resentments, and prospects for "de-socialization" (Hitchcox 1990) would only grow with the passage of time.

The position of long-stayers was therefore anomalous in the eyes of both the camp administration and the other Vietnamese who aspired to—and had reason to expect—timely resettlement. By definition, long-stayers, without meaning or wanting to, breached the most important norm: as quick a departure as possible, with asylum only a temporary arrangement, a way station to resettlement. They were embodiments of what the other Vietnamese did not wish to be; they undermined the "belief in the temporality of camp existence" (Knudsen 1988:90) that sustains asylees and refugees everywhere.

It is the paradox of refugee camps as institutions that those who stayed the longest and who in that respect made up the most stable segment of the population were also the most destabilizing. Where flux was the norm, the relative permanence that long-stayers represented became corrosive.

It is out of these disparate groups of people, seemingly thrown together by chance, that the Palawan VRC community was forged.[12] Shaping the community and being shaped by it were the relations of the groups to each other. The administrative arm exercised the UN mandate and implemented the host country's interpretation of that mandate, which allowed the maximum participation in camp governance from the Vietnamese. The Vietnamese responded by maintaining an internal security that made the Palawan camp rank as perhaps the safest in Southeast Asia (Hitchcox 1990:160–67). The Puerto Princesa community's receptiveness to the Vietnamese made possible an exchange of goods and ideas between camp and town.[13] These conditions left their mark on the give and take of daily life, and on the institutional framework within which people in the VRC made music, listened to it and became creators of and participants in a musical community.

Musical Life in the VRC

An Ethnographic Sketch

Despite—or perhaps because of—the overwhelming sense of loss that refugees share—particularly those in camps of first asylum—there was no lack of music in the VRC. One heard live music in churches, temples, classrooms, and billets, and music in "mediated" forms virtually everywhere else. Many asylees owned radios, cassettes, or boom-boxes; in the mid- to late eighties, those who had been in camp long enough to receive mail often got remittances from friends and relatives already resettled abroad. The CADP maintained a music bank that lent out or allowed use of Western musical instruments. Although I did not find musical instruments of Vietnamese provenance during my visits to VRC, I was told that occasionally, a Vietnamese flute (*sáo*) would show up. The circumstances of flight that brought the Vietnamese to this particular camp ruled out their arriving with larger instruments. The guitar was a general favorite among the asylees, both in its standard acoustic form and in its "Vietnamized" form which asylees produced by doctoring acoustic guitars obtained locally.[14] But with or without musical instruments, the Vietnamese love for singing was evident in Palawan. Virtually everyone who has written about Vietnamese social life— in Vietnam, in camps, in resettlement countries—has noted this penchant for song. Thus, though musical activity may be constrained by other obligations and options and by the number of people sharing limited space, the musical life of Vietnamese was an unmistakable presence in the VRC.

Unlike other Southeast Asian camps where one might hear Cambodian and Laotian music, the VRC offered only two basic musical idioms: one based on Western tonal harmony, and the other, the distinctively Vietnamese idiom characterized by its system of modes and manner of ornamentation (see Tran Van Khe 1980). The former was the idiom shared, used by, and familiar to the camp as a whole. The latter was considered theirs/not ours by the non-Vietnamese. The Vietnamese musical repertory drew from both the Western and Vietnamese musical idioms. The Filipinos and the Westerners (mostly UNHCR personnel) as a rule were conversant only with the Western idiom.

The unfamiliarity of the Vietnamese musical idiom to the non-Vietnamese was reflected in their reactions to that music. Expressed in dismissive and overly generalizing terms, non-Vietnamese described *cải lương*, Buddhist chant, and other distinctively Vietnamese forms such as declaimed poetry (which non-Vietnamese almost invariably take to be song) as "boring."[15] One of the officers likened this music to that made by someone "playing a broken violin." Music in Western idioms recognizable as Vietnamese principally through its Vietnamese texts was waved off by a WESCOM officer as "all Broadway." A volag commented on the "endless tango music."[16] Where there was no Vietnamese text—for instance, instrumental pieces composed in the Western idiom by Vietnamese asylees and played on a regular acoustic guitar—the music was simply taken as Western music appropriated by Vietnamese.

The Vietnamese point of view was characterized both by what they did and did not say about what they performed. They made no overt effort to identify their music as Vietnamese. A UNHCR field officer remarked that in Palawan, asylees felt little need to assert their Vietnamese identity because they were among other Vietnamese in what they saw as a Vietnamese environment. (This can best be appreciated through contrast with the practice in the Bataan refugee camp where there were Laotians and Cambodians, and in the United States where ethnic labeling is almost automatic.) Nor did they identify music by genre or function unless explicitly asked. What they did say about the music they made in Palawan was that it was "mostly 'sad songs' and 'love songs'" (VR Council interview, August 17, 1988), a statement both of fact and of ideology.

"Sad songs" and love songs were true expressions of how asylees felt, as confirmed by their narratives and the growing body of published accounts by former refugees. Vietnamese in Palawan (and elsewhere) offered a historical explanation for the dominance of these songs in their repertory, recalling the years of continual warfare—with the Chinese, the French, the Japanese, the Americans, the Viet Cong—that have made separation and loss part of virtually every family's story. (This sense of loss would emerge as a dominant theme throughout the study as Vietnamese moved from camp of first asylum to resettlement in the United States.)

Statistical support for the factual substance of "sad songs" is suggested by Hitchcox's data. While asylees may have felt ecstatic over the success of their escape and their survival of terrible ordeals, they were soon beset by anxiety and depression. Hitchcox found that for all the "pleasant surroundings of Palawan with its relaxed regime"—some asylees have called it the Ritz of asylum camps—the anxiety and depression level there as measured by the Hopkins Symptom Checklist (HSCL-58) was higher than that at "prison-like" Phanat Nikom camp in Thailand (1990:260–62). This was attributed to the more protracted escape endured by those in Palawan but above all to the importance of resettlement. At the time of Hitchcox's study in the late 1980s, only 11.6 percent were long-stayers in Thailand compared to Palawan's 30 percent.[17]

The ideological grounds for preferring sad songs and love songs lay deeply embedded also in their exodus. Until the late 1980s, the Socialist government of Vietnam had prohibited love songs and songs nostalgic for pre-1975 Vietnam. To sing sad songs and love songs was therefore an act of defiance or self-differentiation from those who accepted the communist prohibition, and by extension, at least in the asylees' view, the communist regime. This was the regime they had risked their lives to flee. Once free—this was in large part what Palawan meant to them—it was not to be tolerated. Being noncommunist was a strong criterion for admission into the Palawan Vietnamese community. Thus an asylee, described as a "good composer" by volags who knew him was marginalized by his fellow asylees because he was believed to be a "communist." In a community that considered itself victimized by communism and still reeling from the vivid memories of what its members had endured, that was enough to warrant censure.

The ideological component of the Vietnamese exodus and the pervasive sense of loss would remain dominant themes in the lives of Vietnamese even as they moved from camp to camp and from status to status—as escapee, then asylee, then refugee, and finally resettler. These would color the choices they would make, both musical and social, throughout their journey. But certain aspects of their musical life would be situational, responding to specific conditions as they moved along a trajectory that was only partly of their own choosing.

An Ethnomusicological Picture

The repertory heard in camp can be arranged according to conventional categories: religious/secular, vocal/instrumental, love songs/work songs, popular/traditional, and so on. But the resulting order, while useful, might reflect the general Western conventions governing musical typology more than those features specific to the VRC. Just as the social hierarchy that obtained in Vietnam had been badly shaken in the process of escape and within the framework of refugee camps, many conventional musical typologies had become altered in meaning and function in this new context.

What seemed more revealing of musical life as an intrinsic part of social life in camp was a contrast between music as private and as public act.[18] Beyond personal tastes and choices, such a contrast illumined Vietnamese and non-Vietnamese attitudes toward each other, their interactions, and hence the nature of the relations between dichotomous (musical) worlds that had to be forged in order to construct the social unit that was the Palawan camp. In this respect—in the integration of the musical and the more broadly social made possible by the response of one to the other—this contrast yields important components of an ethnomusicological picture of the VRC situation.

Privacy is highly relative in a camp as small and as densely populated as the VRC. Asylee huts huddled close together, there were no doors to speak of, and thin walls made audible what they hid from sight. What constituted the private as contrasted to the public therefore carried a strong subjective element. To a large extent, music for public consumption was music deemed comprehensible to all or at least recognizable by all as familiar or as compatible with music they considered their own. Music in the Western idiom responds to this description. But also included is music for or as special event—music on those few occasions that involved the Vietnamese as a distinct musical community, and music, therefore, that the camp administration accommodated as public function. An example is the *cải lương* presentation commemorating the important Vietnamese midautumn festival, which merited public performance in the center of camp. As will become evident, this conception of what is public and what private would find confirmation in a particular fit between repertory and location.

The public-private opposition became notable not only because little was truly private in camp (which would have made the likelihood of the private, as social category, unlikely or of negligible value) but also because no camp regulations defined or ruled on it. It was therefore not the result of observing an existent, labeled, or commonsensical understanding of what is private and what is public. Rather, camp life and the relations within it created the opposition. The public and the private thus seemed to emerge from tacit understandings between the interacting groups and could be said, as a consequence, to be organic to their relations.

Apart from conventions about what is proper for certain places and functions—in churches, temples, and classrooms; for worship, formal learning, and so on—there were no rules that pertained to music making in camp. From 6:00 A.M. to 10:00 P.M., when everyone was supposed to be up and about, people could play or sing whatever music they pleased wherever they pleased. The substance of the opposition therefore lay in the perceptions of Vietnamese and non-Vietnamese about each other's music and the accommodations they made as a result.

I was dismayed when a well-meaning staff member introduced me to the chairman of the VR Council as someone who wanted to know whether music making made life in camp easier. As though responding to a cue, the chairman, apologizing that he could not come up with professional musicians, presented me that evening with a program of Vietnamese folk songs and pieces by Andrés Segovia played on a guitar by a former Saigon Conservatory student. The camp had heard about my arrival through the public address system. An officer of the VR Council told me that some asylees, upon hearing the announcement, had come to him to volunteer to sing and play for me. From that self-selected group he had picked out those who could play what he thought I had come to hear, that is, what he thought my non-Vietnamese hosts had expected me to hear. This conjecture was borne out when I finally convinced him that my interests did not necessarily coincide with those of my official hosts, and that I did not require professional musicians. I was then allowed into the "private" musical sphere—*cải lương,* poetry recitation, singing, and such musical activities as were kept away from the center of things out of consideration for—or protection from—uncomprehending Western ears.

The move from a public repertory with a strong Vietnamese and non-Vietnamese common denominator, which made it potentially comprehensible to both audiences, to a private repertory in a musical language comprehensible only to the Vietnamese was paralleled by a spatial move. When the Vietnamese Refugee Council saw its task—accommodating me—as a response to a WESCOM and UNHCR request, its representative arranged a music session in the VR Council office in the center of camp, part of a complex of offices for camp personnel.

From there, we moved to the handicrafts store, carrying with us some of the office furniture to seat the growing number of music makers, who also represented a wider repertory. Finally, I was introduced to the other end of the public-private continuum in the periphery of the camp where there was no other non-Vietnamese in sight or within earshot.

The walk to the location where these events took place is also symbolic of the cultural distance between the musical idioms involved. At night, when the communal music making took place, the walk, although short, involved picking one's way with a flashlight through informally arranged living quarters and across little drainage canals to a clearing with some partially walled thatched structures. I needed the guidance of a VR Council member to find the way; I doubt that any of the Philippine or Western staff members would have led me to that location at the proper (music-making) time.

During my visit to the Palawan camp in 1988, social and music activities were rather intensive because the Vietnamese community, under the leadership of the Buddhist temple, was preparing for the midautumn festival. Its main feature was to be a full-length *cải lương* on the life of Buddha. In rehearsal were songs and dances for the celebration. But the scene as a whole was not confined to music making, nor was the music making confined to the items intended for the midautumn festival celebration. The scene was more like a gathering in a social club. People played board games, gossiped with each other, or just looked on. Two Buddhist monks supervised the rehearsals, and a solitary guitarist off to one corner played softly to himself. A group of young people sang *vọng cổ* from "Lan và Điệp" to each other.[19]

In one of the structures, men rested on a bamboo platform a few feet off the floor that served, as in many billets, as a bed or eating area. Clothes hanging on a line above the platform and two "scalloped" acoustic guitars leaning against a wall suggested that this was someone's "house." A few feet from the platform was a table about six feet long at which people sat singing, one after another, songs that they said they learned from each other, brought from Vietnam, or composed themselves. My Vietnamese companions, one a woman soon to leave for resettlement in France and the other, headed for Pennsylvania, a former lieutenant colonel and helicopter pilot in the Vietnamese Air Force, gave a running commentary on the activities. In contrast to the individuals who had volunteered to perform after they heard of my presence through the public address system, those making music here were not self-selected for my purposes. They were doing what they wanted to do in an environment of their choice.[20]

As the night wore on, I began to worry about curfew. In other camps, violation of curfew meant time in the "monkey house"—detention quarters—and possible complications in the resettlement process, a situation refugees tried to avoid at all costs. My Vietnamese lieutenant colonel companion assured me that everything would be all right as long as he took personal responsibility; he was a ranking officer of the VR Council at the time. More than an hour after curfew, we finally went on our way, my companion doing the rounds, affording me a view of a "private" life after curfew when people sat chatting quietly just outside their billets or slept in the open air under a tropical sky. The camp personnel whose barracks I shared seemed totally unconcerned about the lateness of my arrival. They said that my companion was trusted implicitly by the camp administration, that he had made it a habit to go around late at night to see that everything was all right, and that everyone, Vietnamese and non-Vietnamese, had become accustomed to his nightly "patrol."

Underscoring the public-private dichotomy was this incident. One of the *vọng cổ* singers I had met in the "private" sphere turned out to be a worker in the office of the WESCOM administration. Jokingly, the secretary in the office (a non-Vietnamese staff member who knew nothing of the young man's singing activities) suggested to the worker that he might wish to sing for me. To the secretary's surprise, he jumped at the chance, ran out to gather some friends, and came back to take over the conference room for our session.

Everyone was excited. The young Vietnamese interpreted the secretary's suggestion as an invitation to sing "his" kind of music—*cải lương*—in WESCOM (public) premises. Frustrated that my tape recorder would not enable them both to enjoy hearing their recorded voices and to have them heard in the center of camp, they decided to borrow the officer-in-charge's boom box. The young man sent on the errand was instructed to say that I was the one borrowing the box. When I demurred, the group argued that it was the only way they could have their music making heard by the rest of the camp under these circumstances. In other words, they recognized this occasion as exceptional—a departure from the unspoken distinction between public and private music making, made possible by my presence and by the "invitation" of a WESCOM staff member.

The mutual accommodation reflected in musical life and evident in day-to-day interaction was, of course, not motivated by altruism or good-will alone. As both Hitchcox and Knudsen have noted, it served both Vietnamese and non-Vietnamese interests. For non-Vietnamese, having the Vietnamese attend to security and internal order was an efficient use of scarce resources. The presence of people who were exemplars of resistance to communism had propaganda value for the Philippine government, until the 1980s grappling with its own problems with alleged communist insurgents (Hitchcox 1990).

The Vietnamese in turn were exercising the utmost care that nothing jeopardize their resettlement. This meant not only strict adherence to regulations and cooperation with those who could facilitate resettlement, but also the suppression of anything that might be misunderstood. Knudsen writes about withdrawal, the avoidance of conflict, "undercommunication," and "privatization" of problems and personal feelings as strategies toward the achievement of resettlement (1988:108–14).

Underlying the distinctions between music as private and as public act, therefore, appear to be factors analogous, if not homologous, to those that motivate Vietnamese to draw distinctions between what they choose to present in public as opposed to what they choose to keep private in the larger social sphere. They are factors that take into consideration important social concerns: How much can the Vietnamese and non-Vietnamese public be trusted to assign the same or at least an equivalent value to what is being offered? Will public exposure enhance self-presentation, or will it invite ridicule? Will it facilitate or will it hinder acceptance in the new and largely unfamiliar milieu? These concerns lie at the core of the adaptive strategies that evolve as asylees become refugees and finally resettlers in their host countries.

CHAPTER 2

Springboard to Resettlement:
The Refugee Processing Center

The drive from Manila to the Philippine Refugee Processing Center (PRPC) in the province of Bataan can take from three to six hours, depending on traffic, road, and political conditions. On my first visit in 1983, it took three uneventful hours to make the trip of 180-some kilometers. In 1988, with the rebel People's Army active in the countryside, checkpoints and tree trunks arranged at points along the way to force vehicular traffic to slow down lengthened the trip to five hours. And in 1991, with Manila's worsening traffic conditions ensnaring vehicles, and the eruption of Mount Pinatubo raising river beds and flooding sections of the highway, the trip took six hours. Compensating for the inconvenience was the spectacular scenery on the stretches of open road—on one side, green mountain ranges and on the other, a breathtaking view of the South China Sea. For miles, a tall white cross stood guard over the landscape, a monument to one of the greatest battles of World War II between the Japanese and the Philippine and U.S. forces under the command of General Douglas MacArthur.

The Bataan and Palawan camps contrasted sharply in all important respects: in size, in the national origins of the refugee population, in function, in the services provided, and in the level of institutionalization. At Bataan, refugees arrived and left by the busload several times a week, giving a quicksilver quality to life at the PRPC: in the first ten years of its existence, it had hosted and sent 310,725 refugees on their way to resettlement.

After the 1979 Geneva Convention, which sought to address the problems posed by the growing numbers of forced migrants from Vietnam, Laos, and Cambodia, the Philippine Refugee Processing Camp was constructed in 1980 on a plateau between the Bataan mountains and the South China Sea, a site provided by the Philippine government. An administrative staff was given charge of basic services, security arrangements, the procurement of

Freedom Plaza in the Philippine Refugee Processing Center in Bataan, where boats in which refugees arrived from Vietnam are memorialized, 1991

food for the refugees, and other day-to-day management matters. As in Palawan, UNHCR had oversight of the camp as a whole. Voluntary agencies provided specific services, ran a wide range of programs, and were funded from a variety of local and international sources.

If Palawan as camp of first asylum was a point of entry into the refugee world, Bataan as processing camp was a point of departure, a final stop on the way to resettlement. If Palawan with its dust roads and nipa-and-bamboo structures exuded a rural village atmosphere, PRPC was a town community with a high degree of institutionalization and a population averaging 15,000 to 19,000 at any given moment—larger than that of Morong, the nearest town a few kilometers away. In its 350 hectares (about 864 acres or 1.35 square miles) were an administration building, a post office, a hospital, a mental health clinic, schoolhouses, libraries, audiovisual centers, two fairly large markets, a guest house, office buildings, staff houses, churches, pagodas, a house of detention ("monkey house"), the

Refugee billets in the PRPC, Bataan, 1991

billets that housed the refugees, and eating establishments that ranged from stalls in the markets to a mess hall and a fast-food kiosk to a Vietnamese restaurant that charged Manila prices.[1] These structures were made of a variety of materials: concrete, cement blocks, corrugated tin, and wood. The major streets were paved and had names like UN Avenue. There was a central square called Freedom Plaza, where boats that had been used to escape were enshrined as memorials and where people gathered for all kinds of activities.

Refugee quarters were clustered in neighborhoods that consisted of long barrackslike living quarters divided into ten or more billets, each consisting of two levels with sleeping space for eight that could accommodate more when the refugee population swelled to above normal. Each billet was approximately ten feet by 16 feet, with a door at each end, one opening to an outdoor space for common activities like sports, and socializing, the other leading to the billet's cooking area. A numbering system gave the refugees an "address": 702-C, for instance, meant neighborhood 7, building 2, billet C. During my first visit, there were nine neighborhoods. By 1988, the number had increased to ten, and in 1991, more quarters were in construction. Knudsen calculated at one point that each refugee was allotted four square meters of living space (1983:5).

Until the late 1980s, two neighborhoods designated Phase I and Phase II flanked the central plaza. With the enactment of the Homecoming Act of 1987 and the resulting influx of Amerasians and their relatives into the PRPC directly from Vietnam, construction began on a Phase III. By 1991, a new facility called Refugee Transit Center housed those who had been "screened in" through the Comprehensive Plan of Action (CPA) but had not yet found a country that would take them in, and those who were waiting for transport to their country of resettlement. Other buildings were still in construction.[2]

Nonrefugee accommodations varied from the dormitory-like or shared housing arrangements occupied by most of the Philippine staff to single-family housing provided by the Philippine government and governments that had personnel in camp.

The People and the Program

As in Palawan, roughly the same three categories of actors interacted daily in camp: the refugees, the Philippine staff, and the international contingent. But the dynamics were made far more complex by the large number of individuals and subcategories created both by receiving countries and by the refugees themselves. The refugees, who at the peak of the exodus numbered approximately 17,000, were Cambodian, Laotian, and Vietnamese. During my 1988 visit, they numbered 13,697, of whom close to 75 percent were Vietnamese. Although a small number of asylum seekers had landed on the shores below the Bataan camp, most of the refugee population had come from other camps of first asylum in Thailand, Malaysia, Hong Kong, Indonesia, and Palawan. As the refugee flow matured, an increasing number came directly from Vietnam through the Orderly Departure Program.[3] In 1988, they comprised approximately 2,700 or close to 20 percent of the Vietnamese population. By the time of my third visit in 1991, the Amerasians were a segment large enough to effect changes in the educational, and other service programs offered by the camp.

The Philippine personnel worked for the camp administration as staff, as security officers, postal employees, or blue-collar workers, for voluntary agencies under contract by other government entities such as the U.S. State Department, or for individuals or families as domestic workers or hired help.

Of the at least fifteen voluntary agencies, the most prominent were the International Catholic Migration Commission (ICMC, which in 1989 employed some 1,300, roughly half of whom were teachers, mostly Filipino), the Intergovernmental Committee for Migration, and the Joint Voluntary Agency. While most of these agencies were funded by the United States, other governments and organizations were repre- sented as well. For example, the mental health clinic was supported with funds and personnel by the Norwegian government, the medical tech- nology services by Japan, and the Red Cross and UNHCR staff by a va- riety of countries.

The PRPC, specifically intended to serve resettlement rather than asy- lum purposes, was highly didactic in function. Its programs, particularly the educational ones, were geared toward preparing refugees for life in the United States.[4] Camp life for the refugees, therefore, was built around what was called the "cycle": for those between the ages of seventeen and fifty-five, six months of English-as-a-second-language instruction, four hours and forty-five minutes a day, four days a week; cultural orientation twice weekly; work orientation six days a week; and two hours a day of work credit activities as volunteer assistant teachers, interpreters, clerical help, maintenance workers, and so forth. Those eleven and a half to six- teen years of age attended PASS, or Preparation for American Secondary Schools, which simulated U.S. school curricula and activities.

To accommodate the constant influx of refugees, a new cycle began about once a month and, according to *The ICMC Refugee Training Pro- gram* (1989), as many as six cycles of classes might be going on at any one time, serving a total of 8,000 to 12,000 students. Upon "graduation," un- less an unforeseen problem developed, refugees expected to be on their way to their country of resettlement.[5]

The linkage between completion of the cycle and the end of life as a refugee or the beginning of resettlement is best symbolized by the Flight List or Departure List posted in the administration building. It contained the departure dates and the names of people who should be ready to leave for resettlement within forty-eight hours. Refugees who had completed the cycle visited the list daily, sometimes more frequently, as though doing so would hasten their posting. The list was on everyone's mind, a major topic of conversation, eliciting jubilation when one's name finally appeared, or tortured speculation when it did not.

The Music

During the day, when the heat required windows and doors to be wide open, the sounds of music met heavy competition from the roar of motor vehicles, machines that maintained the grounds, and the occasional piece of heavy equipment at work on construction. One caught snatches of taped, broadcast, or live Vietnamese, Cambodian, Lao, Philippine, or Western music emanating from classrooms or billets, and boy scout and girl scout songs in the plaza or in one of several open public spaces. But in the evening, when the streets belonged to pedestrians and relative quiet reigned, when refugees were either in their billets or engaged in leisurely activities around camp, and when other camp personnel had either returned to town or gone home for the day, the camp's musical life came into its own.

From the billets emanated the sounds of Vietnamese music, as refugees sang, played musical instruments, or listened to audio cassettes. As in Palawan, this repertory was in the distinctively Vietnamese musical idiom as well as in the Western idiom marked by Vietnamese texts. A wide variety of popular music, U.S. and Philippine, came from the radios. Elsewhere in camp, one might hear Vietnamese and Philippine church choirs in rehearsal, Buddhist ritual music from the pagoda, Vietnamese folk music as children rehearsed for some celebration. On any given evening, one might catch the sounds of a rock band, a solitary singer or instrumentalist, some small-group music making in Freedom Plaza. Very occasionally, one heard items from the Western European art music tradition played live or in recorded form coming from the billets or the staff houses. The relatively infrequent occurrence of Lao and Cambodian music reflected camp demographics: in 1988, these groups comprised some 25 percent of the 13,697 refugees at the PRPC. By 1991, 90 percent to 95 percent of the refugee population were Vietnamese and only a "few hundred" were Lao and Cambodian (PRPC "Fact Sheet" 1991). As in Palawan, therefore, the most frequently heard musical idiom was Western.

These observations belie the complexity of musical life at the PRPC, which begins to emerge in its fullness only with a closer look at the behavior, motivations, and choices of individuals and groups. They shaped a musical life pervaded by a sense of temporariness heavily overlain by expectations of impending departure. A Vietnamese paterfamilias, for instance, who, like many of his cohorts, took his mission to be the conservation of pre-communist Vietnamese culture, had his children instructed in traditional Vietnamese music as part of his preparation for leaving Vietnam. Once in Bataan, he had their performances videotaped and documented so that the tapes could be deposited in the camp's Instructional Media Center. He became known among both the refugees and the volags for the zeal—others called it snobbery—with which he tried to maintain the "purity" of traditional practice, constantly correcting his children and monitoring or restricting their contacts with other refugees.

Others took the opposite tack, looking toward the West as they prepared to begin life anew. Many, particularly those from cities, said that an important part of their planning to leave was to try to learn English secretly. One told me that after having been denied entry into the university because he was Catholic, he earned his living giving private English lessons. In camp, he sang Vietnamese folk and urban popular songs daily, with and for Filipino and Vietnamese friends, and, given the smallest opportunity, talked long and affectionately about the musical life he had known in Vietnam.[6] But he was eager to learn the most current popular songs in the United States. He showed me a notebook that he had begun to keep in Bataan. In it, he had painstakingly written the text of each song he remembered from Vietnam—he said it was his way of reliving his old life—as well as each new American song addition to his repertory, practicing the pronunciation of unfamiliar English words as he went along.

Another refugee who had walked to Cambodia and from there escaped by boat brought with him a book of cải lương songs that he had carefully collected over twenty-five years. Leafing through its pages, deciding on what to sing for me, he handled the book as though it were a sacred object.

Most refugees were unselfconscious musical culture carriers who sang their songs and played their music as part of daily existence. Personal preference for a genre or for items within it determined what they performed. But occasionally the identity of a performer and of his music as Vietnamese became primary considerations.

One such moment came when a very well-known Vietnamese singer, Duy Khanh, and a versatile Vietnamese musician, Cao Phi Long, who played trumpet, Western flute, accordion, and electric keyboard, arrived in the PRPC in 1988. During their stay, the two livened the musical scene. Cao Phi Long collaborated with Duy Khanh and helped to arrange public performances; Duy Khanh not only performed for the refugees but attracted Vietnamese celebrities from as far away as California. Agents resident in the United States pressed him to sign performing or recording contracts, the Voice of America wanted to feature him in a program, and Nam Tran, a TV personality from Orange County, California, who was also well-known to the overseas Vietnamese community, reportedly came to camp to interview him. There was talk of bringing another famous singer, Hoang Oanh, from the States so that the two could give joint performances in Bataan and Palawan.

Because Duy Khanh's performances attracted campwide audiences, because his repertory straddled Vietnamese music in the Western as well as in the historically Vietnamese idiom, and because his celebrity status forced camp staff to take notice, the issue of Vietnamese musical identity came in for closer examination. For the Westerners and non-Vietnamese it was a question of whether music in the Western musical idiom could be Vietnamese music. As in Palawan they assumed almost automatically that it could not be; a member of the international community in the PRPC called it "elevator music to the rhythm of cha-cha-cha." But while Duy Khanh's performances may not have been a sufficient corrective, they offered an alternative, hard to ignore, though fleeting affirmation of the Vietnameseness of this repertoire by a well-known and respected Vietnamese musician.

The ad hoc nature of these occasions was underscored when Duy Khanh's last performance in Bataan never happened because the guitarist got on the departure list and left on the usual short notice. Cao Phi Long assured me that the concert would go on, that a guitarist was likely to come along—but almost as suddenly, Cao Phi Long and Duy Khanh themselves had to leave before the concert's date.

Musical life in camp was affected not only by who came but by what the arrivals brought with them. The variety of sounds that the Vietnamese in the PRPC could summon benefited considerably from the influx of ODPs that began in the late 1980s. This population, which departed Vietnam by plane and grew to outnumber the former boat people in Bataan by the early 1990s, brought musical instruments with them—even bulky ones like electric keyboards and the *đàn tranh*, a sixteen- or seventeen-string zither unobtainable in the Philippines. (In light of the strict baggage allowance given ODPs flown in from Vietnam or to refugees flown out to resettlement countries, what they took along indicated the value they assigned to those objects.)

The impact on the musical repertory in camp was unmistakable. In 1988, my informants and I could not find a đàn tranh in camp even with the help of the office of the Processing Community Organization and Social Services (PROCOSS), which performed clearinghouse and liaison functions between the camp administration and the refugees. By 1991, these instruments had become relatively easy to find. More striking, the arrival of keyboards, saxophones, and other Western instruments meant that the Vietnamese could play rock and other Western-derived popular forms with each other instead of depending on the highly unlikely possibility that they would be asked to play with local Filipino groups.

These musical activities and events were emblematic both of the richness and the seeming arbitrariness of musical life at the PRPC—an arbitrariness that can be made coherent only when placed in context.

PRPC as Context for Musical Life

Bataan is a long way from Palawan not only in terms of physical distance, size, and refugee expectations, but also in terms of a social complexity exacerbated by greater flux. Bataan's cycle, a prescribed period of preparation for resettlement now measurable in days and months, replaced the indeterminate period of hoping and waiting that suffused life in Palawan. Incentives for exploring individual or group initiatives made expedient in Palawan therefore lost much of their adaptive value in Bataan. The refugees showed a pronounced disinterest in getting involved in aspects of PRPC life beyond those requisite for their release or those that they chose to respond to in their own terms. For the refugees, Bataan was no more than a way station, not even a temporary residence as Palawan had been, a turn not so much away from Vietnam as toward the United States. Palawan's active participation in shaping communal life thus gave way to Bataan's unquestioning acceptance of the routines and procedures imposed from outside.[7]

The regularities imposed by the refugees' daily schedule promoted a strong impression of orderliness. At the same time, strong contrasts punctuated the regularities. From lights out at 9:00 P.M. and the stillness imposed by curfew, (9:30 for refugees, 11:00 for the whole camp), the activity that erupted with sunrise was startling. At 6:00 each morning the camp was roused by the sound of numerous five-passenger motorized tricycles revving up noisily as people took advantage of cooler morning temperatures to get their chores done. Soon afterward came the rumbling of buses ferrying refugees from one neighborhood to another to attend classes. During the day, buses loaded with refugees bound for Manila to catch their flight to resettlement or to participate in some activity contributed to the hubbub. Delivery trucks, staff vehicles, and all manner of transport brought in visitors or workers who commuted from their homes outside camp.

In addition to scheduled activities, daily chores included marketing, getting one's share of the distributed food, cooking, and housekeeping. From noon to 2:00, the hottest part of the day, everyone went back to their billets for lunch. Many devoted this period to siesta, to hobbies like jewelry making, or to other activities like giving private Vietnamese, Lao, or Cambodian language instruction. Toward evening, when the regimen was over, refugees and staff took walks and socialized around camp.

Even without a calendar, one could easily distinguish the weekend from weekdays. The bustle of the work week came to an almost abrupt halt or changed in character as many of the camp personnel left the PRPC for the weekend. The refugees seemed transformed, dressed up, some in *áo dài* (the Vietnamese tunic over loose, flowing pants), to go to church or to walk around camp taking pictures. Cows wandered in to graze on the administration building grounds.

The maintenance of this apparent order was remarkable in light of the ongoing changes in the camp population and in policy decisions—local, national, and international. These affected the push and pull of group relations, which were magnified, minimized, or distorted by bureaucratization, undulating funding levels, and overlapping lines of authority.[8] The end result at the PRPC was an intricate mix of goodwill and genuinely warm relations on the level of direct and personal interactions. On the intermediate level, between individual interactions and those with the upper reaches of the hierarchy, the level represented by PROCOSS and the InterNeighborhood Council (INC), which consisted of neighborhood leaders, there was a palpable climate of cooperation. But on a more abstract

The administration building at the PRPC, 1991. Cows graze on the grounds during weekends.

bureaucratic level, serious tensions arose from what Tollefson calls a "hierarchy of nationality" fomenting a "hierarchy of petty privilege" (1989:95–97). The power and wealth of participating nations translated into discrepancies among camp personnel in such things as salary scale, health leaves, housing and transportation privileges, and facilities. Comparisons were inevitable, particularly because the physical structures as well as the behavioral evidence and effects of asymmetrical relations confronted everyone everyday. The effects on relationships all around were expressed by a Filipino teacher who said that one would have to try and ignore these things if one did not wish to go around "with a heavy heart."

The international personnel had their own disappointments. Many had come to work exclusively or principally with refugees—one of the supervisors spoke of visions of saffron robes and temple bells—and found themselves working many hours a day with Filipinos.

Some in staff or administrative positions saw the refugees as clients to be given the necessary services, and while there were doubtless those who acted out of idealistic humanitarian motives, a patronizing attitude was never hard to find.

In the terrace like area in the guest house, which attracted staff, visitors, and refugees for drinks, snacks, and socializing at the end of the workday, for instance, refugees, Filipinos, and Westerners clustered at separate tables as though invisible lines divided the groups.

I inadvertently stumbled into this differentiated world one afternoon when, shortly after I began fieldwork, I found myself in conversation with a visiting UNHCR officer, an American. He had long experience living in the Far East, was educated in a university not far from mine, and shared many of my interests. It was perhaps our animated conversation that pulled into our circle first a Norwegian doctor and then an Indian visitor. As people began to come in, our little culturally unmarked group, encouraged some Filipino friends to join us. Came dinnertime and the American suggested that we all go to the Vietnamese restaurant. Awkwardness crept in as it became evident that what had started out as a casual encounter was turning into a more clearly defined social form. Filipino members of the group begged off, but the friend whose living quarters I shared came along. Dinner at the restaurant was followed by dessert at the doctor's house, luxurious by local standards and, the doctor noted, paid for by the Norwegian government.

On the way to our quarters just a few steps away, my friend, who held a responsible position in the administration, remarked that this had been a most unusual evening with a most unusual group of people. Despite having been neighbors for a long time, despite being social and professional equals, each in her own sphere, and despite their both being socially adept and gracious, she and the Norwegian lady had never socialized. PRPC's highly complex social and bureaucratic structure, tied to and controlled by local, national, and international bodies, had conditioned relations between the various groups in camp.

Among the refugees, a number of criteria for differentiation and stratification existed, some of them pre-exodus in provenance and already evident in Palawan. Other grounds for differentiation and potential conflict were postexodus, specific to camps like the PRPC. Boat people distinguished themselves from the ODPs and vice versa.[9] Boat People had experienced untold hardships and survived; many took pride in their stamina and resourcefulness. The ODPs were, by implication, soft. But these were often people who had the resources, the know-how, and the connections to push their papers through the bureaucracies that governed ODP procedures. The early ODP population also contained more urbanites, who had easier access to those bureaucracies. The combination of resources and an urban way of life underscored the contrasts between most ODPs and boat people of rural origin. When, in addition, the personal effects that ODPs were able to bring with them gave evidence of that contrast in the narrow confines of the billets, the lines that separated ODPs and boat people gained in definition.

From the standpoint of camp personnel, ODPs on the whole were healthier psychologically, having been spared the hazards and traumas of escape. They were more likely to have kept their families intact. Frank DiGiacomo, a member of ICMC's teaching and supervisory staff, explained the contrasts from another perspective: "ODPs are a positive, positive force here because they have not learned to behave like refugees. A successful refugee learns strategies for how to behave to get through those awful camps. You learn what the boss wants and that's what you do. . . . refugees quickly become institutionalized and there are big problems of self-esteem and self-sufficiency because self-sufficiency has been discouraged for so many years. But the ODPs, despite the fact that they have taken a great deal of grief from the Vietnamese government . . . have not been shredded by that institutionalization. . . . This is a good thing for the land and boat people to see again"(interview, July 20, 1988).

Other observers, however, were more in accord with the boat people's perceptions. Hitchcox cites a number of sources (Eitinger and Schwarz 1981; Furnham and Bochner 1986; and Keller 1975) who support the view that "refugees are more politically committed and therefore more highly motivated than other migrants." Eitinger is quoted as stating, "A person who has just escaped a really dangerous life-threatening situation in his own country of origin will more easily and often gladly cope with all the problems of adjustment in his new surroundings, considering them unimportant trivialities" (Hitchcox 1990:251). Dr. Lulu Pablo of the Community and Family Services International, who had worked for eight years in the camp's mental health clinic, admired the boat people and particularly the unaccompanied minors. She viewed them as survivors; many, deeply aware that they have been chosen by the family to be helped to escape, have a great sense of responsibility to help their family.

Whichever of these generalizations proved accurate, the differentiations applied and were perceived as important diacritica by both the Vietnamese and the service providers as they established relations with each other. These perceptions of difference colored the way individuals and groups related to each other. But as in Palawan, the refugees' part in maintaining the social equilibrium was made easier by the high cost of doing otherwise: forfeiting a resettlement already within reach.[10] Despite the many grounds for conflict, therefore, the predictable duration of the refugees' stay in camp and the detachment it made possible acted as strong forces in favor of playing by the rules.

But the PRPC's social order was always a work in progress, continually tested by political, economic, and demographic changes. Both its vulnerability and its strength were revealed by the arrival of the Amerasians shortly after the enactment of the Homecoming Act of 1987. (Amerasians are "born of American fathers and Vietnamese mothers during the Vietnamese war" [Felsman and Felsman 1986:57], at that time ranging in age from seventeen to thirty.) By 1991, most of the camp's population consisted of the Amerasians and their relatives; the rest were ODPs and screened-in refugees from camps of first asylum.

The new majority, although technically refugees (as defined by U.S. government legislation), had not experienced a hazardous escape, or life in a camp of first asylum with an uncertain resettlement outcome. The Amerasians, in most cases, had not been fully integrated into Vietnamese society, partly because of the stigma of suspected illegitimacy and fear on the part of the general Vietnamese population of being associated with the Amerasians' American fathers, and partly because many Amerasians had Caucasian or African American phenotypical features that set them apart. Most, therefore, arrived in the PRPC with at least a three-year deficit in schooling, little if any knowledge of English, and the consequences of having lived a fatherless and marginal existence in a society where family ties are central to one's identity. Many came with relatives they barely knew, leaving behind in Vietnam those who had actually raised or sheltered them, often their grandparents, because they could not or did not wish to leave.[11]

At the same time, the Amerasians came with a newfound sense of power. Through them their relatives had found a way to the United States. They were aware that facilities and programs had been set up in camp especially for them. Unlike the other Vietnamese in camp who, to attain the status of refugee and to avoid repatriation, had to undergo the screening process mandated by the UNHCR's Comprehensive Plan of Action, the Amerasians left Vietnam with their entry into the United States assured. This dramatic change in their circumstances proved highly disorienting socially and psychologically. It also underscored their difference from the rest of the Vietnamese in camp. They had not been participants in Vietnam's political life, had little or no experience of a precommunist Vietnam, of a free society, and had no deep sense of allegiance to any government. Their experience of migration, therefore, the reasons for their being in camp, were radically different from those who had to justify leaving by invoking political ideology.

In that they, too, did not have to justify leaving Vietnam in the same terms as the refugees before them, the relatives who accompanied the Amerasians differed from the majority of the earlier ODPs in camp. Not only did they not have to undergo the hazards that marked the boat people's journey; neither did they need to use wealth or suffer the long, arduous, and often punishing procedures that qualifying for ODP involved.

Thus, the differences in the characteristics of the camp population before and after the enactment of the Homecoming Act, and the differential effects of policies like the Comprehensive Plan of Action, created corresponding changes in the dynamics among the refugees, and between them and the camp personnel.

Public and Localized Music Making

While musical life in Palawan was created in an environment that, as safe haven, could be regarded as a destination, musical life in Bataan was a response to this camp as a way station meant to prepare people for quick and certain departure. No account of musical life as PRPC-specific can make sense without recognition of this central fact.

As in Palawan public music making in the PRPC referred to those events known to be occurring by the general public and accessible to all: music in churches and pagodas, the musical activities that institutions sponsored or supported, and musical events that were part of the camp's programs and were intended for campwide involvement.

Palawan's private music making, however, had no conceptual counterpart in the PRPC. Music performed by refugees in the privacy of the billets or on the periphery of camp was virtually impossible to observe systematically, given the unpredictability of its occurrence, the size of the camp, the distribution of space, and the turnover of the population. The category that best contrasts with public music making I labeled localized music making, defined by the size of the space within which the music took place, the reach of its sound (no amplifiers), the size of the group participating, and a certain level of compatibility among the participants that drew them to interact in the first place.

Localized music events took place in private, public, or semi-public spaces like the small squares in front of neighborhood billets, in principle open to all but, in practice, extensions of private space, as for instance, when refugees slung hammocks there for their noon siesta. Localized music making, even when planned, was casual and marked by an absence of protocol-governed behavior. All the conditions surrounding localized music making encouraged spontaneity and ease of communication.

Public music making, with its campwide scope and institutional nature, and localized music making, with its individual or small-group initiatives, combine to provide a fairly balanced view of the small-scale and large-scale social pressures that shape Vietnamese life in the PRPC.

For a camp with the cultural diversity and the size of the PRPC, events open to all about which information was to be disseminated campwide required permission and support, if not direct sponsorship, from the camp administration or the established institutions within it. Only these could provide the space, security arrangements, audio and other equipment, and, if needed, dispensation from curfew that these events called for. In this respect, public musical events in the PRPC were analogous to those in Palawan but with an important difference. Whereas public music making in Palawan was built on common sentiments and was a manifestation of a sense of community, public music making in Bataan pulled disparate groups together; it represented an aspiration for the coherence Palawan already had.

Three public music making events, each supported by a different kind of institution, serve as examples: the song contest, the Vietnamese Roman Catholic mass, and Vietnamese Buddhist ritual worship.

Arranged by PROCOSS through the InterNeighborhood Council, the song contest, according to Josie Matol, the PROCOSS officer-in-charge

The Catholic church in the PRPC, 1991

during both my 1988 and 1991 visits, had the following objectives: (1) to identify and showcase talent among the refugees; (2) to promote cama-raderie among the various groups; and (3) to help develop English skills (texts of the songs had to be in English.) Richard Engelhart, field repre-sentative of UNHCR, which funded these activities, said that the contest sponsors' stated intent was to help refugees adjust to life in resettlement countries.

In the summer of 1988, sixteen contestants from the Cambodian, Lao-tian, and Vietnamese groups competed. The first round eliminated seven; of the six finalists, three, all Vietnamese, won the top prizes. All the judges were camp personnel or were invited by the sponsors; none were from the refugee population, although the input of an estimated 2,000 refugees in the audience during the final round was apparent through their applause and reactions to the contestants. All performers presented U.S. songs from the 1960s and 1970s. The winners sang "Love Story" (first prize), "Yesterday Once More" (second prize), and "The Great Pretender" (third prize).[12] The first two prizes were won by women.

The 1988 contest became a major undertaking for all concerned. Refugees who knew English were sought out by potential participants and asked to help with pronunciation and interpretation. Neighborhood residents banded together to provide accompaniment for "their" contestants. People with stage experience were recruited to coach participants on stage behavior. Perhaps even beyond the expectations of the contest organizers, a huge infusion of Western influence—in music, language, and forms of social behavior—effectively found its way into refugee camp life and reinforced the hegemony of the Western musical idiom by publicly showcasing and rewarding its users.

The Vietnamese Roman Catholic mass could count on the services of at least two choirs. Like the Catholics in Vietnam, those in the PRPC saw themselves as part of the larger Catholic hierarchy whose boundaries transcended those of the locality and extended ultimately to Rome. At the PRPC, they worshiped in a church and in a smaller chapel used by the camp community at large. Adaptations to Vietnamese worship, particularly in the form of the Vietnamese-language mass into which some features of Buddhist ritual had been incorporated, were not intended to exclude non-Vietnamese Catholics, who did attend this mass.[13]

In the mid- to late 1980s, there were as many as three Vietnamese church choirs: a children's choir for what the Vietnamese priest, Father Tri, called a "secularized and casual" children's mass; a youth choir consisting of male and female members in their teens; and a smaller mixed choir consisting of people with some musical training who, in general, could read Western notation. The choirs sang with electric organ accompaniment complemented by whatever other instruments were available—in 1988, a violin; in 1991, a Vietnamese bamboo flute (sáo) and a clarinet.

Besides the institutional structure that lent stability to these choirs, the structure of the Catholic mass governed what was to be sung when and by whom. While the choir sang during the offertory, the sanctus, and the communion, the congregation chanted prayers in Vietnamese before, at certain points during, and after mass. Helping maintain continuity through the changes in choir personnel was a collection of mimeographed scores (see Figure 1) brought from Vietnam by refugees or contributed by Paris's longstanding Vietnamese community. Some of these scores offered only a one-voice melody; others, more elaborate, included

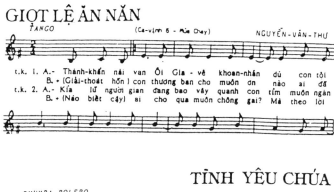

FIGURE 1. Samples of religious songs sung in the Catholic mass. Note the use of dance rhythms for tempo indications.

soprano, alto, tenor, and bass parts and đàn tranh, sáo, *song lang* (foot clapper), and organ accompaniment.

All the texts were in Vietnamese, including those to adaptations of works by G. F. Händel and J. S. Bach, and most of the compositions were by Vietnamese. The influence of the Western art music tradition was much in evidence, particularly in the choral conducting and in the harmonic and contrapuntal elements, but the influence of Western popular music was unmistakable in the rhythms. Where tempo indications are conventionally to be found in the score, such terms as "valse" and "slow rock" appeared. Often, the rhythmic patterns used were the prerogative of the organist, whose choices leaned strongly toward slow rumba (or "bolero").

A third public music-making event was the Buddhist ritual worship. At the PRPC, the Vietnamese Buddhist presence was signaled by an imposing pagoda, distinctive in its architecture, with grounds that had accommodations for Buddhist monks, and landscaped sections that invited meditation. In contrast to the larger Catholic hierarchy within which Vietnamese designed their own activities, the Vietnamese Buddhists and their pagodas had a considerable measure of autonomy. Dramatically politicized during the Vietnam War (see Karnow 1983), Vietnamese Buddhism was also particularized as specifically Vietnamese. I was told that the chants I was hearing in the pagoda were the very ones being heard in the pagodas in Saigon. I, of course, could not verify this, but it brought back the words of a Vietnamese who had resettled in Jersey City, New Jersey: "Around here, there is a Chinese pagoda and there is a Japanese pagoda, but we have our own."

The wide range of musical types represented in these three distinct institutional contexts was a measure not only of the Vietnamese willingness to adapt and of the adaptive behaviors at their command but also of their understanding of what was expected at each type of public event. The song contest, understood to be a UNHCR-PRPC initiative as well as a competition between individual singers, elicited a Western repertory of songs and behaviors that were intended to win not only the sponsors' approval but also a personal prize. The Catholic mass, a global practice adapted to the needs of the Vietnamese congregation at the PRPC, elicited a repertory that ranged from the strictly Vietnamese congregational chanting of prayers, to the Western European musical tradition represented by Händel and Bach, to the secular popular rhythms of Latin

Photograph taken in 1987 of the inscription on the wall of the Vietnamese Buddhist Temple, PRPC: "You, O Refugee will change/America, Just as it will/Change you./But do not fear. Know/Yourself. And where you/Are from. Take care, how-/Ever, That the change is for the better and not/For the Worse./East is least/West is best./Is that so?/No, no, no!!"

music, all of them identified by the Vietnamese as Vietnamese. The Vietnamese Buddhist ritual music was as Vietnamese as the song contest repertory was American. Clearly, choices had been deliberately made out of a wide range of options ready to hand to meet institutional expectations while serving group and individual interests as well.

In contrast to such public music events, localized music making, despite its richness, was elusive: one caught it whenever and wherever one could, with no assurance that it would happen again in the same place with the same individuals. Yet it was the most direct way of getting at personal musical expressions, the closest one could get to an unalloyed, unmediated manifestation of music in everyday life. And, as Clifford Geertz has pointed out, "meaning is use, or more carefully, arises from use, and it is by tracing out such uses as exhaustively as we are accustomed to . . .

that we are going to be able to find out anything general about them. . . . This is . . . a plea for . . . turning the analytic powers of semiotic theory . . . away from an investigation of signs in abstraction toward an investigation of them in their natural habitat—the common world in which men look, name, listen, and make" (1983:119).

To get a sampling of that "common world" I supplemented visits to the billets and to places where Vietnamese tended to congregate by arranging opportunities where music making might take place and then sitting back to see if anything would happen. I set these up wherever friends and I could find space that would accommodate a group of from three to five without creating too much of a disturbance or disrupting other people's activities—my accommodations when the weekend afforded some space, rooms in the camp's facilities when they were not in use, or a room at the guest house where we could share some snacks and chat. I hoped that by inviting people whom I knew liked to make music and by allowing them to invite their friends, I would come as close as possible to venues that had become familiar to the refugees at the PRPC—the informal encounters in their neighborhoods, the moments when they chose to make music by themselves or with others.

On these occasions, the refugees performed whatever they wanted whenever they felt moved to do so. People stopped and started, reminisced, chatted, consulted with each other as they tried to recapture songs momentarily forgotten, or sang songs straight through one after the other. In the course of my visits to the PRPC, thirty-one individuals consented to be tape recorded and subsequently interviewed. Many of the participants at these get-togethers came with friends or acquaintances; some were meeting for the first time, but the degree to which they shared a common repertoire was notable. For reasons I did not come to appreciate fully until I did the Orange County fieldwork, many items were so often repeated by different performers that I ended up with a total corpus of not more than sixty-nine discrete items.[14] `

Classificatory Ideas

In the course of conversations about the music they were singing, the participants suggested operative terms and criteria for differentiatng categories of music that they found relevant or significant in the camp context.[15]

As in Palawan, the name of the genre or type—cải lương, vọng cổ, quan họ (a responsive vocal form), tân nhạc (Westernized popular music), and so on—was seldom offered. More frequently, music makers made distinctions in terms of *traditional, popular,* and *folk music,* which, despite their specifically Vietnamese application, did not escape the confusion that these terms create when used in a more general ethnomusicological sense.[16] Predictably, arguments about the application of the terms were inconclusive, but the frequency with which the terms were used indicated that the inconclusiveness could not be taken to mean irrelevance. The consensus among participants, with some vọng cổ performers dissenting, was that traditional music is for the elite or for the intelligentsia—one can learn it in the conservatory—while cải lương, of which vọng cổ is a part, is close to a vernacular and is not a prestigious form. As one of the Vietnamese told me on July 22, 1998, "Cải lương can be heard everyday in Vietnam. Just turn on the radio and you can hear it. But traditional music is heard only on special occasions, and popular music, everyday, but in public only when sanctioned by the government. Otherwise you must do it very quietly or you can be put in re-education camp."

To bolster her contention, this Vietnamese participant in the discussions said that even in the PRPC, you can hear popular music and folk music just about everywhere, but traditional music is a rarity. She cited an event in one of the neighborhoods—extraordinary because traditional music as ensemble performance (nhạc tài tử, South Vietnamese form of chamber music in this case) requires the right mix of musicians and instruments. But in a discussion on August 7, 1988, one musician contradicted the conception of traditional music as music for the intelligentsia: "traditional music is the tears of the people to express their heart."

Enjoying the strongest consensus was the identification of folk songs, while the identification of popular Vietnamese music proved more problematic. Some items such as songs by Pham Duy resisted categorization; his "Vietnam, Vietnam," for example, was simply called *patriotic song.* Many items were identified as love songs on the basis of their texts, even when their musical features could yield to identification as Western or Westernized popular music in typical two-part or three-part song form.[17] But despite the strong overlap in musical features between "Vietnamese popular" and Western popular music, the Vietnamese were never ambivalent about distinguishing one from the other. The language of the text superseded melodic content and other formal musical features as determinant of the music's identity as Vietnamese. When, for example, Vietnamese texts replaced the English texts in familiar items from Händel's "Messiah," these items were almost invariably identified as Vietnamese.

Musical distinctions were also drawn according to the major regions of Vietnam with which the music is associated: north, central, and south. Sometimes the regional designations refer to provenance, sometimes to characteristic musical features. Perhaps because vocal music predominated in the PRPC, regional terms were often used to describe what they called "voice," as in: "He [or she] sings with a northern [or central or southern Vietnamese] voice," or "I can only sing with a northern voice; I cannot sing with a southern voice."

From the usage and the illustrations, the term *voice* meant a combination of features that included stylistic elements such as the use of ornamentation, regional linguistic accent, and a manner of singing for which "soft" was constantly used to describe a marked and highly desirable attribute. This feature was most closely associated with music from Central Vietnam, especially Huế. It referred not to volume but to the use of ornamentation in a manner and with such subtlety that it "softened" the melodic line.

Questions about regional distinctions for folk music prompted one singer to say with a touch of petulance, "Folk songs are Vietnamese and not from north or south."

Particularly before 1988 when the majority of the camp population were boat people, nothing engaged the Vietnamese more powerfully or aroused passions more readily than the criteria for what was to be admitted into their musical life. "Before 1975" and "after 1975" permeated the refugees' speech, not only as marker of historical or autobiographical events but as indicator of what constituted the truly Vietnamese in the realm of human relations, art, music, politics and social life in general.[18] These expressions were taken to be synonyms for "non-communist" and "communist," respectively, which, in the PRPC, carried particular significance: (1) for the refugees—as code words that encapsulated those events that transformed them from Vietnamese citizens to stateless refugees; (2) for the resettlement countries, particularly the United States, which favored those who "voted with their feet" and fled communist regimes; and (3) for intragroup relations among the Vietnamese in camp, for whom being a communist was tantamount to being a traitor.

Many of those who consented to being tape recorded made clear that their repertoire included only pre-1975 songs. At one of our gatherings, a young man volunteered that he knew a post-1975 song and sang it for us. I never saw him again. Discreet inquiries suggested that he was being ostracized.[19] In the early stage of my fieldwork, before the significance of these expressions had become impressed upon me, I asked a very talented singer who had a wide repertoire if he knew any post-1975 songs. He fixed me with an almost hostile glare and said that he would "never remember" such songs because they were communist.

Recognizing communist versus non-communist music, apart from the date of composition, was difficult, although Vietnamese seldom failed to make the distinction.[20] A clear indicator lay in the text and the events and places to which it refers. Government guidelines, until they became more flexible in the late 1980s, forbade texts that dealt with romantic love and related personal feelings. They recommended instead texts glorifying collectives, labor, Uncle Ho, love of country, and communist ideals. Some of the Vietnamese claimed that post-1975 music can also be recognized in the music itself (not just the text or subject matter), but upon closer questioning, they also agreed that strictly musical criteria have become difficult to apply because, as I was told on July 23, 1988, "composers from the north have began to imitate composers from the south," thereby reducing the strictly musical distinctions. Another reason, repeatedly cited in California but which I did not hear in Bataan, is that pre-1975 tunes were used by government functionaries for post-1975 texts.

In any case, my refugee friends insisted, the restrictions go against the grain because Vietnamese like to sing about the immediate and central: their loves and their losses. A singer who has sung in public professionally as well as "in secret" with other musicians, whose arrest persuaded her to flee, simply protested the situation where music "is limited by the law of those who have the power to control or correct all songs."

The composer's ideological orientation, taken as fact or imputed, can also be a criterion for inclusion in the acceptable repertoire; the work of one refugee-composer believed to be communist was rejected in the PRPC. The ambivalent reaction to the work of Trinh Cong Son, one of the best-known composers of the generation following Pham Duy, reflected the suspicion that he was communist.

Music and Ethnography: Intrinsic Relations

What emerged from these discussions were intuitive judgments—on-the-ground, moment-to-moment, everyday-life responses rather than carefully considered, theoretically or historically grounded, logically argued propositions. They were elements of musical life-in-the-making sounded against the musical life in Vietnam that the refugees were struggling to reinterpret in a new and transient context. Out of these came indications and patterns of significance that in turn led to classificatory ideas—grounds for differentiation and ordering upon which description on a more abstract level can be constructed.

What seemed to matter most—the pre- and post-1975 distinction and what to the Vietnamese was its semantic equivalent, communist/non-communist—was congruent with that part of their identity of greatest import in the PRPC: refugee. Not that the identity as Vietnamese was less dearly held; rather, in this particular context, it was not what needed most to be communicated. The refugee identity—multifaceted, complex, tough yet vulnerable under these circumstances—is what held refugees together as they descended into the centrifuge that was the refugee experience.

Vietnamese identity in these camps put three of its constituent parts into play, giving greater or lesser prominence to each according to changing conditions: (1) national identity (Vietnamese); (2) regional identity (North, Central, or South Vietnamese); and (3) situational identity (asylum seeker, refugee, ODP, or Amerasian). In Palawan, these did not need to be separately articulated. All three parts were bound together in a unitary identity that the Vietnamese shared and that the non-Vietnamese understood, within a cohesive social unit and in an environment that was consciously constructed and maintained as a Vietnamese village with the consent of all concerned. To the Vietnamese and the non-Vietnamese, the refugees' or asylees' very presence in camp signified repudiation of the communist government.

In the PRPC, however, the legal challenge to Vietnamese identity as refugees had to be met to qualify for "processing" in this camp; they were in the company not only of Laotians and Cambodians but of ODPs and Amerasians the basis of whose identity as refugees differed from those who had risked their lives to achieve it;[21] and the presence of Vietnamese from different parts of the country could trigger memories of ideological, political, and social fissures. Here there was a stronger need to make explicit those parts of their identity that meant most to them at this point in their journey. Each part had to be separately addressed not just in terms of its substance—What made one a refugee? a Vietnamese?—but in terms of the dynamics of self- and other identification: one identifies oneself not only as someone in par- ticular; one also identifies oneself *to* someone as different *from* someone else.

Of the highest priority both to the individual and to the authorities was the legality of the individual's claim to be a refugee; to the authorities, the clearest formulation of that claim, particularly before the end of the cold war, was flight from communist repression or persecution. Hence the priority and the unequivocal value assigned to the communist/ non-communist identity as it applied both to individuals and to their musical expression.

It became clear to the Vietnamese, however, that the pre- and post-1975 markers communicated little to the non-Vietnamese. When a group of refugees, former ARVN officers, brought their grievance to PRPC camp authorities after someone sang a post-1975 song in public, the authorities failed to understand the gravity of the accusation.

Similarly, regional differences had relevance only among the Viet- namese, who associated them with social, political, and aesthetic charac- teristics; hence, the value placed in the "voice" of Central Vietnamese music and the southerners' wariness toward northerners until suspicions of communist sympathy or affiliation had been dispelled.

The wider Vietnamese identity was an important marker of difference *from* the "others" in camp—primarily the Laotians and the Cambodi- ans—a message addressed *to* the camp personnel, not to the Laotians and Cambodians, who were already aware of the difference. The importance of being identified as Vietnamese by camp personnel in contradistinction to Cambodians and Laotians was indicated by the Vietnamese choice of music when the refugees were asked to bring examples of their music to class. While the Laotians and Cambodians brought what to their teachers sounded like Laotian and Cambodian music—that is, it did not sound like Western music and thus met their expectations of what these refugees' music should sound like—the Vietnamese brought music that sounded Western to Philippine and Westerners' ears.

The Vietnamese choice of music partly reflected the dominance in camp of Vietnamese popular music, with its strongly Western harmonic and Latin rhythmic features. But it may also have been a strategic choice:

the historically Vietnamese musical idiom might have been mistaken for Cambodian or Laotian by untrained Philippine or Western ears. To the Vietnamese, the greater risk was being identified with the Cambodians and Laotians; hence, the preference for that part of the Vietnamese repertory that would communicate their difference *from* Cambodians and Laotians *to* the camp personnel, even at the risk of being identified as non-Vietnamese.

The blurred boundaries between popular and traditional music were the consequence not just of the growing arbitrariness with which these boundaries are drawn almost everywhere. The ambiguities seemed to serve the Vietnamese well as they grappled with the conflicting loyalties that make forced migration such a wrenching experience.

At the Bataan stage of the Vietnamese journey, ostensible efforts to sort out the differences between traditional, folk, and popular music usually became occasions for jogging the memory into descriptions of musical life in Vietnam. It did not seem to matter much which way the discussions led; the apparently rambling conversations, the comments on these kinds of music, seemed to converge on Vietnam as home, as nation, as object of their patriotism. Borrowing between the repertories in each category is not only commonplace but proudly acknowledged by both performers and composers. I have not met a Vietnamese who did not know the name Pham Duy, Vietnam's best-known composer, and his use of folk and traditional materials in the music he created and performed— music subsequently heard all over Vietnam as a powerful rallying cry around Vietnamese nationalism during the war against the French. At the PRPC, Duy Khanh took pleasure in playing for me tapes of his performances and compositions, which combined folk, traditional, and popular materials.

Over and over again, the infusion of folk and traditional elements (arguable though the categories might be) into musical repertories became professions of nationalistic fervor and justified identification as Vietnamese. Nationalism thus became the counterpoint to those discussions of traditional, folk, and popular music, the positive side of Vietnamese refugee identification as not-communist. Borrowing from traditional and folk music to proclaim Vietnamese identity may also be the flip side of the trend in Vietnamese music at another time in its history: when, under the influence of the French, Vietnamese composers began to use features of Western popular music in their work to advance the cause of Vietnamese music, they were, as Jason Gibbs noted, "not trying to create 'popular music' but to create Vietnamese music" (1997:30). Nationalism, after all, was not just recurrent in the speech and musical behavior of Vietnamese refugees.[22] It had become integral to their existence as refugees—as people who had installed at the core of their self-definition their opposition to those whom they perceived as enemies of the "true" Vietnam.

The Amerasians provided an illuminating contrast to these images of the Vietnamese refugees' social and musical life in the PRPC. Marginalized in Vietnam for most of their lives, then suddenly sought after by relatives who hoped to accompany them to the States; refugees only technically, exiting Vietnam without the risks the classical refugees had to take; assured of admission to the United States, the Amerasians as a group had no motivation for seeking the refugee community's approbation in Bataan. They did not fear to lose what most of them never had. Apolitical and with little direct experience of pre-1975 Vietnam, they were not bound by the strictures imposed upon musical and social life by pre- and post-1975 evocations of Vietnam. All of this, for the Amerasians, diluted the power of anti-communist sentiment that bound refugees together in the shared conviction that they were all victims of an unacceptable political regime or protectors of the "true" Vietnamese culture. This contrast was made more concrete by a survey conducted in 1991 by an ICMC staff member on reactions to the possibility of a normalization of relations between the United States and Vietnam. Boat people, older people, and the military were aghast; for them the schism between democracy and communism was irreconcilable. For young Amerasians who had had no participation in Vietnamese political life, however, it was hardly an issue.

The congruence of the ethnographic and the musical thus seems evident. The classificatory ideas drew from one and lent order to the other. In both Palawan and Bataan, situational identity was paramount, hence the significance to musical life, and to social life in general, of the pre- and post-1975 and the communist/non-communist distinction. Vietnamese identity supported by nationalistic fervor was that situational identity's complement as well as its motivation. In this scheme of things, regional differences and pinning down distinctions among folk, popular, and traditional music faded in significance.

PART II

THE TRANSPLANTED LIFE

Prologue

Damn it, we have too many Orientals.

—*Congressman Bruce Talcott*

Let me say this, the Americans have done a lot for us, but whatever we think we need, they don't provide, and whatever we don't need, they provide. —*Vietnamese evacuee*

In the United States, Vietnamese refugees confronted a new set of conflicts only hinted at by the remarks that introduce this prologue. Quoted in *Time*, May 12, 1975 (p. 24), Bruce Talcott was registering his strong opposition to admitting Indochinese refugees into the States. The sentiment was reflected nationwide in a 1975 Harris poll showing that only 36 percent of Americans thought they should be admitted into the country (Kelly 1977:18; Montero 1979:4; Rose 1985:205).[1]

In different ways and for different reasons than those of the Vietnamese, Americans had been torn by a war that defined a generation. "The Southeast Asians were reminders of an unpopular war" (Haines 1985:23). "We hated losing, and still hate the Vietnamese for it. Nobody knows how much" (Leo Cawley, quoted in Isaacs 1997:103). And, apart from being reminders of the war itself, "the size, suddenness, timing and context of [the Indochinese] entry into the United States . . . complicated their reception. They arrived en masse (fully 450,000 during 1979–82 alone), and at the worst possible time: the peak of their arrival (1980) coincided with the highest domestic inflation rates in memory, followed during 1981–1983 by the most severe recession in nearly half a century, and by an accompanying socio-political climate of intensifying nativism, racism, xenophobia and 'compassion fatigue' " (Rumbaut 1989:143).

A sense of unpreparedness and of being in less than full control of the situation contributed to the country's attitude toward the refugees. No legal or social service apparatus was in place to handle the influx in other than an ad hoc manner. President Gerald Ford had created an Interagency Task Force for Indochinese Refugees on April 18, 1975, less than two weeks before the fall of Saigon. Within a few months, reception centers hurriedly set up in Guam, the Philippines, Wake Island, Thailand, and Hawaii were filled to capacity. Centers opened in the United States— Camp Pendleton in California, Indiantown Gap in Pennsylvania, Eglin Air Force Base in Florida, and Fort Chaffee in Arkansas—ceased to function by December 1975. The Indochina Migration and Refugee Assistance Act of 1975, which provided funding for moving and resettling refugees, was enacted to expire after two years; by then, it was believed, the problems that the act was meant to address would have been resolved. All this was taking place against the backdrop of the 1960s reform of immigration law, which had brought the growing Asian population to the attention of the U.S. public. The recognition of the legal status *refugee*, which was part of the Refugee Act of 1980 and guaranteed federal assistance to refugees, raised concerns that assistance given to refugees would be assistance denied to U.S. citizens (Haines 1985:10).

Within a larger historic framework, the ambivalence toward migrants, born of conflicts between U.S. idealism and pragmatism and between moral and political interests, had been working itself into the country's psyche over a long period of time. As Nathan Glazer has pointed out, "We have for a hundred years struggled with the question of 'whom shall we welcome,' to use the title of a major report on immigration policy issued in 1953 by a commission appointed by President Truman. . . . [I]t is clear we will be struggling with the question for many years to come" (1985:3).

The suddenness and seeming arbitrariness of forced migration exacerbated the national ambivalence. Responses to the arriving refugees ranged from altruism and a genuine desire to help, to hostility and violence. Confusion and ignorance were constant threats to the order of things.

The Vietnamese had been introduced to most Americans only through the media in the context of the Vietnam war. Until 1966, the Immigration and Naturalization Service had no demographic designation for Vietnamese; they were subsumed under the category "Other Asia" (Wright 1980). In 1964, there were "only 603 Vietnamese living in the United States . . . students, language teachers, diplomats . . . from South Vietnam" (Takaki 1989:448). American altruism—or self-interest, as the case may be—in the form of the costliest and most comprehensive resettlement program in the history of the United States (Montero 1979:68) was largely uninformed about the people it was supposed to help.

Without a community of settled Vietnamese to ease adaptation among the newcomers, and with a long and powerful tradition of family cohesion as their primary and often sole source of support, the Vietnamese were denied the company of their cohorts by a policy that, in the early stages of the migration, dispersed them throughout the states and thrust them into uncomprehending U.S. communities for resettlement. The full impact of this policy can only be imagined from one refugee's understated comment: "The worst thing they have done to us since we came here was to put us in different places all over the country. We depend on each other. . . . We have been through so much together."[2] The policy was guided strictly by U.S. logic: the refugees' care should be shared by the states, and placing the refugees in an overwhelmingly American environment would best help them assimilate (Kelly 1977).

It would be some time before U.S. policymakers realized that the cost of depriving the refugees of the support of kin and fellow Vietnamese was far greater than the cost of dispersal. It would be some time before it would be understood that Vietnamese efforts to adapt to U.S. society or be integrated into it could not be mandated. The instinct and the will to hang on to Vietnamese culture cannot be eradicated or replaced through institutionalized programs for "cultural orientation." These programs did not take full cognizance of the fact that "coerced homelessness" engenders in refugees a longing for home that acts as a deterrent to Americanization.[3] Refugees tend to hold on to old ways against the day of their return.

Pham Duy, Vietnam's pre-eminent composer, who had a huge following in Vietnam gained through his songs during the country's fight for independence from the French, escaped on the very last day of the Vietnamese evacuation and found himself in Fort Indiantown Gap in Pennsylvania. There, along with camp offerings of Herb Alpert and the Tijuana Brass, he sang about home, "evoking many strong emotions from his

[Vietnamese] audience" (Kelly 1977:85). Once resettled in Orange County, California, he wrote a major work, the suite *Songs of the Refugee's Road*, which gives voice to Vietnamese aspirations: "We escaped and here we've come, Bringing the soul of Viet Nam." It ends with a sentiment that is thematic: "We will return and take our stand."[4]

The dream of return also serves as coping mechanism. Vietnamese refugees arrived in the United States greatly disoriented by their flight from Vietnam, by the years most of them had spent in camps that fostered dependency and passivity (Hitchcox 1990; Kelly 1977; and Knudsen 1983), and by the long geographical and cultural distance they had traversed. Under these conditions, they had to confront two monumental crises: the "'crisis of loss'—coming to terms with the past—and the 'crisis of load'— coming to terms with the present and immediate future" (Rumbaut 1991:57), one crisis heavily encumbered by the other. The hope that these travails would be temporary and would end with the restoration of the status quo ante was a sustaining one to which many refugees clung.

Thus, while the Vietnamese staggered under the weight of their coerced homelessness, the host society too was feeling coerced and unprepared to receive them. While the Vietnamese were feeling both beholden and misunderstood, Americans were struggling with a complex mix of idealism, guilt, resentment, and generosity. Through this maze of tangled feelings, Vietnamese and Americans needed a common ground upon which they could jointly build a modus vivendi.

Ironically, that common ground was there from the beginning of U.S. involvement with Vietnam. Portes and Rumbaut identify it as the strong anti-communist feelings that are the common denominator not only among Vietnamese and Americans as a whole but among refugee groups admitted into the United States during the cold war period (1990:24; see also Zolberg, Suhrke, and Aguayo 1989:163).

The legal structure governing the assignment of the label *refugee* had made that stipulation: the Refugee-Escapee Act of 1957 defined refugee-escapees as "persons fleeing persecution in Communist countries." Even with the enactment of the Refugee Act of 1980, which "repealed the ideological and geographic limitation which had previously favored refugees fleeing communism" the preference continued in practice, (Leibowitz 1983:15,18). In 1987, of a total of 91,474 refugees admitted to the United States, only 10 percent came from the non-communist world (Portes and

Rumbaut 1990:23–24). Those who voted with their feet provided the host society with propaganda material, vindication for its own anti-communist ideology, and political grounds for admitting the refugees into the country. Anti-communism as the basis for granting refugee status was also the basis for creating a "bureaucratic identity" for the migrants, which made them easier to stereotype, standardize, and, hence, control (Zetter 1991). Until the late 1980s, "refugee" was a class designation given to individuals not as individuals but as members of a group.

For the Vietnamese refugees, anti-communism, however defined, provided a heterogeneous population with a basis for intragroup solidarity and continuity with a remembered life.[5]

Out of anti-communism as the encapsulation of a long and painful history and as symbol for something shared at great mutual cost, the terms of Vietnamese interaction with Americans in the United States emerged.

Much remained to be sorted out to reestablish order out of the chaos that is the refugee experience. Issues of self-identification, survival, community building, relations with those with whom they must live in the new environment—Vietnamese and non-Vietnamese alike—had to be addressed. How to proceed? What symbols should be used? Which of the old would continue to function and what would replace the rest? What role would expressive culture—music, dance, the arts in general—play in the construction of a transplanted life?

Each group would find its own way, according to the opportunities that presented themselves, according to how the group defined itself and its needs, and the inner and outer resources at the group's command and their deployment in the new environment. But all refugee groups in resettlement—and the individuals within them—would be engaged in "a process of constructing a world of choice and not of fate. For all of them, the process [would] be a lifetime occupation" (Rumbaut 1991:88).

CHAPTER 3

Vietnamese in New Jersey:
The Birth of Community

Shortly before the fall of Saigon in 1975, a U.S. company began relocating some of its Vietnamese employees from South Vietnam to the Jersey City–Hoboken area in New Jersey. These became the state's first Vietnamese who came as a group. Within a very short time, these evacuees—educated, highly skilled, relatively affluent men and women, most of whom had come from the Saigon area and had left with their families—were followed by members of what has been called the first wave of Vietnamese refugees, those who fled in the wake of Saigon's surrender.[1] Similar to the Vietnamese who preceded them, these were also well educated, many of them Catholic, relatively young urbanites who had extensive contact with Americans in South Vietnam. For most of these early arrivals, departure from Vietnam and resettlement in the United States was interrupted only by a short stay in U.S. holding centers either in Guam or on the U.S. mainland. In this respect, their experience of forced migration differed considerably from that of subsequent arrivals—the so-called boat people, the second wave of refugees, and the vast majority of those who fled Vietnam after 1977.

With the latter influx, the relative homogeneity of the Vietnamese population in New Jersey was supplanted by the heterogeneity of post-1977 arrivals, among whom were large numbers of farmers, fishermen, people who lived in coastal areas and therefore had access to boats, people of different ethnicities who came from a much wider area than the urbanites before them. Joining them were other Vietnamese similar to the early arrivals but whose qualifications for joining the new exodus were not education, U.S. contacts, or white-collar skills but the possession of the wherewithal to flee—access to boats, the ability to leave at short notice, stamina, motivation, and the currency (preferably gold) with which to bribe authorities and to pay for a place on a boat.[2] Such "qualifications" made it difficult for whole families to escape. Many people escaped alone, and these would subsequently suffer the lack of family support—paramount in Vietnamese culture—and in many cases bear a burden of guilt and loss on top of that imposed by forced migration and resettlement in an unfamiliar milieu.

Once in the United States, refugees were dispersed throughout the country so that their care could be equitably shared by the states. The implementation of this policy, sometimes referred to as the scattered resettlement policy, was assigned to voluntary agencies. National organizations like the American Council of Voluntary Agencies, the American Council for Nationalities Services, and the United States Catholic Conference allocated refugees to different states through local affiliates such as the International Institute and the Catholic Community Services, which then assessed the local capacity to meet refugee needs. Where refugees were resettled, therefore, depended on such local factors as the availability of housing for large families or for single individuals. The institutionalization of aid that this process entailed, while understandable and useful under the circumstances, reinforced the sense of helplessness and loss of control that had taken root and grown in refugee camps. For most adult refugees, these psychological and emotional injuries would fester for a long time.

Most of the early Vietnamese refugees assigned to New Jersey were resettled in Jersey City and the surrounding areas, where there was an adequate stock of low-cost housing. As the hub of a wide network of public transportation, Jersey City offered relatively easy access to services that refugees would need. And in Jersey City, one of the most culturally diverse areas in the region, they might be spared the discomfort of being different.

By the early 1980s, with the growing controversy over the 1975 scattered resettlement policy and the rise of secondary migration, Vietnamese increasingly sought their own places to live.[3] By 1983, William Beebe, director of the Adult Learning Center, estimated that 60 percent to 70 percent of the pre-1977 arrivals had moved out of the Jersey City area. Their wider range of skills, familiarity with U.S. culture, and more adaptable work experience, put them in a better position to seek out and take advantage of opportunities as these arose.

But soon others began to move for reasons of their own. Those in search of relief from the harsh northeastern winters left for more congenial weather in southern states like Texas and California. Others came to New Jersey attracted by the proximity of New York City and Manhattan's Chinatown. To those who found New York City rents prohibitive, New Jersey, a few minutes away by public transport, offered reasonable alternatives. Ethnic Chinese, particularly those who could speak Cantonese, saw prospects for work in Chinatown. Some Vietnamese came to New Jersey in response to invitations from friends and relatives. Still others, having tried other places, decided to return to the state.

Mobility was not only interstate but intrastate as well. As family members were reunited and families grew, as they became more financially secure and more confident in their ability to function within the wider society, Vietnamese began to broaden their sphere of activity within the state.

The immediate effect of the freedom to move was a heightened sense of transiency that hampered or delayed community building. Ten years after the first Vietnamese came to New Jersey, the Vietnamese population was still in flux. There were other barriers to social cohesion. Religious, ethnic, educational, and class differences that went back to life in Vietnam were compounded by different rates of adaptation to the new environment and by growing segmentation along generational lines. Problems stemmed from differences in the experience of forced migration—the evacuees' relatively direct and safe journey in contrast to the risk-laden, protracted, convoluted route that others had followed; the refugees' experience of life under communism, which the evacuees had not had; the long periods spent in refugee camps. What bound the New Jersey Vietnamese together as a group at this point, therefore, was more a keen awareness of their cultural difference from the larger society than consciousness of what they shared with each other: a common language and a common homeland.

The Stirrings of Community

In time, voluntary associations, the early and unmistakable signs of a community in the making, began to emerge. Some of these associations were frail in their infancy; others showed promise of survival and fruitfulness.

Two years after the first program for Vietnamese was initiated in Jersey City in 1976, Minh Tran, an energetic and highly dedicated Vietnamese counselor working for the Adult Learning Center, capitalized on the fact that the majority of the Vietnamese population were young, single, and male. He organized a group called Thao Viet(Vietnamese Sports). Every weekend, weather permitting, members met in Lincoln Park, centrally located in Jersey City, to play soccer, volleyball, basketball and track and field. An important incentive for joining was that participants were eligible to compete with other Vietnamese teams from Canada and the United States in the Vietnamese North American Games, which took place in either country on the Fourth of July. These sports-centered activities expanded to include picnics, dances, the celebration of Tet, and other social events that served both to raise funds for Thao Viet and to encourage the Vietnamese to get together.

Thao Viet was essentially self-funded. Outside of contributions from some small businesses, which rarely exceeded fifty dollars each (in 1980 dollars), the group received little or no support from public or private sources. Often, for such items as transportation or the purchase of uniforms, members had to dig into their own pockets. The group's existence was therefore precarious and its survival highly problematic.

Religious institutions also recognized the desirability and the need for a sense of community. In New Jersey, where most Vietnamese were Buddhists, even if only nominally, Buddhism's public participation in Vietnamese social life was largely ceremonial (e.g., the homage to ancestors that opens the celebration of Tết).[4] A small pagoda was established in Jersey City, but Buddhism's role in public affairs remained modest. In contrast, Roman Catholicism, which ministers to a minority of the Vietnamese population, sought to fill both a religious and a social niche.

In 1983, Bishop James H. V. Cua of the Phu Cuong diocese in what used to be South Vietnam came to Jersey City as part of a countrywide visit to reinforce ties among Vietnamese locally and regionally. Almost immediately afterwards, Fr. Joseph Nguyen Tri Minh became the first Vietnamese priest appointed to the Newark Archdiocese. One of his first acts was to set up a Vietnamese-language mass at Our Lady of Victories Church in Jersey City. Like Thao Viet's sports activities, the weekly mass became an occasion for Vietnamese to get together. Here the ministry could reach out and address social and cultural concerns. Father Minh outlined how he hoped Vietnamese communal sentiment and involvement would grow: "I think that the people who come here every Sunday for the services, they begin to know each other. After that, they come to appreciate the good will of each other. Then they can work together. When they are together, there are new needs, new preoccupations: how we can teach children Vietnamese, who can teach them. . . . What can we do for next Christmas, for the party, for the theater. We are thinking now of how to work together, and people tell me who will be the best to work on these programs. So they will sit down, talk, know and appreciate each other better and that is the way, I think" (interview, March 15, 1984).

Shortly after Father Minh's arrival, people from surrounding areas— Hoboken, Nutley, East Orange, Newark, South Amboy—began to attend the weekly Vietnamese mass in Jersey City. In an interview on May 1, 1984, Khanh Nguyen, who had assumed the duties of Vietnamese choir director, told me that the original 70 or so people who attended the liturgy had now grown to 150, and Father Minh had begun to say mass in other churches in the archdiocese. Instead of going home immediately after mass, people began to socialize. Classes in Vietnamese for children were initiated, and parents brought them from miles around. As a choir of around twenty people began to meet regularly, the Vietnamese masses added choral to congregational singing.

While the impact of his work was felt most strongly by New Jersey's Vietnamese Catholics, Father Minh was optimistic that the sense of community he had begun to build would eventually extend to non-Catholic Vietnamese as well. Without religion to draw people together, however, and with the accumulation of factors that kept people apart, Father Minh's optimism would be repeatedly put to the test. The effects of scattered resettlement and secondary migration continued to be felt well into the 1980s. But more urgent were the demands of adaptation and survival, from learning how to use the telephone to gaining some competency in English to contending with the complexities of public and private bureaucracies. Above all, Vietnamese needed to earn a living, not only to support family members in the States but to help those left behind in Vietnam. Over and over again, one heard the plaint, "We have no time . . . to socialize, to spend time even with our families." Vietnamese were in a state that has become familiar to service providers and students of refugee phenomena called "survival mode."

In the secular sphere, initiatives similar to those in the religious sphere were beginning to take shape. State government offices like the Office of Ethnic Affairs, city councils, and sponsoring agencies tried to help promote a sense of community by facilitating celebrations of important holidays. Their assistance was enthusiastically accepted, and Vietnamese set up their activities. These, however, were highly localized and episodic; attempts to reach out to the wider community were tentative at best and were largely individual and private initiatives. Until the mid-1980s, Vietnamese did not participate in major regional or statewide events such as the annual Liberty Park Ethnic Festival.

But other Vietnamese voluntary associations were even then struggling to be born. Some were succeeding, although knowledge of their existence was slow to spread among their potential constituencies. In 1983, two voluntary associations began to be visible to the Vietnamese in the state: the Association of Free Vietnamese, and the Federation of Vietnamese and Indochinese Mutual Assistance Associations of New Jersey.[5]

While initially differing in their core constituencies and aims, the associations' membership pool, their tasks, and the nature of their activities overlapped. Both targeted the Vietnamese population of New Jersey for their membership, although the federation made it a point to include Laotians and Cambodians. Both aimed to draw the Vietnamese of the state together and to awaken a sense of community among them. Both recognized the importance of making public the celebration of major events in the Vietnamese calendar, creating occasions and powerful incentives for Vietnamese to meet. Both associations expressed the desire to make their celebrations accessible to non-Vietnamese as well to enhance mutual understanding. To this end, they gave state public officials and private non-Vietnamese citizens active roles in those celebrations. But differences between the associations were signaled by the date on which each celebrated Tết, their most important holiday.[6]

The Association of Free Vietnamese began when twenty-four Vietnamese got together in 1980 "to generate community involvement among the Vietnamese in New Jersey, to assist newcomers and create opportunities for them." In 1981, the organization was formally set up around the rallying cry, "We do not accept the Communist government," as I learned from one of its founders, Mrs. Thanh Cong Nguyen, January 20, 1984. By 1986, however, the association's Tết program reflected changes in empha-

sis: "As a non-profit organization formed in May 1981, the Association actively seeks to provide services to the Vietnamese community in New Jersey, to preserve the Vietnamese cultural heritage and to create opportunities for Vietnamese to meet and discuss their experience with life in the
U.S." Its newsletter, *Gio Nam*, announced funding from the State Department of Human Services, expansion of its constituency to include "newly
arrived Indochinese Refugees," and "promot[ion] of the Indochinese cultural heritage" (4[2]:19–20).

The federation was born about a year after the association, between
1982 and 1983, after Dr. Can Ngoc Hoang (who became the coordinator
of the association) attended a technical training session sponsored by the
Indochinese Refugee Action Center in Washington, D.C. In March, 1983,
representatives of the Indochinese Mutual Assistance Associations of
New Jersey formalized the federation, committing themselves "to the essential role of the refugee organizations in the provision of services to
members of our respective communities and in strengthening our social
and economic base in order to achieve self-sufficiency within the realis-
tic American society" (Can interview, February 25, 1984).The federation
set for itself the objective of coordinating the efforts of twelve mutual aid
associations (MAAs) in the state, ten of them Vietnamese, one Laotian,
and one Cambodian. And while its focus was service to the Indochinese
community through technical assistance (conducting workshops on
such concerns as job training, transition problem solving, financial assistance, and language learning), it also sought to engage in advocacy
regarding federal, state, and local government policies affecting refugee
resettlement.

Dr. Can Ngoc Hoang was keenly aware of the difficulties of coordinating the twelve groups, each with its own interests.[7] "Survival mode"
was a persistent theme. An official of the Association of Free Vietnamese
put it this way: "There are some 6,000 Vietnamese in New Jersey, and
while many do volunteer to help, only 30 have become members of the
Association. . . . everybody is busy." Leadership and its exercise, crucial
to community building, suffered from cynicism born of recent Vietnamese experience. As Scott Wasmuth of the International Institute
observed, "Vietnamese are suspicious of people who aspire to be leaders.
They have had their share of corrupt leaders in Vietnam" (interview,
October 12, 1983).

Only in rudimentary sense therefore can one refer to a New Jersey Vietnamese community in the mid- to late 1980s. Such a community was just beginning to feel and act upon the stirrings of a sense of communal identity. The concrete forms that were to represent common interests still lacked clear definition. The Vietnamese as a collectivity had not yet had the time for organic growth and evolution toward a critical mass that could trigger social cohesion. The story of the Vietnamese in New Jersey thus far had been a string of ad hoc responses to a sense of impermanence that could not be put to rest as long as memories of their exodus were kept fresh by the continuing influx of other refugees.

The Musical Life

In the 1980s, the Vietnamese in New Jersey gravitated around the public celebration of Tết. No public occasion attracted as many Vietnamese. Perhaps none was as powerful a reminder of their being away from home, of their status as overseas Vietnamese, for in Vietnam, Tết is above all family centered, integral to Vietnamese social life, requiring no adjustments to the schedules or protocols of a larger, non-Vietnamese society.[8] More than any other event, the observance of Tết brings together many facets of their communal life—the secular and the religious, that part of their history that was lived in Vietnam and that part evolving away from the homeland. Music, as an important part of the Tết celebration, therefore affords important clues to what that life may be at this point in the New Jersey Vietnamese story.

Tết in Woodbridge, New Jersey

Like most of the Tết celebrations I attended in New Jersey in the 1980s, the 1984 event in Woodbridge took place in school premises (Woodbridge High School) and consisted of two distinct parts. One had the character of a performance in an auditorium: an audience seated in rows facing the stage where the action was taking place. The other was a party—a dance with a live band or two, food, and active participation by all. The performance segment consisted of a ritual and ceremonial portion (the "Procession of Flags," with the U.S. and former Republic of Vietnam flags held aloft at the head of a solemn procession into the auditorium; homage to the ancestors; and speeches by Vietnamese and local and state officials) and a secular entertainment portion—songs, dances, skits, and musical performances of various kinds.

In 1984, the Woodbridge Tết was sponsored by the Association of Free Vietnamese. On the basis of ticket sales and invitations, the audience was estimated to number between 1,000 and 1,200, at least 90 percent of whom were Vietnamese. The performance portion featured Pham Duy's *Con Đường Cái Quan*, also called *The National Road* and, less frequently, *Journey through Vietnam.*[9] Supplementing this centerpiece were short numbers, such as Vietnamese folk songs.

Composed as a suite of nineteen songs—six each for North, Central, and South Vietnam, and the nineteenth symbolizing the country unified—*Con Đường Cái Quan* was staged as a musical in Woodbridge. According to Vu Thanh Vinh, who produced the show, this format was suggested in Pham Duy's introduction to the work. The story line (a wayfarer who sets out from North Vietnam and travels south to unite the country), Vu believed, was particularly apt for Tết, when Vietnamese turn their thoughts to the homeland and to those left behind.[10]

Vu described the contents of this program as "traditional": Pham Duy uses Vietnamese folk material, the rest of the songs in the program—texts and music—were conceived or written by Vietnamese, and the musical items were part of a past that all shared. "We make it [the presentation] more traditional through costumes, scenery, slides of Vietnam [projected on a scrim or used as backdrop], folk songs, etc. . . . [I]n a traditional program, there is always a song about the country, the love for country, and since we are abroad, there are always songs about nostalgia for the country" (interview, February 11, 1984).

But while he would have liked to use traditional musical instruments, Vu stopped short of what he called "strict traditional music": "I feel that if you go into strict traditional Vietnamese music . . . you will not have a very wide audience. . . . You have to understand and appreciate and be very knowledgeable of [traditional] music to like it." What Vu had intended was something that "can be enjoyed by a wide variety of people . . . we had in mind also to entertain our American friends . . . something they can relate to"(interview, Februrary 11, 1984).

It was obvious that certain accommodations had been made for the general audience. Three well-known Vietnamese folk songs—one from each region of the country—were sung by Mary Ellen Dougherty, a non-

Vietnamese colleague of Vu's at Bell Labs. She learned the text phonetically from Vu, whose wife then sang the songs on tape so Dougherty could learn them by rote. The song "Vietnam, Vietnam" that ends the musical and has achieved almost the status of a national anthem to overseas Vietnamese was followed by "America, the Beautiful," because, as Vu put it, "we feel that this is our second country". His arrangement of the instrumental accompaniment for Pham Duy's work was realized with the help of non-Vietnamese friends: Curtis Lee, a Chinese American, at the piano; the "sound man," Joe Clark, who handled microphones, tapes, and other sound equipment; and the drummer, Chuck Swierad. As a consequence, Western harmony, which had been implicit in the score, became explicit (Figure 2).[11]

Vu Thanh Vinh said that he borrowed many production ideas from Broadway and particularly from *Nicholas Nickleby*, tapes of which he had studied closely. This accounted for an end product that was professedly Vietnamese in content and motivation but presented in a manner reminiscent of Broadway.[12] Incipient Western influences were coaxed to the surface as much by favorable social circumstances, social incentives, even social pressures, as by the lack of access to and even interest in what Vu called "strict traditional Vietnamese" materials.

At this Tết celebration, themes emerged that were to recur not only in other Tết celebrations but on other musical occasions as well: the refugee-exiles' nostalgia for home, and the need to identify themselves with and adapt to a host society. In playing out any of these themes, the refugees would inevitably collide with the demands of the survival mode. As Vu remarked: "We are a very young group in this country and there is a lot of pressure to make good, so we have not had much time to build a real community. Some people have to work two or three jobs and do not have much time for anything else." (This sentiment found expression in some of the skits. Although the texts were in Vietnamese, a smattering of English was thrown in: "work all the time," "my bones hurt.") Participation in the stage presentation was therefore a measure of the value the performers attached to Tết and to the particular manner of celebrating it in the New Jersey context. The cast, many of whom had never been onstage before, spent weeks at rehearsal and learned their songs while commuting to and from work from tapes that Vu had recorded for each of them.

Inevitably, too, in dealing with adaptation and self-identification, Vietnamese would confront the question of what is Vietnamese and how to

FIGURE 2. Fragment of Pham Duy's score, *Con Đường Cái Quan,* which gives only the melodic line. Vu Thanh Vinh, who very graciously gave me a copy of the score from which he worked for his stage production of this work, claims that this was the original score to which he added the chords in his arrangement for instrumental ensemble to accompany the singers. On page 87, the corresponding fragment from the 1989 edition of the work (Midway City, CA: PDC Productions & Pham Duy), which begins with the arrow at the end of the second line, shows considerable differences in harmonization.

FIGURE 2. *Continued*

effectively address this in the U.S. context. Just as the stage presentations during Tết underscored the theme of nostalgia for homeland and the presentation of the self to the public as Vietnamese, the party segment, which came to being only in the States, highlighted the problem of communicating their distinctiveness through music and behavior that the larger society were likely to take as Western if not American.

Music for the Woodbridge Tết was provided by the Lang Du Band, a family ensemble consisting of a lead singer and three instrumentalists,

TABLE 1   Lang Du Band's Response to a Questionnaire

Name of Piece	Composer	A	V	O	Type	Singer(s)	E	V	O	Topic
		Kind of Music					Lyrics			
Ngày Về Quê Cũ			x		Paso doble	Phoung & Loan		x		Return to home-town
Blue Tango		x			Tango					
Nhúng Biồc Chan âm Thâm	Y Van		x		Boléro	Tuan & Thang		x		Lonely steps
Saigon			x		Cha-Cha	Phuong & Loan		x		Saigon City
Rock 'n' Roll Is King	Jeff Lynne	x			Rock 'n' roll	Phuong & Loan	x			
Saigon ơi Vĩnh Biệt	Nam Lòc		x		Slow	Thang		x		Goodbye, Saigon
Blue Danube				x	Waltz					
Hoa Soan Bên Thềm Cũ	Tuan Khanh		x		Rhumba	Phuong & Thang		x		Flowers on the old door step
Oh Carol		x			Cha-Cha	Phuong & Thang & Loan	x			

A = American; E = English; V = Vietnamese; O = Other.

Note: This first page of a questionnaire lists the repertory the Lang Du Band played during the Tết celebration of 1984. The form was filled out by the group's keyboardist and arranger, who functioned as music director.

their father, and two of his sons-in-law. The ensemble consisted of three guitars, electric keyboards, a drum set, and, occasionally, additional percussion such as the maracas. All the instruments except the drum set were electric or amplified. All except the percussionists used handwritten musical scores. Most song texts were Vietnamese.

More than half of the numbers (see Table 1, under "Type") were placed by the musicians in some category of Latin American dance music. This identification was reinforced by the dancers on the floor, who danced stylized tangos, cha-cha-cha, and rhumbas on the numbers so designated in Table 1. Ambiguities crept in, however, when one compares numbers identified as "American," "Vietnamese," or "other" with the language of their texts.

Seven of the twenty-four items were strictly instrumental, leaving seventeen with texts or ("Lyrics" in Table 1). All of the items with English texts were identified as American. One item with no text, however, was identified as a tango as to type and American at the same time. Nine of eleven items with Vietnamese texts were marked Vietnamese as to kind of music; one was marked Latin/cha-cha; the other (an arrangement of Schubert's "Serenade"), Latin.

Worth noting in light of the information from Lang Du is the claim, repeatedly made by Vietnamese I have spoken to on the east and west coasts of the United States (including the Lang Du Band members and despite the discrepancy indicated by the items above), that an important marker of Vietnameseness in song is its text. As to the older Latin American dances like the tango, their Vietnameseness was justified on the grounds that they are part of the Vietnamese cultural heritage that came with them when they left their country. These spontaneous claims were often revised in the light of more thoughtful discussions on what constitutes Vietnamese culture and musical tradition. But that they are made so frequently by a large cross-section of Vietnamese hints at the complexity of these issues, particularly in light of the new contexts within which Vietnamese refugee-resettlers try to reconstruct their lives and their cultural identity.

Tết in Plainfield, New Jersey

The weekend after the Woodbridge Tết celebration in 1984, Tết was celebrated in Plainfield High School under the sponsorship of the Federation of Vietnamese and Indochinese Mutual Assistance Associations.

This was a more informal celebration—"just for fun" as Nghia Nguyen, then president of the Rutgers University Vietnamese Student Association put it. Nonetheless, its framework, consisting of a performance and a party, closely resembled Woodbridge's except for a fair-like arrangement opened in the afternoon. Booths were set up to sell snacks and traditional Tết foods and to display typical Vietnamese crafts such as lacquered plaques, vases, and boxes inlaid with mother-of-pearl. Young and old alike tried their hand at a variety of board games and games of chance.

The entertainment section of the staged segment consisted of songs, dances, and instrumental performances followed by an áo dài fashion show with canned music in the background. (Since the áo dài invariably consists of a tunic with long sleeves and a high collar worn over loose flowing pants, variety is introduced through differences in fabric, hand-painted designs, and other decorations on the tunic.) Besides the more informal atmosphere, with children running up and down the aisles and people with cameras rushing forward to get better shots, this event differed from that in Woodbridge in the inclusion and active participation of Laotians and Cambodians. The audience was invited to join the Cambodian and Laotian dancers on stage, and some Vietnamese did. Taped music accompanied the dances. Live music came in the form of Vietnamese folk songs sung with guitar accompaniment; a Vietnamese choral number sung in unison and accompanied by two electric guitars and an acoustic guitar; a guitar solo; and a piano piece played by the young Vietnamese woman who composed it.[13] American officials spoke, from Governor Thomas Kean's representative to Plainfield's mayor, the latter proclaiming the week "Vietnamese Heritage Week" in the city of Plainfield.

Three bands for the dance—Vietnamese, Laotian, and Cambodian—took turns playing sets. The Vietnamese band showed its predilection for Latin dances. Song texts were Vietnamese. There was, however, a higher incidence of disco-type dancing partly because the Laotian and Cambodian bands' repertoires were not as laden with Latin American rhythms, partly because of the greater number of Americans among the dancers, and partly because this celebration attracted a larger audience than Woodbridge's and a correspondingly larger proportion of younger and more Americanized Indochinese.

The point of the Tết celebration, and its changing form and function in a new environment, was summarized by Dr. Can Ngoc Hoang, coordinator of the Federation of Vietnamese and Indochinese Mutual Assistance Associations, and his wife during an interview on February 25, 1984 (see also Reyes Schramm 1986). Although intended for the Vietnamese and other Indochinese who have few chances to get together, Dr. Can said,

> It was also structured so that others—non-Asians, our American friends—can understand our culture a little bit more. . . . [T]he artistic part [i.e., the stage performance] is an accommodation to the non-Indochinese. We tried to choose certain traditional dances. Also we tried to show them what is most characteristic of the nation as a whole. It's very difficult to separate one from the other. . . .
>
> I wouldn't say that [the dance part of the celebration] is a tradition. . . . [U]sually practicing Tết in Vietnam really means family celebration, and. . . you are looking back to the past, to what your ancestors have done for you, and you try to commemorate their memories, and you want their protection for the coming year. . . . Now, coming to this country, what all of us see Tết to be is more than that celebration. . . . It is a means for people to get together once a year, to know each other, to exchange wishes and greetings and also for the young to learn more about culture. And because of the involvement of all those young people, the dance has become part of the celebration—to tell them that we also think of them and not only of the seniors and older people in the community.[14]

Dr. Can spoke for the majority of Vietnamese when he said that they are unable to do the things they used to do in Vietnam to celebrate Tết. His wife interpolated: "Like now, on the first day of the New Year, I had to go to work. . . . And when you go to work I don't think you can control what happens or what you want to do. . . . It is very hard to keep [traditions] when you are living in an environment which is not yours. So you have to adjust" (interview, February 25, 1984).

Adjusting or adapting, the need to keep traditions alive, and a perception of themselves as a community still in the making echoed in verbal and musical expression.[15] There are frequent comparisons to the situation in Orange County, California, where the size of the Vietnamese population and its stability as a community are frequent reference points. Vu Thanh Vinh, for example, held up dance bands in New Jersey as the principal examples of organized musical groups in the state, noting that these Vietnamese bands do not consider their music making a profession. "They don't intend to 'make it' in a general popular sense because this is tough. . . . These bands do get paid when they play for dances. But all of them have other jobs . . . music is just a hobby and if they make a buck when they do it, that's fine." He contrasts this situation with California's, where Vietnamese music is an "industry," where music tapes are made "strictly for Vietnamese consumption, and they make money from this. In fact there are people [in California] whose profession at home was in the performing arts and when they came over here that's what they do" (interview February 11, 1984). Father Minh made a similar observation: "Videotapes and cassettes are brought from California where there is a big Vietnamese community and a concentration of musicians and of musical production" (interview, March 15, 1984).

The members of the Lang Du Band, who had played for dances in New Jersey as well as for the Woodbridge Tết celebrations, confirmed Vu's observations. Loan Nguyen and two of her siblings had received extensive formal piano instruction in Vietnam: scales, Czerny, Bach, Mozart, Beethoven, and Chopin, as Loan put it. A younger sibling, Phung, and her mother are violinists. But when they tried to resume lessons in New Jersey with a teacher they had known in Vietnam, he advised them that they would do better getting the family to form a band. They did so "as a hobby," and now that they were being invited to play for a variety of occasions, they practiced as an ensemble at least once a week, bought tapes produced in California and sold in Chinatown to keep abreast of what was going on in the overseas Vietnamese musical world, and watched MTV for ideas from the musical world at large.[16] These activities, they felt, they owed their audiences out of respect and to maintain their good reputation. But they would not have this band if they were in Vietnam. Loan prefers her Western European art music, and the others feel that they are not of a professional calibre—that in Vietnam, others would be doing a better job with this repertoire than they (interview, March 4 and 10, 1984).

The hobbylike, almost incidental character of these bands became more apparent in the reply to my inquiries about how many Vietnamese bands there were in the state. Loan, consulting her husband, sister, and brother, said that there are "five, six, seven bands . . . some of them die, they keep changing names. . . . [M]ost of the professional bands are in California where there is a large [Vietnamese] population. . . . They can make a living out there." The bands in New Jersey do not play regularly.

"During the holiday months—Thanksgiving, Christmas, New Year—they play once a week, twice a month, something like that."

As a consequence, Vietnamese can be persuaded to congregate in large numbers around a strictly musical event only by "importing" a well-known Vietnamese performer like Khanh Ly, whose popularity goes back to Vietnam before the fall of Saigon and who now resides in Orange County, California. In Loan's words, "in this state only people will get together like when they have a band forming and they invite singers from California because most of our famous singers settle there. That's the only time they [Vietnamese] come together, to listen to the music, listen to the lyrics . . . that holds the people together." Hoang Oanh, one of these famous singers, lived in New Jersey until the early 1990s when she moved to southern California, but few Vietnamese in the state seemed aware of her presence among them. In contrast, once in California, she has had such public exposure that she needs sometimes to hide behind big dark glasses when she goes out, to avoid being recognized.

The nebulous character of the New Jersey Vietnamese musical—and the more broadly social—community was underscored by the ambiguity of attitudes toward the form the community should be taking and toward the markers of communal identity. The remarks of Vu Thanh Vinh and of Dr. Can Hoang Ngoc and his wife explaining the choice of the musical activities to celebrate Tết exemplify the struggle to address a fundamental question: What forms are recognizable to the Vietnamese as Vietnamese and at the same time acceptable to the larger society as both an expression of distinctiveness and an expression of what might be—at least potentially—the American side of the hyphenated Vietnamese-American identity?

This concern underlies the constant references to the traditionally Vietnamese in tandem with the continual articulation of the need to adapt and to be understood by the non-Vietnamese. That traditional music is a symbol of cultural identity was taken by the Vietnamese I spoke to as axiomatic. The problem lay in finding the sounds—the musical equivalents—of the label *traditional music* that would be meaningful in the U.S. environment. It involved establishing or reconciling relations between the Vietnamese past and present—away from where that past and present were born and from where their meanings came into being and evolved.

These difficulties were evident in the following comments from Dr. Can: "I would say that our traditional music does not have Western resemblance at all. . . . Like we have instruments which in no way resemble Western musical instruments. . . . Then I guess when you come to the '60s and the '70s, music evolved everywhere, and Vietnam is no exception. So it became more modern and it was more under the influence of Western music . . . I don't know many Vietnamese people coming to this country who are still playing those classical or traditional instruments" (interview, February 25, 1984).

Vu Thanh Vinh pointed out that "it is extremely difficult to find performers of . . . strictly traditional music in this area. These kinds of music have no market and can hardly survive. Those who know how to perform this music can only do it occasionally and thus their performance lacks polish" (interview, April 18, 1984).

Fr. Joseph Minh, the only Vietnamese priest in the Newark Archdiocese said, "The traditional [music]—perhaps the people don't know. . . . It is very difficult to find someone who has the ability, the desire, and the professional knowledge to present a truly traditional concert" (interview, March 15, 1984).

The members of the Lang Du Band got into quite a discussion on the topic, triggered when Phung remarked: "Old people like my grandmother have their own kind [of music]—very traditional, very hard to sing. And the musicians, they don't play the instruments we play. That's not the music people would expect to hear when they ask for Vietnamese music. They would give you the popular singers of today who only sing the modern songs. You could ask for Pham Duy songs and you would get that." Another band member added, "Performers of old traditional Vietnamese music and Vietnamese instruments are very rare." (interview, March 10, 1984). He struggled hard to recall the name of a traditional musician, only to come up with the name of the man who encouraged them to form the band. (This was not unusual. A founding member of the Association of Free Vietnamese could not come up with the name of a traditional musician either.)

Initially, Phung seemed not to consider traditional music rare. It turned out that she had a very different conception of what traditional music is: "They are for ballroom dance [tangos and waltzes which the Vietnamese dance in a highly stylized manner]. Those are the ones that old people like the most." But when I inquired about music played on traditional instruments, she said: "That's completely different. That's gone." Her father, however, qualified her statement: "It's not completely gone. There are still some. But we don't have musicians who play those kinds of instruments."

Asked whether a Vietnamese claiming to be a musician today would be expected to play Western or Westernized music, Loan replied: "I don't think so. . . . We pretty much stick to our traditional music. If you go to different bands and other groups, they might play more American or Westernized music, but there still are Vietnamese songs. People still want to listen to Vietnamese music." The band members agreed on one point articulated by Loan: when one says "Vietnamese music" now, one is thinking of music with lyrics that have to do with Vietnam and are in Vietnamese (Lang Du interview).

The linkage of Vietnamese traditional music and Vietnamese music, and the confusion of one for the other, thus became unmistakable. On one level, the apparent contradictions found resolution in the *concept* traditional as a historical reality, distant and abstract, and as a present-day reality assigned a contemporary function. As historical reality it has become rare, strikingly so and deserving comment in the New Jersey context, with few practitioners and users, hardly accessible in daily life. As contemporary reality, it was considered an important element of what is Vietnamese—a shared heritage, a symbol of community in a society where what is Vietnamese needed to be defined. Yet *as sound*, traditional music remained elusive. Perhaps, I thought, I might gain access to it through what was called simply "Vietnamese music," with which it was so often associated and at times even identified.

When I asked Khanh Nguyen, the Vietnamese choir director of Our Lady of Victories Church in Jersey City, what I might expect to hear if I asked a Vietnamese musician to play me some Vietnamese music. He said: "Probably the kind of music that is after 1954, because the music written before the war is very difficult. After the war we had two different kinds of music, one to talk about the war and love of country, and the other is romantic, about love" (Khanh Nguyen interview, April 9, 1984)—a reply that brought me back to the sad songs–love songs "typology" from the Palawan camp.[17]

To a considerable extent Khanh Nguyen's statement was reinforced by members of the Lang Du Band, although they put the burden of Vietnamese identification on the lyrics: "It's the lyrics. Mostly about the country, our love for the country and how we miss it, love songs." And Vu Thanh Vinh, who defended the traditionality of his Tết programs even as he described most of the music that Vietnamese listen to as "Westernized," called attention to the texts, to Vietnamese origin, and to what Edward Shils called "pastness": "The texts of the songs are Vietnamese.... The lyrics are very Vietnamese.... Many of these songs were very popular at home before we came here, so these are old songs for us" (interview, February 11, 1984).[18]

Trying to build a historical bridge, Fr. Joseph Minh recalled a musical movement called "Get into Life," which meant getting nearer to the culture, the daily life of the people. "I remember that in 1945, 1950, there was something between traditional and occidental, Western European music, and the inspiration was limited to traditional practice of liturgy . . . to the church life.... In 1965, 1970, there began the new musical movement which tried to get into something outside of liturgical life but belonged to our life. . . . It integrates religious and secular life"(interview, March 15, 1984).

But Father Minh's bridge led not to the sounds of traditional music but to a restatement of the problem: "Music belongs to life, and life in Vietnam is not the same as forty or fifty years ago. It is more European, Americanized, so also the music, the music composed by Vietnamese, sung by Vietnamese in Vietnamese. But we can ask if this is really Vietnamese or not." He is torn between the Vietnameseness of this "European, Americanized" music and what he cited as examples of traditional music, "a basis of our Vietnamese soul": Buddhist liturgical music and *hát bội* (a form of Vietnamese theater from North Vietnam with strong Chinese elements), both of which, he acknowledged, barely exist in New Jersey (Minh interview).

A consensus about what music is Vietnamese emerged with mention of the music of Pham Duy, the composer, who came to national attention when his songs were widely broadcast during the Vietnamese fight for independence from the French. In contrast to the blank that I frequently drew when I asked for the name of traditional musicians, virtually every Vietnamese I spoke to in New Jersey immediately responded to the name Pham Duy with the remark that he is a famous Vietnamese musician. While opinions differed on the merits of his later works, particularly those created in California after 1975, there was general consensus on his work before then. Father Minh expressed that consensus: "Pham Duy's music was really the music that renewed and awakened our national search for independence—our longing. . . . His songs during the revolution would be classified as the avant-garde of the modern music, and at the same time, he composed songs inspired by traditional music."

Thoughts of Vietnamese music, for the New Jersey population, therefore, seem to invoke not the sounds of an ancestral past expressed in a distinctively Vietnamese musical idiom through the medium of distinctively Vietnamese musical instruments, although they know this is part of their culture and acknowledge it as a representation of who they are. But thoughts of Vietnamese music invoke rather the *concept* of the traditional, while reaching for sounds that emanate from a more recent past that binds them through a set of painfully remembered common experiences: the fight for independence from the French; the division of the country into north and south, which was prelude to the flight from their country into the world of forced migration; the "love songs" and "sad songs" that represented these and were proscribed by the government they had repudiated.

The themes suggested by the Tết celebrations now emerged more clearly. The first is the primacy of a Vietnamese identity based on *a Vietnam the New Jersey Vietnamese remember.* This was the Vietnam that aroused their nostalgia, the Vietnam they sang about in their sad songs and love songs. It is the Vietnam indicated by their choice of specific items for the most public and most admittedly Vietnamese of their celebrations—Tết: Pham Duy's highly suggestive *Con Đường Cái Quan,* dances based on Vietnam's harvest routines, songs about beloved cities (Saigon, Da-Lat, and Hanoi, this last pertaining to "separation of loved ones between the two capital cities of the divided country"), skits using ancient Vietnamese legend (e.g., that of Son-Tinh, god of the mountains, and Thuy Tinh, god of the seas), a musical trilogy about Vietnam's three famous rivers (the Red River in the north, the Perfume River in Central Vietnam, and the Nine Dragons River in the south), a song called "Nostalgia" that "portrays the many tender images of the beloved homeland in the heart and mind of the one in exile," and songs that "speak of the longings for the Motherland and the commitment to a united and free Vietnam," the "true" Vietnam, that the communists are believed to have destroyed.

The second theme is a keen awareness of the larger U.S. context within which they must define themselves in terms understandable to all. This was consistently underscored by their conscientious inclusion of U.S. public officials and the adoption of Western elements to render the celebration understandable to a non-Vietnamese audience. (The same Western elements in music from Bataan, where they were used to distinguish the Vietnamese from the Laotians and Cambodians, in New Jersey were used to establish a common denominator with their U.S. hosts.)

Among the consequences of acting on these themes were the blurring of distinctions between the more generally Vietnamese and the specifically traditional Vietnamese in music—a distinction that, under the circumstances, seemed not particularly significant. In theory and in principle, the significance of that distinction had given way to the pragmatic. The need was for a symbol of Vietnamese identity that could be called traditional and that was accessible to Vietnamese and non-Vietnamese alike. Filling that need was a music that was: (1) traditional in Shils's sense, that is, it drew from the past to serve a function in the present; (2) Vietnamese in its content, that is, the subject matter of the "love songs" and "sad songs," the folk songs and the legends; (3) Vietnamese in its texts when texts were involved; and (4) accessible to non-Vietnamese through the use of the Western musical idiom.

How comprehensible was this to the non-Vietnamese Americans and the larger society to whom Vietnamese were identifying themselves?

Those who had the most extensive exposure to Vietnamese in the state—the voluntary agencies, the state government officials who attend to ethnic affairs, those who had friends among the Vietnamese community and came to participate in their celebrations—indicate that the ambiguity on the part of the Vietnamese was received with at least an equal degree of uncertainty by the larger society. Guests to Tết and other occasional Vietnamese celebrations almost with one voice took the music to be Western except for the text. Nick Montalto, director of the International Institute, remarked on his various experiences with Tết celebrations: "The music, to my ears, sounded highly Westernized. It was performed in Vietnamese [i.e., sung to Vietnamese texts] but in rock rhythms. It is hard for me to distinguish anything unique about the music." Later, however, he revised his view. "Vietnamese music is syncretic; the cadences and rhythms are Western but the content is Eastern" (interview, September 27, 1983).

Scott Wasmuth, also of the International Institute, echoed the "typical Western music" impression but qualified it at the same time: "They tend to like Western music but of course they try to give a Vietnamese or Chinese touch" (interview, October 24, 1983).

The strong tendency even among thoughtful observers is to equate Westernized sounds, just as they do Western dress, hairdo, and other aspects of material culture, with assimilation into U.S. society. But those who have had the opportunity for longer exposure sound an emphatic vote of caution.[19] William Applegate of the Joint Voluntary Agency office in the Philippines recounted that as a frequent visitor to Vietnam before 1975, he found U.S. popular music commonplace in that country. In one of his visits between 1969 and 1972, he said, he found Vietnamese in a village with a couple of car batteries hooked up to a phonograph, listening to an Elvis Presley rendition of "I Ain't Nothin' but a Hound Dog." "But I think that's a deception. . . . With the Vietnamese, they are fiercely nationalistic, exceptionally so, and also very regionalistic" (interview, November 9, 1983).

Indeed, in New Jersey, it was easy to be blind to all but the Vietnamese "public face," partly because the Vietnamese have strong ideas of what must be kept private and partly because they were a minority new to the state—one that had not yet become "visible" for reasons of secondary migration, fluctuating numbers, and moves within the state to find jobs and adequate housing. And the Vietnamese ambiguity can be taken as nothing more than the functional ambiguity of the label Vietnamese American, and the dual identity that it stands for. But what was then specific to the New Jersey Vietnamese was the tentativeness with which they sought to identify themselves to the larger society even through their music. (One recalls their nonparticipation in the state's Liberty State Park Ethnic Festival, the tortuous discussions on Vietnamese music, the description of their musical activities as a "hobby," their constant deferring to the Orange County, California, community as the proper representation of a Vietnamese musical community). For a form to become a symbol requires the consensus of users as to the symbol's meaning. As this account has shown, the Vietnamese themselves had not as yet arrived at a common perception of who they were or, more accurately, how they wished to be perceived both by themselves and by their conationals in the U.S. context. The musical and the ethnographic voices were delivering the same message: the Vietnamese in New Jersey were still a community in search of itself in a territory they were still trying to map. In this sense, they were still an incipient community, one that, as was the case with the Quebec City Vietnamese described by Dorais, Pilon-Le, and Nguyen Huy had not attained social cohesion since they had yet to "reaffirm their specific identity to themselves and to the rest of society" (1989:40). Replicating the life they had left would be impossible, nonfunctional, and probably undesirable under their new circumstances. The task was one of sorting through an inventory of familiar and commonly held symbolic elements and of achieving a common understanding as to which would be made to serve in the new environment. While the resulting choices might appear arbitrary, a larger perspective suggests that they were not actually so.

Father Minh's juxtaposition of the Paris Vietnamese community that he had served for many years and the New Jersey Vietnamese population (he came to the Newark Archdiocese in 1984) suggests what the grounds for choice might be. For him, despite the diversity of the New Jersey Vietnamese, the Paris community was differentiated even more deeply by the refugee experience: members of the old Paris community had not "known the same difficulties to get out [of Vietnam]." In New Jersey, he thought, despite a few years' difference in their arrival, Vietnamese came under the same or similar circumstances at approximately the same time. As a consequence, the refugees in Paris "don't have the same past and possibilities as those who had left before." From this perspective, the major cleavage is between the community of voluntary migrants and the collectivity made up of forced migrants.

Bousquet (1991) made explicit the distinctions that Father Minh was putting delicately: those between *immigrant* and *refugee,* those, that is, between the Vietnamese who came before the 1975 reunification of Vietnam (the immigrants), and those who came after. The distinction was a matter not just of chronology and legal status but, more importantly, of political allegiance. The immigrants, according to Bousquet, tended to be pro-Hanoi, which at one point in the Vietnamese struggle for independence was equated with being nationalistic; the refugees were anti-Hanoi, which to them was synonymous with anti-communism. The issue was central to Vietnamese self-identification in Paris and, as will become evident, in California. Its centrality, in turn, was deeply rooted in the trauma of displacement, caused in no small part by political ideology. Bousquet underscores the broad and long-term implications of such political alignments: "It would be misleading to believe that these [political] organizations will fade away as soon as their [ex-South Vietnamese] leaders withdraw from the political scene. The torch has been passed to a younger generation" (1991:6).

The crucial difference that may explain a great deal is thus the difference between the experience of voluntary and forced migrants. In New Jersey, although Vietnamese may have come "from different parts of Vietnam— and every part of Vietnam has a different way of seeing and feeling—they are more uniform . . . they have the same *preoccupation*," namely, survival, and its attendant concerns, manifested in the nearly compulsive need to achieve, to acquire, in concrete and measurable terms (interview with Father Minh, March 15, 1984; emphasis added).[20] This common preoccupation that binds the forced migrants vies with a common history and a common culture—the more common bond among immigrants—as the center of gravity that holds a population together and binds them into the entity called community. The salience of this preoccupation—impermanent when compared to the depth and the long-term nourishment that make "roots" a frequent metaphor for cultural origins—marked the New Jersey Vietnamese as a transitional or emergent community, one in the early stages of defining itself both to itself and to others. This stage in the evolution of a community and in the process of self-identification becomes even clearer when examined in the light of the Vietnamese community in Orange County, California.

CHAPTER 4

Orange County, California, and the Vietnamese

Twice a refugee and now resident in Orange County, California, Pham Duy speaks not only for himself but for most Vietnamese in the United States in "O Saigon, Wait for Me!"—"I'll be back to kiss the streets of Saigon/Sharing with you joy and pain./Though they have changed your name/Saigon, I'll never forget you."[1] His outburst, part of his song cycle *Songs of the Refugee's Road* (1988), is tribute to the Vietnamese refugee-resettlers' strong attachment to Vietnam and particularly to Saigon. In words more sober but no less indicative, Pham Dong Long Co, president of the Vietnamese Chamber of Commerce, echoed that sentiment in a letter published in the October 1992 newsletter of that organization:

> Many of us still remember vividly the touching moments of the ceremony [in 1988] at the Asian Garden Mall where a freeway sign of Little Saigon was unveiled. Some . . . could not hide their tears. For them being thousands of miles away from their homeland, they could still associate their beloved City of Saigon with Little Saigon. Ever since Saigon was renamed Ho Chi Minh City, we all felt that we had lost the old name for good and that we needed to revive the name in one form or another. That is the reason why the Vietnamese community had chosen [to] rename the the so-called "Capital of the Vietnamese Refugees in America" Little Saigon. . . .
> Only by adhering to our tradition will we [be] able to retake our beloved city and rename it Saigon.

Little Saigon in Westminster in California's Orange County covers a mile-long stretch of six-lane Bolsa Avenue and spills over onto tributaries that run down intersecting streets and avenues.

The Asian Garden Mall, Little Saigon, Westminster, in Orange County, California. The huge U.S. flag is hung for Independence Day, July 4, 1990.

With pagodalike structures, symbolic dragons, and other mythic figures incorporated into buildings and mall entrances, Little Saigon suggests a more general Asian identity—a Chinatown perhaps—but the directory listings in front of the malls and the signs along the buildings are overwhelmingly Vietnamese. They announce supermarkets, professional offices, restaurants, fast-food stores, bake shops, banks, a post office, beauty salons, optometrists, herbalists, karaoke centers, mom-and-pop stores, a senior citizen recreation center, a wide variety of retail stores, travel agencies, realtors, laundromats, recording studios—virtually any secular service that one would need for daily living.

Little Saigon's architectural centerpiece is the Asian Garden Mall with its towering front entrance set back from the street and framed by landscaping, its upward-curving green-tile roofs supported by red columns framing and sheltering statues of the gods of longevity, prosperity, happiness, and good fortune. More mythical figures adorn the sides of the building—two-story-high nymphs or fairies rendered in what looks like fine green tubing, achieving the effect of line drawings on the light-colored walls. No one driving by, regardless of speed, can miss this imposing structure.

Pagoda on Bolsa Avenue that flies the flag of the old Republic of Vietnam, 1990

Within, the large space encourages socializing. Tables and chairs spill out from food shops all over the main floor, and there is a permanent public stage for ceremonies or performances of various kinds. Here, Vietnamese friends have told me, they come sometimes to see if they might find people they had lost track of since leaving Vietnam who may also have found their way to this part of the country. (I witnessed two such meetings. One Vietnamese friend, concerned about not being recognized because steroid therapy had rounded out her face, was rewarded when a friend she had not seen for the fifteen years since she left Vietnam did recognize her. Another friend bumped into an old classmate from Saigon; neither knew that the other had left the country.) Here too, some people come to be seen, to give evidence of their success in the new environment. A Vietnamese friend visiting from New York told me that although at home she did not bother to dress up if she did not feel like it, she had to "put on her face" to go to Little Saigon.

The people who come to Little Saigon represent a broad cross-section of the Vietnamese population in Orange County, from the well-to-do who frequent the jewelry stores to those who must use food stamps; from the grandparental generation who sit for hours at the tables set out on the floor of the Asian Garden Mall to the teenagers, many of them born in Vietnam but raised in the States; to the infants who are brought in by their parents. Some regularly visit and linger in the bookstores, some browse in the video and audio stores, and some care mainly for the latest fashions. Some are fluent English speakers, true bilinguals who switch easily to Vietnamese as they make their rounds of the stores. And some speak little or no English—shoppers, business owners, and employees who clearly do not see their inability to speak English as a handicap in Little Saigon.

The musical soundscape that matches this physical presence greets visitors as soon as they step inside the Asian Garden Mall where, of the approximately one hundred shops and establishments, six are audio and video stores. The continuous stream of music that pours from the stores as they compete for the public's attention is overwhelmingly what the Vietnamese in Orange County call Vietnamese music, Vietnamese popular music, *tân nhạc,* or, as one of my informants preferred, *musique légère.* Most songs played have Vietnamese texts and the rhythms of cha-cha-cha, bolero, rhumba, tango, and occasionally rock.[2] From time to time there is the sound of strictly instrumental music: Western instrumental ensembles, sometimes spiced with Vietnamese instruments like the đàn tranh or sáo. Westerners mistake it for Western popular music, but Vietnamese take it for Vietnamese, particularly when they recognize the melodic materials. Occasionally one hears a vọng cổ or a smattering of Vietnamese folk songs. All in all, they reflect what cassettes or CDs the Vietnamese buy or can be induced to buy, and what most Vietnamese therefore listen to in their homes or their cars.

What made Orange County's symbolic Saigon the "Capital of the Vietnamese refugees in America"? What made it the musical capital of overseas Vietnam, a major producer of sound recordings distributed and heard worldwide, a small geographic space with a disproportionate number of Vietnam's best-known musicians?

The story can be best told from three vantage points: from outside the Vietnamese community by those who observe the newcomers in their midst; from within, using Vietnamese perspectives; and from those junctures at which Vietnamese and Americans interact, each group leaving its mark on each other's lives. In combination, these vantage points afford a full view of Vietnamese community life in Orange County and provide the context within which the music that will be discussed in the next chapter can be best understood.

The View from Outside

Although there had been a trickle of Vietnamese to the region previously, not until 1975 did the story of Vietnamese in Orange County really begin. The fall of Saigon in April of that year brought the first sizeable group of Vietnamese into the country. Camp Pendleton just outside Orange County was one of four reception centers in the mainland United States set up to give the arriving Vietnamese temporary shelter. Many Vietnamese were subsequently sponsored by people in the surrounding areas and eventually settled in Orange County. Attracted by the temperate climate and by the prospect of being closer to relatives and friends, later arrivals and secondary migration from other parts of the United States augmented the population. In the early 1980s, the Orderly Departure Program (ODP) raised the number of Vietnamese in Orange County to the present level.[3]

The 1990 census recorded 71,800 Vietnamese in Orange County, the largest nationality group after Mexicans.[4] Of the total county population (2,410,556), the Vietnamese represent less than 3 percent, but their concentration in the area covered by Cypress, Fountain Valley, Garden Grove, Midway City, Santa Ana, and Westminster makes them visible to each other and to the rest of the non-Asian population.[5] By 1992, Orange County's all-news radio station, KFWB, in its coverage of the coming elections, repeatedly announced that Orange County had the largest Vietnamese community outside of Vietnam. Its growing participation in the county's political life was made evident by the candidacy of three Vietnamese Americans for public office. One of the three, Tony Lam, won a seat on the Westminster City Council.

Despite the concentration of Vietnamese in certain areas of Orange County, however, clear residential patterns had not emerged. The tendency to cluster or to form enclaves on the model of early Chinatowns, where public and private lives are lived largely if not exclusively within a few city blocks, had been countervailed by the need for affordable housing wherever it could be found, by the diversity of tastes and means among the Vietnamese, the kind of life-style made possible by California's car culture, and, on the part of the market and the society as a whole, the greater openness to Vietnamese (and other ethnic) buyers and neighbors.

Among the Vietnamese, the diversity that was exacerbated by the circumstances of flight and the conditions in camp was again reconstituted, redefined, and reconfigured in Orange County. Anchored by the commonalities they know they share (their language, their Vietnamese identity) and by the commonalities made obvious for them by the larger society (principally that they are not mainstream Americans), Vietnamese worked those differences into the fabric of daily life, making possible the sense of community that is translatable into political and more broadly social action in the U.S. arena.

The View from Within

To highlight social interaction among the Vietnamese in Orange County, particularly as it has been affected by forced migration, I focus on contrastive pairs of categories that entered the lives of the refugee-resettlers as a consequence of their departure from Vietnam. Of these pairs, four have special significance: pre-1975 and post-1975 arrivals; evacuees and refugees; sponsors and the sponsored; and communist and non-communist. I take them as pairs rather than as individual categories to underscore the dynamism of the relations between the constituent groups: one member of each pair defines or illumines the other.

Pre- and Post-1975 Arrivals

On July 10, 1990, Loc Nguyen, the Refugee Coordinator of the Orange County Vietnamese Community Center, told me in an interview that the number of pre-1975 Vietnamese was too insignificant to make a difference in the community.[6] Nonetheless, they turned out to constitute a perfect example of the power of contrastive categories to clarify each other. Almost totally ignored in accounts of Vietnamese life in California and in the country as a whole, they not only help foreground features characteristic of the subsequent arrivals, they also strongly suggest the differences between voluntary and forced migrants.

The relative homogeneity of the early (pre-1975) migrants threw the heterogeneity of the later arrivals into sharp relief. Arriving in the early 1960s as U.S. involvement in Vietnam accelerated, these early arrivals were mostly young and educated. Most came for advanced studies or for language or military training. They saw themselves and were seen by others as members of an elite, by virtue of both the traditional Confucian value placed upon intellectual pursuit and the economic success they were seen to have achieved in the United States. While making it clear that he did not share the sentiment, one of the pre-1975 Vietnamese whom I interviewed quoted a cohort as saying: "Anyone can come as a tourist or as a refugee; not anyone has the qualifications that brought us here."

The post-1975 arrivals' perspective was represented by the interviewee who described the pre-1975 arrivals as aloof and reluctant to be associated with those who came with or after the fall of Saigon. Nonetheless, to the post-1975 arrivals, the pre-1975 Vietnamese were somewhat like role models; they demonstrated the adjustment and success possible in the new environment.

Hoang Thi Tho, a musician and producer who has become almost as successful in the States as he was in Vietnam, believed that those who came before 1975 identified with the Vietnam of that time (interview, November 29, 1992). It was the Vietnam they would have expected to return to had the war not intervened.

The differences between the pre- and post-1975 arrivals, therefore, centered on: (1) their respective views of homeland and their relation to it: the Vietnam of the post-1975 arrivals was not the Vietnam of the pre-1975 arrivals; and (2) their social distance from each other. This distance was demonstrated by the remark on the different qualifications that gained pre- and post-1975 arrivals entry to the States. The contrasting views of homeland were exemplified for me by an incident involving a pre-1975 and a post-1975 arrival.[7]

One evening, a Vietnamese singer whom I will call Ms. A invited me to go out to dinner. At the appointed time and place, she showed up with a friend, Ms. B, whom she introduced as the social worker who had taken her under her wing when Ms. A arrived as a refugee some ten years ago.

Over dinner, the conversation turned to the subject of travel to Vietnam. Ms. B, who had been in the United States since 1969, had just come back from Vietnam and was brimming over with stories about her trip. Ms. A, a former boat person, became increasingly quiet. She said she had sung for the Voice of America before 1975, did not think she would be welcome under the current regime, and would not want to go anyway until Vietnam no longer had a communist government. Her tension, evident in the tightness around her mouth and her virtual withdrawal from the conversation, contrasted sharply with Ms. B's animated comments on life in Vietnam—how inexpensive a good hotel room is, how Air Vietnam's service is improving, how she was planning to make the trip again, and so on.

The emotional content of returning to Vietnam differed dramatically based on the divergent trajectories these women's lives had taken as a result of events defined by 1975.

Evacuees and Refugees

Tri Nguyen, a counselor at Golden West College in Westminster who had advised hundreds of Vietnamese students since 1976, emphasized what he felt was an important distinction. He divided the 1975 and post-1975 arrivals into evacuees (those who either were evacuated from Vietnam by the Americans or who left with the Americans in the chaos of the fall of Saigon) and refugees (those who escaped from the communist regime on foot or by boat). The former were a more homogeneous group: urban, mostly skilled professionals who have had considerable contact with the West, having been trained by or having worked with the French or the Americans.

Nam Tran, a well-known TV personality who for years had worked with refugees, shuttling tirelessly from refugee camp to refugee camp and thence to Orange County, helping separated family members and relatives reestablish contact, outlined the difference this way: "Those who came later are always scared. They feel they have to protect themselves. They feel worse than we [the evacuees] did. We feel mostly lonely and empty. They feel scared. They have experienced life under communism, and then this freedom. That is a major difference between them and us" (interview, July 17, 1990).

To the experience of life under communism must be added two crucial elements that may help explain further why the refugees "are always scared": they "have experienced protracted and dangerous escapes, often after several attempts; and they have usually spent lengthy periods in refugee camps both before and after acceptance by the U.S." (Haines 1989:10).

The differences can cut deep, particularly among members of the same family. Nguyen Qui Duc, an evacuee, has written of the chasm between himself and his father, who had spent twelve years in Viet Cong prisons before finally making it to the States: "[A]fter a mere month together, there was a grievous rupture between parents and son. Anything they said wound up being about how terrible the Viet Cong were. And as long as I failed to agree with them . . . it was their duty to continue to criticize. I had not lived with the Viet Cong and I couldn't know how bad it had really been. . . . I came to accept that for my parents, Viet Nam had been destroyed by cruel men blinded by Communist propaganda. For me, however, Viet Nam still existed. . . . It was my homeland" (1994:214).

Sponsors and Sponsored

The distinction between those refugees who left by boat *("ô đi ghe")* and those who left on foot *("ô đi bộ")*, which had considerable immediacy in the refugee camps, had lost much of its impact in Orange County.[8] For most Vietnamese families, the new distinction lies between former refugees and those whom they have sponsored under family reunification rules.

Vietnamese refugees were entitled to government aid for a predetermined period. Such aid came directly, in forms like welfare and medical care, or indirectly, through the services of voluntary agencies. When refugees subsequently changed their legal status to permanent residents or citizens and undertook to sponsor family members for immigration to the States under the ODP, they assumed substantial responsibilities at a time when they were themselves still adjusting to a society much different from their own. Sponsors paid for their sponsored family members' transportation from Vietnam, their subsistence, and their medical care until they could take care of themselves.

The following three cases, which focus on sponsors, provide a glimpse of the realities that lie beneath the generalizations.

Mr. A was a former pilot in the Vietnamese Air Force. His outstanding qualities had gotten him assignments to the United States and to Australia before 1975. Although entitled to leave Vietnam under the ODP, he could not wait out the five years or more that he calculated it would take to get his papers processed. After ten attempts to escape, he finally succeeded in 1987 and arrived in Orange County the following year.

Quickly realizing that downward mobility was in store for him, he took a job as technician in an electronic-electrical company and enrolled in evening courses as a first step toward earning a U.S. degree.[9] A fluent English speaker and an avid learner, he got excellent grades and was soon preparing to enter a university. Meantime, his family's application to qualify for the ODP, originally filed in 1980, finally came through, and he was reunited with his wife and two children in December 1991.

Holding a full-time job and trying to study full-time finally took its toll; Mr. A was hospitalized for hypertension. He has now given up his academic aspirations so that he can help his non-English-speaking wife adjust and his children prepare for college.

Miss B, another sponsor and the daughter of a high-ranking former officer of the ARVN, left Vietnam while the rest of her family opted to await the processing of their application for the ODP. Shortly after arriving in Orange County, she received word that her father, who had been in reeducation camp for fifteen years, had obtained "ten passports": ten members of her family had been cleared to leave for the United States.

Although there would be some aid on account of her father's former military status, she assumed that she would be responsible at least in part for her family's subsistence. People her father's age—he is in his late fifties—expect to be retired in Vietnam, and long confinement in reeducation camp, according to Tri Nguyen, so disorients people that adjustment to a new and alien environment is particularly difficult if not impossible.

A very attractive young woman, Miss B resolutely said she had no time for any romantic involvement. She did not even have a social life. A good singer who won second place in a song contest for Indochinese refugees, she had no time to sing. She worried that she might not have enough to help support her family when they arrive. She had a full-time job as cashier on the graveyard shift in a casino while she went to school full-time. Four days a week, she worked from 2:00 A.M. to noon, went home to sleep until 5:00 P.M., and got up to attend to household chores and get some studying done until 8:00. She then tried to get some sleep before she went off to her job or did some school work that could not be scheduled for the other three days of the week. She was suffering from excessive hair loss, which, she said, had been attributed to severe nervous tension.

Finally, Ms. C, an evacuee, is a musician who had won fame in Vietnam before 1975 and remained among the better-known and -loved performers among overseas Vietnamese. She performs extensively in the United States and abroad and produces her own CDs and audio and videocassettes. These activities, however, had to give way to family obligations, particularly because she is the oldest among her siblings. Besides being a mother of two teen-age children at the time of our interview in 1992, she felt obliged to see that her parents and five siblings, whom she had finally succeeded in bringing from Vietnam, were settled before she felt free to devote herself once again to her musical activities. The whole process took seventeen years.

These three cases were not exceptional. Although the considerable stamina, skills, and resourcefulness required to bring family members to the States from Vietnam might be expected to limit the number of people who would assume sponsorship responsibility so soon after their arrival in this country, the sense of obligation to family is so deeply ingrained that sponsorship was the rule rather than the exception.

In many ways, the sponsor-sponsored relation repeated the pattern of earlier migrants who paved the way to the United States for the rest of their families. But the Vietnamese case (and, to some extent, that of other refugee groups who came after them) differed in the institutionalization of the aid given to them—a consequence of the legal status of refugees—and in the effects of the sweeping government policies that followed.[10]

Finally, the differences between sponsors and the sponsored approximated those between forced and voluntary migrants: "[F]ew refugees were prepared for life in the United States. The abruptness of the evacuation left most refugees psychologically unprepared to start life anew." The ODP immigrants, on the other hand, had the advantage of "anticipatory socialization," learning English, seeking information about the United States, and adjusting themselves to the idea of leaving Vietnam while they waited for their applications to be processed. (Montero 1979:30;60). (Egon Kunz distinguishes "anticipatory" from "acute" migrants [1973:132].) In addition, the entry of the ODP's into an unfamiliar culture was eased by relatives who had already traveled that road and were able to give emotional and psychological support.

Communist and Non-Communist

While most criteria for differentiation among groups changed with changing contexts, one set remained constant and, until recently in Orange County, among the most powerful: those criteria that invoke, feed into, or derive from the communist-non-communist contrast.

In 1990, as I prepared to do fieldwork in Orange County, I expected the strong anti-communist sentiments particularly palpable in the refugee camps (see Hitchcox 1990; Knudsen 1983; and Reyes Schramm 1989) to have abated as resettlement proceeded and as the government of Vietnam eased some of the restrictions on social and economic life in that country. I was therefore surprised by the continuing strength of those sentiments. When I returned in 1992, I was told that, if anything, they had intensified.

Contributing to the collective memory of a Vietnam changed by communist rule were three factors that fortified anti-communism's role and gave it its enduring strength, particularly in Orange County. The confluence of two of them—Roman Catholicism and the large number of ex-military personnel among the Vietnamese population, one religious and the other secular—accounted for the tenacity and power of the communist/non-communist dichotomy, couched in ideological terms. The third factor, introduced from outside the Vietnamese community, ensured that the full power of the dichotomy would be mobilized, eventually exerting tremendous pressure on anti-communists to flee to the States: U.S. involvement in Vietnam and a foreign policy that favored refugees from communist countries.

In 1954, when North Vietnam came under communist control, Vietnamese Roman Catholics in huge numbers—"entire Catholic villages," according to Karnow (1983:58)—fled to the south, aided by a U.S. airlift (Zolberg, Suhrke, and Aguayo 1989:163) and by U.S.-spread "rumors of a bloodbath if the Catholics stayed" (Strand and Jones 1985:27; see also Zolberg, Suhrke, and Aguayo 1989). The influx of two-thirds of North Vietnam's Catholic population into the south tripled the number of Catholics in that region. With the landlords who had also been driven south by communist land reform programs and by persecution, the Catholics became the "pillars of the Southern regime whose raison d'etre was to prevent the consolidation and spread of communism in Vietnam" (Zolberg, Suhrke, and Aguayo 1989:163).

The anti-communist sentiments of Vietnamese Catholics were stronger even than those of the Roman Catholic Church of the 1950s (Kelly 1977:13). This was dramatically manifested when the vast majority of Catholics comprised the evacuees and refugees who fled the country when it fell into communist hands. Entire parishes are said to have fled under the leadership of their parish priests (Kelly 1977:14, 202; Kessner and Caroli 1981:36). And while the number of Roman Catholics relative to the number of escapees was said to be largest among the first wave, Caplan, Whitmore, and

Choy report that of the second wave of refugees, in 1978 and 1979, a fifth were Roman Catholics, double their representation in Vietnam's population at the time (1989:25).

In Orange County, Vietnamese Roman Catholics showed up in force at Vietnamese feasts such as the commemoration of Vietnamese martyrs. On November 22, 1992, this affair was held at the Santa Ana Stadium to accommodate the number of participants and to provide adequate space for the ceremonies, which included a parade showing the colors of the old (non-communist) Republic of Vietnam, Vietnamese dances, choral music, and a mass.[11]

There was at least one Vietnamese priest to every major Catholic church in the area (compared with one Vietnamese priest for the entire Newark Archdiocese in New Jersey), and the regularly scheduled Vietnamese masses offered each Saturday or Sunday were very well attended.

While the initiative for the Roman Catholic presence came largely from within the Vietnamese heirarchy, the strong South Vietnamese military presence in Orange County is largely the result of U.S. policy. Realizing that former military personnel were at high risk of punitive action by the communist government, the United States facilitated their entry into the country. As a consequence, they are strongly represented in the Vietnamese population throughout the country.

The major underlying cause for leaving Vietnam since 1975—the communist victory—has therefore been kept alive in the minds of refugee-resettlers by Catholic and military perspectives. But its emotional charge and its effectiveness as a mechanism for social control is perhaps greater in Orange County than elsewhere in the country because the awareness of community particularly strong among the Vietnamese here has made them sensitive to the fact that the actions of members are observable by other members, and that those actions are expected to conform to generally understood standards.

Thus, Vietnamese daily life in the county has been punctuated by reports of what happened to individuals or groups who, for instance, were believed to have openly supported communism, or who were audacious enough to have shown the current Vietnamese regime's flag, or whose visit to Vietnam was purely as tourists and therefore contributed needlessly to the coffers of the present government. Some establishments were said to have been set on fire or bombed for offenses of this nature (see Bousquet

1991:6–8). A Vietnamese who came to California in 1972 and who has provided his family with capital to open what is now one of the most popular restaurants in Ho Chi Minh City expressed his ambivalence about closer ties between Vietnam and the United States. Interviewed while he was visiting Vietnam, he asked that his name not be mentioned. "There are a lot of extremists among the Vietnamese in the United States who think I am betraying them, and I have my family there" (Erlanger 1990:22). Vuong Tran, a travel agent in Westminster, Orange County, recounted that "when Hanoi first opened the door for returnees . . . he escorted groups of five or ten people on visits to [Vietnam, which] so angered militant Vietnamese anticommunists that his office was fire bombed" (Mydans 1994:6).

Community disapproval of those who support normalization of relations between the United States and Vietnam prompted strong Vietnamese support for the Bush-Quayle ticket in the 1992 election; in Little Saigon, large banners proclaimed "Vietnamese for Bush-Quayle." Clinton was seen as someone who would more quickly normalize relations. The same issue has divided the business community. Some factions supported normalization for economic reasons, and others opposed it for political or ideological reasons.

Conversely, those who were outspoken in their opposition to the present Vietnamese government feared reprisal. Vietnamese in Orange County still believe that there are communists among them who continue to actively support the communist cause and are capable of punitive acts. When a well-known anti-communist writer accepted a dinner invitation from me after having met me just once, her family, she told me, was extremely upset. How could she be certain that I was not out to do her harm, perhaps even kill her? When I came to pick her up, I was asked to provide a telephone number where she could be reached while she was with me.

Some of the incidents involving violence and ostracism were said to be rumors, but that such rumors persisted is symptomatic of the degree to which communism has acted as a prism through which the community views human behavior. The starkness of the contrasts that a consciousness of communism can draw was made evident by Viet Hung, one of Vietnam's eminent and highly respected cải lương actors now living in Orange County: "It is a pity. We are all one people, we have one language, but we are fighting one another. Now we come over here and we're still fighting; there are still Communists" (interview, June 25, 1990).

Communism's capacity to occupy so much space in the lives of Vietnamese in Orange County by now owes less to its substance as ideology than to the wealth of personal experiences with which it has become associated. As many of my Bataan and Orange County friends explained, communism is to blame for their painful separation from their families, the loss of property and prestige, the risks that they had to take to escape, the loss of life at sea, the pirate attacks, and the rape of women.

To these, James M. Freeman adds the deep sense of betrayal that came with the realization that "they were being treated not as brothers and sisters under one flag but as a conquered people looted and terrorized for the benefit of their new rulers. . . . That is why those who fled Vietnam become so emotional about communism." Indeed, Freeman goes so far as to say that the impact of communist domination "seems to be a defining feature of the Vietnamese refugee experience" (1989:200).

Attitudes toward communism, with its accretion of meanings specific to the Vietnamese refugee situation, thus color Vietnamese attitudes toward their culture and their traditions. A strong desire to conserve these is shared by Orange County Vietnamese with their conationals elsewhere. It is a pre-1975 culture, however, the one they feel was destroyed by the communist regime, that they must keep alive abroad against the day communism is finally driven from Vietnam, when they can reinstate that culture in its native land (see Hitchcox 1990:65).

This theme has taken its place beside the theme of longing to return, but not to a communist or totalitarian country. They are themes reinforced and nurtured through various means, most notably and regularly by television.

During my visits to Orange County and in the periods immediately preceding and following, the two-hour Saturday Vietnamese program on TV (KSCI, Channel 18) served as common denominator to the different segments of Vietnamese in Orange county. I met no one there who did not know the program and did not watch it at least sporadically.[12]

Heavily laden with commercials, most from establishments in Little Saigon, the invariable components of the program were: the opening, which featured the national anthem of the former South Vietnam serving as background for scenes of pre-1975 Vietnam—old film clips of military parades, the flag of the Saigon regime, scenes of war, soldiers saying goodbye to children, old landmarks; the display of the program logo at about half-hour intervals, during which time a patriotic song like Pham Duy's "Vietnam, Vietnam" played and some of the same scenes flashed on the screen; the newscast, a one-on-one interview often conducted by a well-known TV journalist like Nam Tran, or a panel discussing an issue; songs and dances. Many of the song texts dealt with loved ones left behind and with the Vietnam the Orange County Vietnamese had known. The format for the presentation of these songs was virtually uniform: shots of the singer alternating or in combination with (through double exposure or split screen) shots of the loved one or the Vietnamese countryside, sometimes in dreamlike slow motion, sometimes in sepia tints to suggest flashbacks. The juxtaposition of images was consistent: away from Vietnam and remembering Vietnam, then and now, spring and winter. According to Vietnamese viewers, this format had remained consistent over at least five years, as of 1992.

Almost all the Vietnamese I spoke to agreed that the permanent inclusion in the program of the opening segment with its musical and visual components, and of the half-hour interval breaks with their patriotic songs, was intended to reinforce identification with pre-1975, non-communist Vietnam. One added that these were also intended to honor the military, of whom there are many in Orange County. The one dissenting though not wholly contradictory note was sounded by a man who left Vietnam before 1975. He explained the whole presentation as part of one big commercial intended to make its potential clients receptive by showing solidarity with them. The message as he saw it was: "I know that you are attached to pre-1975 Vietnam. I want you to know that this is also where I stand. I share this sentiment with you." The intent, however, was "promotional. If you want to sell a product, you have to make your potential customer want it. And, of course, you already know that the sentiment against communism is strong in this area, so you show these [the flag, the parades, etc.] to attract people and to say, 'See, I'm on your side' " (interview, November 24, 1992).

Everyone agreed that those emblems invoke, promote, or reinforce ties to pre-1975 Vietnam. The discrepancy lay in what they imputed to the images and sounds. The majority saw genuine sentiment being represented; the dissenter saw the representation of that sentiment as a means to a commercial end. The majority saw an attachment to the past and to another place; the dissenter saw a pragmatic attachment to the here and now. But these attachments, viewed either way, dovetailed into an attachment to the idea of a pre-1975 Vietnam and an inducement to reject what has been put in its place.

Vietnamese and Americans: Contrapuntal Relations

The shape and quality of Vietnamese social life in Orange County was the result not only of Vietnamese action, motivations, and aspirations but also of Vietnamese interaction with the social environment—in particular, the larger U.S. society. For refugees, the problems "are compounded by the nature of their immigration and the expectation of the host population. . . . The status of the involuntary immigrant and the divergent expectations of the host population create a differential in resettlement outcomes" (Strand and Jones 1985:129).

And just as departure was swift and precipitous for the majority of refugees, for "the host population [there was] little preparation for the effects of the refugees' presence" (Straud and Jones 1985:132; see also Conover 1993:75). The legislated linkage between U.S. society and the Vietnamese refugees—the programs designed or financed by the government to ease entry into the United States—were "complex, divers, and subject to change over very short periods of time" (Haines 1989:12).

All these factors—the internally diverse populations, both U.S and Vietnamese; the constant changes in policies and in legislation; the circumstances of flight on the part of the Vietnamese and of their reception by U.S. society; the apparent rates at which adaptation proceeds in the private and public spheres—make describing the resulting social organisms a challenge. But certain segments of life are amenable to observation and, through them, access to other areas becomes possible.

The Economic Sphere

The signs of adaptation are most easily observed in the public arena, and Vietnamese adaptation is particularly evident in the economic and academic spheres. The business community, in fact, is probably the sector of the Vietnamese population that has been most effective in making its presence felt in the larger society. The Vietnamese Chamber of Commerce in Orange County, through its newsletter and other means, has repeatedly made explicit its awareness of the need to expand Vietnamese markets beyond its own social group. At the same time, the Vietnamese have been aware of the contributions they have made and are making to the economy of Orange County. Few dispute Vietnamese claims that they, with the help of Chinese capital, deserve the major share of the credit for the development of Westminster and Garden Grove.[13]

Little Saigon is testimony to Vietnamese participation and success in the economic life of the larger Orange County community. It is also a response to the American part of their experience. While the facades of the major buildings or the entrances leading up to them serve as distinctly non-American diacritica, the general layout and basic function of these buildings are those of the U.S. shopping mall with its huge parking areas and its conglomeration of shops and businesses in an indoor space. Beneath this level of functionality and significance, Little Saigon's power as symbol derives as much, if not more, from its U.S. context, which reinforces Vietnamese identity by providing the backdrop against which the Vietnamese can see more clearly the one thing they have in common: their difference from the American mainstream.

The Academic Sphere

The academic performance of the Vietnamese has provided educators, sociologists, and American society at large with an exemplar of what can be achieved despite poverty, unfamiliarity with U.S. society and culture, and considerable initial difficulties with language.

Using such measures as grade point average (GPA), school transcripts, records, and performance on standardized achievement tests, Ruben G. Rumbaut, in his study of Indochinese refugees in San Diego, California, found that "drop-out rates for Indochinese students are significantly lower than for other students." In addition, these students, most of whom are Vietnamese, rank only behind U.S.-born Chinese, Japanese, and Koreans (who, in San Diego City Schools, constitute the category "Asians") in the percentage of students with GPAs above 3.0 (1989:168).

Caplan, Whitmore, and Choy, whose study (begun in 1981) focused on Boston, Chicago, Houston, Orange County, and Seattle, corroborate Rumbaut's findings and add a statistic that helps support their view of Indochinese scholastic performance as "stunning." Most of the students studied had lost one to three years of schooling in refugee camps; the majority knew little if any English upon arrival. But "in Garden Grove,

Orange County, for example, [where] the refugee community made up less than 20% of the school population at the time of data collection . . . 12 of 14 valedictorians had Indochinese backgrounds" (1989:vi,69).

Since much of this achievement is often attributed to internal cultural factors—family structure, work ethic, the high value placed on learning—the topic seems to characterize Vietnamese more than their interaction with the larger society. But Rumbaut suggests external forces at work: "There are strongly held traditional values and a sense of ethnic pride and identity. . . . [T]he more convinced the parents were that as Asians they would never have equal status with [white] Americans in the United States, the higher the GPAs attained by their children" (1989:171).

Caplan, Whitmore, and Choy contend that there is an extra-Vietnamese component to Vietnamese scholastic success: the opportunities that the larger society makes available. The match between those opportunities and the attributes that the Vietnamese bring to bear upon them account for Vietnamese educational achievement (1989:131).

Levels of Adaptation and Integration

This very success, however, introduces elements that bring conflicts between Vietnamese and the larger society into the private sphere. As the younger generation gains proficiency in English and becomes increasingly comfortable with U.S. culture, while the parental and grandparental generations remain monolingual or learn English at much slower rates, frictions arise at home. One interviewee complained that when he and his wife come home from work, they seek relief from the effort of having to live their "American life." They want to retreat to a Vietnamese haven where Vietnamese is the language spoken and where Vietnamese customs prevail. But the children speak English, watch American TV, and develop American tastes in food, clothing, and entertainment.

I have seen this classic generational disjunction dealt with in three ways. In one household where children and teenagers are put in the care of their grandparents, the grandparents (who do not speak any English) insist that only Vietnamese be spoken in their house, a policy they contend is essential if Vietnamese are not to forget their culture.

In another household, the parents (who speak English with some difficulty) insist only that the children speak to them in Vietnamese. The children may speak to each other in English if they wish.

In the third household, the parents (who are quite comfortable with English) say that they have given up insisting that the children speak Vietnamese. Both parents work, are very tired when they get home, and, while admitting to misgivings, are quite relieved that the children entertain themselves with U.S. television programming, at least until the parents have had a chance to catch their breath. They express fears that their children are forgetting their cultural heritage, but they see the process as inevitable. They continue to speak Vietnamese and to maintain such traditions as keeping an altar in their home to honor deceased members of the family, and celebrating Vietnamese feasts such as Tết, in the hope of countervailing what they see as their children's growing Americanization.

These three responses to what is seen as the encroachment of things American into the Vietnamese private sphere provide a clue to the diversity of adaptive strategies. While Vietnamese concede the necessity and even the desirability of adapting to U.S. ways in the public sphere, they tend to be guarded about concessions within the home. But the various segments of life cannot be kept insulated from each other. The ambiguities that fuel the search for ethnic identity—Vietnamese/American in the public/private spheres—are as powerful and wrenching, if not more so, among the Vietnamese as among earlier migrants whose cultures were closer to the American. They are especially wrenching for those who cannot—or believe that they cannot—return to their homeland at will.

Thus, while there are analytical and methodological grounds for statements such as Bruce Dunning's, that despite being thrown "quickly into predominantly American settings, their private lives retained a strong Vietnamese flavor" (1989:77), or Nguyen Manh Hung's, that the economic success of Vietnamese in general has not been matched by their social and psychological adjustment (1985:203), one must also keep in mind Young Yun Kim's (1989:91) insistence upon the interrelatedness of various levels of adaptation—the personal, the communal, and the more broadly social.

The very size of the Vietnamese population in Orange County and the degree to which its members have achieved self-sufficiency affect their adaptation to the larger society. Their options are wide-ranging. They may choose to socialize or do business only with their conationals. Or they may choose to keep such contacts to the barest minimum. Individuals can confine their Vietnamese associations to family if they wish or seek out non-Vietnamese for other parts of their life.

The result is the together-but-separate dynamic that underlies much of American and ethnic group interaction, each case made distinctive by what one brings or means to the other. Emphasis shifts periodically between the together and the separate aspects as contexts change and as individual options are exercised.

Emphasis on what is shared, on proximity, has been signaled by the Vietnamese through such gestures as the adoption of the functional aspects of design incorporated into Little Saigon, and the display of a huge American flag that dominated the facade of its Asian Garden Mall in July to commemorate Independence Day. Solidarity with U.S. society has also been signaled by the scenes of the White House, the Washington Monument, and the Lincoln Memorial that were used to foreground the "Happy Thanksgiving Day" message flashed on the TV screen while "God Bless America" played in the background—all part of the Vietnamese newscast on that holiday. Housing and schools have been integrated in Orange County and Vietnamese have adopted U.S. fashions in clothes and cars enthusiastically.

But these readily identifiable signs of integration shade off into ambiguity. In the Saturday Vietnamese TV program's opening section, for example, as the scenes of the Vietnamese countryside, parades, and landmarks unfolded, a voice would break in with "Gooood morning, Vietnam," à la Robin Williams. The juxtaposition of an imagery that was intended to keep fresh the memories of the Vietnam that overseas Vietnamese have wished restored, of a Vietnam in control of its own destiny, and a voice whose distinct association is with a war-torn Vietnam and American military presence at its most controversial point is polysemic to say the least.[14] And although some Vietnamese have told me that they prefer the *Orange County Register* or the *Los Angeles Times* for their daily news, dependence on English-language news media has been attenuated by some twenty Vietnamese publications in Orange County. Three are daily newspapers (Loc Nguyen, personal communication, July 10, 1990), and others are magazines or tabloids like *Kich Anh*, a biweekly published in Westminster that is devoted to entertainment, or newsletters distributed free in places like Little Saigon.

The separateness of the larger Orange County world and the Vietnamese world indicated by the minimal participation on the part of non-Vietnamese in the economic life of Little Saigon has also been reflected in the English-language newspapers. One would not suspect from reading the *Orange County Register*, the county's leading newspaper, that in 1990, the Asian population comprised nearly 17 percent of the Orange County population, of which nearly 30 percent were Vietnamese.[15] In one of the major public events of the summer of 1990, the two-week-long Orange County Festival, there was no Asian representation noted beyond some karate and kung fu events. And on a local level, Vietnamese claim that when they called police from Little Saigon, the police were slow to respond and reluctant to intervene because they considered conflicts there a "domestic matter."

In the dynamic process that seeks some form of integration or adaptation, in the tension between togetherness and separateness, the latter, according to Peter Rose, will tend to have the upper hand. Rose sees the Asians assimilating extrinsically, "taking on the superficial trappings of dominant groups—speech, dress, musical tastes—while remaining socially separate." "For many Vietnamese families, especially those ensconced in such places as Orange County and San Jose, California . . . it all seems to be happening at once. The older people still 'stay behind.' Older children . . . often go through a rapid course in resocialization, learning . . . to walk the tightrope between the two worlds. Younger children, even some of those born in Indochina or in the camps . . . take on the dress, manners, and many of the mores of the new society. Yet, even those in the last group (the 'third generation') seem to maintain some sense of identity, though it is hardly one their relatives back home would comprehend." In the end, Rose contends, owing to their non-Caucasian appearance, the Vietnamese, like other Asians, "are now and will remain hyphenates" (1985:183, 209–12).

The situations and perceptions described fuel the interplay of forces that shape the Vietnamese community of Orange County. That interplay pulls the Vietnamese community and the rest of Orange County apart and brings them together as each responds alternatively to group interests and to the demands of the larger society of which each is a part. Social cohesion, as they demonstrate once again, is a fluid state of affairs that is activated by and that responds to interaction. It is this state of affairs to which music making contributes and in which it partakes. To remove music from this milieu is to decontextualize it and to deny it the sustenance that gives it its particular character.

CHAPTER 5

Vietnamese Americans in Orange County:
The Musical Life

If Vietnamese music is born of Vietnamese life, then the music should vary as widely as the life.

To ensure attention to local circumstances (a cliché that conceals much, from the monotony of the mundane to the violence that cuts a people off from their homeland to create variations on the indigenous life) and to give due respect to the integrity of music as social act, I once again looked to the people—music makers and users, formally trained or not, professionals and lay persons—what they did, what they said, and what they thought about their music. I listened to Vietnamese argue about *real* Vietnamese music, about music that is claimed to be Vietnamese because it uses Vietnamese sounds (vocal and instrumental) although it may lack the "Vietnamese soul," about the Vietnameseness of American music whose texts have been translated into Vietnamese so that they can be performed and listened to by Vietnamese. Of particular interest was not just that the Vietnameseness of this repertory was a matter of debate among its own makers and users—matters of musical identity almost always are. Particularly revealing were the grounds for imputing that identity. They were both historical and contemporary—an invocation and reinterpretation of the past in light of a present that was focused on reconstructing a life and building a community that they can label Vietnamese, in their own terms, in a different land, in Orange County.

The local in this case has global implications. Many of Vietnam's most famous musicians now reside in Orange County. The presence of Pham Duy, Thai Thanh, Hoang Oanh, Hoang Thi Tho, Viet Hung, Duy Khanh, Khanh Ly, and Kim Tuyen, among others—luminaries in the Vietnamese musical firmament by the time they left Vietnam—has led overseas Vietnamese to call Orange County the musical capital of Vietnam. These musicians are or have been recording artists or producers, and their names come up time and again in discourse about Vietnamese music. Many of the younger generation of stars—Y Lan, Son Ca, Thai Hien, Nhu Mai, and Elvis Phuong among them—have also been nurtured in Orange County. Thus, a significant number of recordings disseminated throughout the States, exported to overseas Vietnamese worldwide, and copied even in Vietnam have been produced in Orange County.

To evoke images of this complex and vibrant musical community, I begin with the specifically Vietnamese—the venues, the music that takes place therein, both in its social and hence, human, context. I then move on to the Vietnamese community interacting with the American society of which it has become a part.

Venues for the Vietnamese Musical Community

On a regular basis, the most common venues for public music making by Vietnamese are clubs, churches, and pagodas. On occasions like Tết or for special purposes like lecture concerts, parties, or weddings, schools, university campuses, restaurants, parks, and stadiums become settings for music making. Taken together, these sites offer a composite picture of Vietnamese musical life in the public sphere, evidence of the rich tapestry of that life in Orange County.

Clubs

When I asked Vietnamese friends where I should go to hear live Vietnamese music, the ready reply was "clubs." But that reply was as quickly qualified. Most clubs, they said, are for dancing and may be too noisy for listening. Clubs in Orange County are not part of daily life: they are open only on weekends. Musicians have to work at other jobs during the week to support themselves and to meet other family obligations. Furthermore, most clubs—those for dancing—are rather expensive and do not attract the average Vietnamese in search of weekend entertainment. It is too bad, people told me, that there are not more clubs or tea- or coffeehouses like those in Vietnam, where people come principally to listen. Khanh Ly, one of the best known Vietnamese singers now living in Orange County, reminisced about one such club, her own, in Saigon.

Friends—composers and singers—would come and perform and then move on to perform elsewhere. In an evening, one got to listen to a variety of performers.[1]

Why then the spontaneous reference to clubs followed by the quick reconsideration? Clubs, it became clear, were going to provide more than an exposure to Vietnamese music making. I investigated two, the Caravelle and Đêm Đông Phương, polar opposites in the range of Vietnamese clubs in Orange County.

The Caravelle, perhaps not coincidentally the name of a well-known Saigon hotel that used to be a favorite meeting place for political discussions, was a "listening club," the only one I found in Orange County. Located in Anaheim, the club was unprepossessing in appearance. It occupied space in a row of shops and business establishments that formed a mini-mall.

The modest admission fee varied according to the number and reputation of the artists presented that evening. Inside, a dimly lit intimate space, rows of tables faced a large screen onto which were projected images that complemented the music being played on the adjoining stage. As each table was occupied, the small candle that decorated it was lit, so that when the house was full, rows of flickering candles complemented the bright lights on stage.

No hard alcoholic beverages were served. Fruit juices, soda, tea, and beer were the staples. The clientele spanned a wide age range, from little children who were sometimes carried off in a parent's or grandparent's arms asleep when the evening was over, around midnight, to people in their sixties or over. Attire varied from informal street clothes, which predominated, to suits for men and dressy outfits for women. Almost everyone stayed for the entire event, between three and four hours of nonstop performance by instrumentalists, singers, and the stand-up comics who gave the musicians a chance to rest.

In 1990, Rick Murphy, a non-Vietnamese American who spoke fluent Vietnamese and sang Vietnamese folk songs, ballads, and vọng cổ, served as "permanent singer" and master of ceremonies, cracking jokes, inviting responses from the audience and, in general, livening up the atmosphere.[2] He always wore an áo dài, complete with long scarf and hat—the only male on stage who did so—because, he explained, the Vietnamese owner wanted to simulate as closely as possible a Vietnamese teahouse.

He succeeded, if my Vietnamese research assistant was any indication. She said that once inside the club, it was easy for her to think that she was back in Saigon.

Typically, there were six featured singers in addition to the "house singers," Rick Murphy and Nguyen Kim Long, the owner of the club. With few exceptions (among them Rick Murphy and Lyn, the Australian wife of Vietnamese singer Cong Thanh, with whom she sang duets), all the performers were Vietnamese.

The images on the screen were as much a part of the program as the music. For the love songs and the occasional folk song, the images were romantic depictions of rural or nature scenes, pagodas, flowers. For vọng cổ, abstract shapes moved like figures in a kaleidoscope. For patriotic songs, shots of parades and military scenes that looked as though they were archival footage in black and white or sepia tints, provided documentary reminders of a real past.

The same features marked the program for special occasions, exemplified by that for July 6, 1990, a celebration of Independence Day, with more featured singers and additional personnel in the band. There was also a somewhat wider variety of songs (see the Appendix). Of a total of fifty-six items, thirty-eight—more than two-thirds—were love songs, all but five of which had Vietnamese texts. Seven of these songs were sung twice, once on each of the two evenings I attended. All were love songs, all but one (sung in French) with Vietnamese texts: "Túp lều lý tưởng," "Tạ từ trong dem," "Bao giờ biết tương tu," "Em di," "Lôi về xóm nhơ" "Trúc đào," and "Aline." The songs in other languages were "Aline" and "Main dans la main" in French; "It's a Kind of Hush," "You're My Heart; You're My Soul," and "I Can't Stop Loving You" in English; and "La Bamba," in Spanish. All but five of the Vietnamese songs were composed after 1975, two of them ("Trúc Dào" and "Hạnh phúc lang thang") in the United States.[3]

Đêm Đông Phương was one of the largest and best-known Vietnamese nightclubs in Orange County in 1990. A victim of the economic recession in 1992, it contrasted with Caravelle in just about every respect: physical appearance, size, personnel, cost of admission, and the principal activity that the clubs were intended to serve; Đêm Đông Phương was for dancing.

Considered a more festive and more special occasion, a night out at such a club called for evening or party attire. The sense of the club as a special place was heightened by highly visible security personnel. After paying for admission at the box office–like window by the door, one handed over keys and handbags to one of the guards who stood by a metal detector through which one entered the club. One was then led past a lounge decorated with posters advertising forthcoming Vietnamese events, to be seated at one's assigned table in the elevated area ringing the dance floor.

The background to the large stage looked like a wall of sequins, with a multitude of small lights blinking like stars. Around the dance floor were pairs of lights that rotated as they moved continuously from side to side. Above the area were large grids framed by zigzagging neon lights and checkered with spotlights of various colors, which rotated as the grids were raised and lowered. The general effect was of multicolored lights in perpetual motion, changing the colors on the dance floor and on the stage every moment. Special effects created an air of illusion or unreality: from time to time puffs of smoke or mist rolled onto the dance floor.

The music played nonstop for more than four hours. A succession of singers performed, each announced by the MC. Each sang two or three songs. At the end of the series, the singers came back in more or less reverse order for a second round of songs (see the Appendix). On Independence Day, shortly past midnight, the management invited everyone to celebrate with some complimentary champagne.

The dominance of Latin American dance rhythms was evident not only from the number of pieces played and from the fact that the dance floor was fullest during the Latin numbers (tango, rhumba, cha-cha-cha) but also from the consistent fit between the performances onstage and on the dance floor. This was underscored by the discrepancy between dance and music in the New Wave items, to which people danced the boogie or the cha-cha-cha.[4] During the "valse" numbers and to a lesser extent during the paso doble numbers, the dance floor emptied considerably to be taken over by couples—almost all of the parental or grandparental generation—who used virtually the entire floor to do their wide turns and highly stylized waltz dancing.

The listener expecting a novel musical experience from Vietnamese clubs is likely to be disappointed. Apart from the occasional vọng cổ in the listening club and the Vietnamese song texts that were the general practice, the music was invariably in the Western musical idiom, the instrumentation was Western, and the dance music could serve the purpose of ballroom and contemporary forms of social dance in the wider American society. Differences in vocal style, particularly in the renditions of love songs, might easily be attributed to individual predilection or the requirements of language rather than to differences in melodic treatment and ornamentation that stem from Vietnamese musical tradition.

What clubs revealed, therefore, was less the distinctiveness of the music-making than the construction of a cohesive musical life, and the disjunctions—social and musical—that are confronted in the process. The dominance of love songs and pre-1975 songs was strikingly reminiscent of the repertoire of "sad songs" and love songs on Palawan. The major alterations in Orange County were situational: instrumentation took advantage of the availability of the full range of Western musical instruments, acoustic and electronic, and the rhythmic treatment of the music responded to the function of the clubs, in particular the dancing clubs, where the music was performed.

The roles and activities of the performers were defined by the club's primary function. The MCs in the listening club must engage the audience and keep them entertained. They must know the featured performers, the audiences, and the culture well so that they can banter effectively, and they must be performers themselves. These talents were less necessary, even dispensable, among MCs in the dancing clubs, whose primary function was to introduce the performers. The back-up musicians in the listening club consider their first obligation to be to the singer, whose performance they must complement and enhance. The back-up musicians in the dancing clubs must keep the dancers in mind; the rhythmic features of any song must be made palpable to induce the audience to dance.

The adjustments imposed by differences in club functions were described by Kim Tuyen, a singer who performed in both kinds of clubs. When she sang at listening clubs, she tried to "balance between styles of singing by including a love song, a cha-cha-cha type, a slow bolero, a vọng cổ" in each set. For performances in dancing clubs, she submitted a list of songs, and what she sang and in what order were decisions made by the band and the club manager (interview, June 23, 1990).

Attempting to discover who the clientele of nightclubs or dancing clubs might be, I asked a number of Vietnamese on what occasion they would go to a nightclub. The respondents were two couples who were pre-1975 arrivals, two former refugees (one a man in his early forties, a

1980 arrival who now owns two houses in Orange County and works for a large U.S. corporation; the other a former pilot in his mid- or late forties), a writer in her late fifties, and four young men in their late teens and early twenties. None of them said they go to Vietnamese nightclubs. One of the young men said that when he felt like dancing, he went to American nightclubs because he did not care for the ballroom dancing that dominates the Vietnamese nightclub scene. One of the former refugees said that he would go to a Vietnamese nightclub to entertain someone whom he thought might enjoy it.

While these responses were statistically insignificant, they indicated the location of clubs in Vietnamese life in Orange County. There were few, if any, regular nightclub patrons. Those who went did so occasionally and tended to be in their thirties and older, interested in ballroom dancing, and members of at least the middle class. Clubs therefore—particularly listening clubs—were centrally located in the Vietnamese *recollection* of their musical world.[5] They quickly rose to consciousness when one asked where to go for live music. But things remembered quickly clashed with reality, which forced memory to reconsider, for clubs have clearly become marginal to Vietnamese daily existence in Orange County.

Just as cohesive elements represent continuities with the past or conflicts resolved, disjunctions represent conflicts that must either be resolved as part of the resettlement process or accommodated as social fact—simply the way things are. Three sets of disjunctions were immediately evident in Đêm Đông Phương. The first was the mismatch between the club's physical features and both its surroundings and the cultural identity of its clientele. Đêm Đông Phương, a structure that, in the pitch of its roof and in its use of thatching and exposed beams, suggested the South Seas touched by a Hollywood wand, stood out on busy Harbor Boulevard in Santa Ana's central business district, announcing its Western offerings in French ("Nuits d'Orient") to a Vietnamese clientele. The constellation of disparate elements from widely divergent cultures and geographic locations strung together and displayed in this corner of Orange County seemed to mirror the experience of its Vietnamese patrons and clients—dislocated from Vietnam, passing through the corridors of different cultures, and accumulating a variety of cultural influences on their way to resettlement elsewhere.

I saw a second set of disjunctions in the behavior of dancers and musicians. The mostly young singers, whose costumes and onstage demeanor would have been appropriate for MTV, seemed to belong to a time and a place different from that of most dancers on the floor, who were doing ballroom dancing from decades gone by. These two groups of Vietnamese, most if not all Vietnam-born, were separately (one group as musicians onstage, the other as dancers on the floor) yet simultaneously representing the different rates at which they let go of old cultural habits.

A third disjunction was suggested by the audience's response to one of the performers. In surroundings replete with the latest in technology, the most applauded singer and the one who seemed the biggest draw was also the oldest—Thai Thanh, the mother of four professional singers, one the well-known Y Lan. Thai Thanh brought down the house with her rendition of Johann Strauss Jr.'s "By the Beautiful Blue Danube" with Vietnamese text, sung in a lyric soprano voice and embellished with coloratura passages, her vocal quality and style diverging strikingly from the rest of the evening's performers.'6

Churches

Although pagodas or Buddhist temples and Protestant churches are important musical venues, the overrepresentation of Catholics among the Vietnamese population made Catholic churches perhaps the most important locus for large gatherings of Vietnamese on a regular basis. These churches, in fact, had spawned a number of choral groups—as many as fourteen in 1992—some of which performed outside the church context. At least as important as the religious affiliation was the specificity of the context as Vietnamese: when the Vietnamese gathered on Saturdays or Sundays, they did so in the context of a mass that was announced as Vietnamese in church bulletins and other public venues. The officiating priest was Vietnamese, the language of the service was Vietnamese, and the congregation was, with very few exceptions, Vietnamese.

Music came from two sources: the congregation and the choir.

In the many Vietnamese contexts where I have had a chance to observe the celebration of the Roman Catholic mass—Ho Chi Minh City's cathedral, the refugee camp churches in the Philippines, churches in central New Jersey, and churches in Orange County—congregational participation in what is arguably the musical domain centered on certain liturgical passages and responses during the mass, and on prayers before and after it. This participation has been variously called chant, prayer, and,

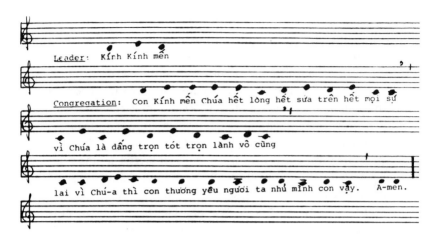

FIGURE 3. Fragment of chanted prayer before the Roman Catholic mass. Note correspondence of linguistic tone and melodic contour.

rarely, song. (Tran Van Khe [1980], for example, puts it in the same class as declamation of poetry, which, in Vietnamese practice, might be described as straddling speech and song.)

The musically ambiguous character of this practice (see Figure 3) arises from the fact that the requirements of Vietnamese phonemic tone are exceeded in ambitus, and the rhythms of normal speech are constrained by the almost uniform durational value given to each syllable—hence, the argument that it is not merely speech. At the same time, the practice boils down the musical aspects to the minimal requirements of melody: the pitch inventory seldom exceeds three basic pitches. This feature, added to the rhythmic austerity, constitutes the core of the argument against the practice's being regarded as song.

Predictably, this practice, perhaps above all other forms, has manifested the greatest stability in acoustic features and in function, despite the dislocations to which it has been subjected. Its melodic contour has been determined largely by the linguistic rules of Vietnamese as a tone language, and it enjoys the protection of the conservatism that characterizes much of religious ritual, reinforced by habits deeply embedded in communal practice.

The musical repertory of church choirs was as diverse stylistically as the congregational repertory was not. Unlike other masses in the area, the

Vietnamese mass relegated the singing of hymns, of special songs during the offertory and the communion, and of certain parts of the liturgy almost entirely to the choir. The range extended from monophonic singing that uses the Vietnamese pitch system, to original Vietnamese compositions written in four parts for soprano, alto, tenor, and bass, to what one of my informants called "Vietnamese polyphony"—strongly Vietnamese influenced in pitch system and polyphonic in the Western European sense—to Christmas carols and instrumental and choral works by J. S. Bach and G. F. Händel.[7] The texts were invariably Vietnamese; those originally in another language were often replaced by Vietnamese rather than translated, to avoid the difficulty of reconciling Vietnamese phonemic tone with a melodic contour that was not intended for it (see Figure 4). The organ, when available, was the preferred accompanying instrument, followed in frequency by the guitar and piano, and on occasion, joined by the đàn tranh and the violin.

The richness of church songs from Vietnam is worthy of note. In Bataan, in Jersey City, and in Orange County, I have seen mimeographed collections of songs composed and disseminated in Saigon after 1975, when doing so was considered subversive, when religious activity was being discouraged, and when it was illegal to own duplicating or printing equipment without government permission.[8] Composers used different names to disguise their identities. Cat Minh, the composer of the "Ave Maria" in Figure 4, is a nom de plume of one of the foremost composers of Vietnamese polyphony. One young contributor, whose songs used to be sung at the Saigon Cathedral and whose work I encountered in one of the many mimeographed booklets in circulation, used the name of his brother, who at the time had already escaped and resettled in the United States.

The choice of what the choir sang depended on liturgical need and on the tastes of musical and choral directors, as well as on the strongly expressed preferences of choir members, the talent available, and the motivations of those who joined the choir. People joined for social, musical, religious, or linguistic reasons; some choir members told me that they sought to reinforce or retain Vietnamese language skills through singing songs with Vietnamese texts.

Since choir members were volunteers, what each brought to the activity and each member's degree of commitment varied enough to

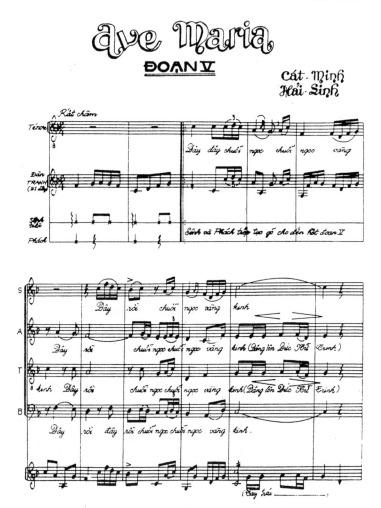

FIGURE 4. An example of what was characterized as "Vietnamese polyphony."

influence each choir's repertory. Attendance at rehearsals depended upon personal schedules and individual inclinations. Inevitably, the quality of performances varied, and, as is common in groups whose members differ substantially in musical skill and sophistication, a serious consideration in programming was navigating between the expectations of the highly trained and the limited capabilities of those with little or no musical training.

Other Venues

Vietnamese musical events took place only sporadically or occasionally in most venues outside of clubs and churches. The few occasions when one or two musicians or groups performed in concert or lecture-recital format were likely to take place on college or university campuses. Large events that included music and pageantry, such as the celebration of the feast of Vietnamese martyrs, took place in stadiums. Restaurants that cater to wedding or birthday celebrations often also provided facilities for bands. But school auditoriums, because they are affordable, accessible, and likely to have adequate parking space, were the most common sites for events that ranged from "festivals," to dances sponsored by Vietnamese organizations, to theatrical presentations.

A typical event at a school auditorium was the International Festival, billed as "Dại Nhạc Hội" (big music festival)—listed in Pham Duy's *Music of Vietnam* as a form of variety show that came to being in the 1950s (1975:113, 115). Organized by the Vietnamese Student Association of Long Beach University, the festival took place at Valley High School in Santa Ana. It combined songs, dances, comedy skits, and an áo dài fashion show followed by a Western-attire fashion show in a program that, as was not unusual, lasted four hours.

The audience consisted almost entirely of Vietnamese ranging in age from infants to the grandparental generation, although most were eighth- to twelfth-grade students, the population eligible to compete in the tests on Vietnamese history and literature that the International Festival was promoting and to which its proceeds would go. It was also an occasion for promoting Vietnamese culture: reading lists that were announced as aids to reviewing for the test were distributed.

The musical portion consisted of twenty-eight songs: three comic songs (sandwiched between jokes and humorous stories), fifteen love songs, five "descriptive songs" (on such topics as the harvest, fishing, what it is like to be sixteen), one vọng cổ, and one American song (Stephen Foster's "Oh, Susanah," which was not sung but played on the nhị, a two-stringed fiddle. This item was the only purely instrumental piece.)

All but one of the performers (Rick Murphy) were Vietnamese, many of them well-known in the Vietnamese musical world: AVT (a trio that goes back to pre-1975 days in Vietnam), Y Lan, Son Ca, Thai Hien, and Nhu Mai. All the song texts were Vietnamese, and while I could elicit dates of composition for only eighteen of twenty-eight, only one of these was composed after 1975 ("Em đi roi," attributed to either Duc Huy or Lam Phuong). The preponderance of Latin rhythms, particularly the "slow rhumba" or "bolero," was emphasized by an almost intrusive *clave* from the band that accompanied all the singers except AVT and Rick Murphy.[9] AVT accompanied itself with the nhị, the *đàn nguyệt* (a moon-shaped, two-stringed plucked lute), and the Western acoustic guitar. Rick Murphy accompanied himself with an electric scalloped guitar or *lục huyền cầm*.

Music

Phong T. Nguyen has listed six genres of Vietnamese music that have survived transplantation to the United States: "*đàn ca* (folk song), *nhạc tài tử* (chamber music reserved largely for connoisseurs of music), ritual music of the Buddhist liturgy, *cải lương* (reformed theater), *tân nhạc*, (modern, Westernized music) and *châù văn* (music for sacred text singing and dancing in shamanist temples)" (Nguyen 1989; Nguyen and Campbell 1990:36). All these, with the exception of chầù văn, I heard live in Orange County. But what Phong T. Nguyen had designated tân nhạc was the music that one was most likely to hear in the public sphere in Orange County and the music that permeated Vietnamese homes in forms delivered by the media—audiocassettes, CDs, television programs, and videocassettes.

A distant second in frequency of occurrence were folk songs, which could be heard in a variety of forms and contexts—sung a capella by schoolchildren or arranged for singers and instruments and stylized to a lesser or greater degree for variety show or club formats. Rick Murphy, from his vantage point as MC at a listening club, confirmed in our interview June 15, 1990, the lack of enthusiasm for folk songs and genres in the Vietnamese musical idiom, even among older audiences. As chamber music for connoisseurs, nhạc tài tử is the most specific in what it requires of performers and listeners and is the least accessible not only to Western listeners but to Vietnamese as well. As public event, it was extremely rare. I heard nhạc tài tử only once in a private home, performed by three gentlemen who insisted that the genre was alive and well in Orange County even if they could not direct me to where I could hear more.

Access to Buddhist ritual music was easy, since it is performed frequently in the many pagodas in Orange County—there are at least ten—all of which are open to the public. In contrast to listening to or performing nhạc tài tử, exposure to Buddhist ritual music may or may not be musically motivated. Such music may be taken as an inevitable complement to Buddhist worship—hence the relatively large audiences—active or passive listeners—that Buddhist music can claim.

Cải lương was seldom heard in full; twice a year was about the limit. But one might hear segments of it, in particular vọng cổ, in clubs, festivals, and demonstrations in academic settings. And while the dominance of tân nhạc is based on its ubiquity in the daily lives of Vietnamese in Orange County, the importance of cải lương derives more from its role in the refugee-resettlers' past, more from a life remembered than from the one here and now. Popular as live theater and on television in Vietnam, cải lương's part in the musical life of Orange County can only be inferred. As Pham Duy reportedly told Rick Murphy, Vietnamese culture is dead when cải lương is no longer remembered or performed (Murphy, personal communication, July 11, 1990).

Two of the genres Phong T. Nguyen named (tân nhạc and cải lương) and one concept (traditional music) reflect most closely the flux and adaptations that forced migration and resettlement have wrought. Cải lương's adaptations have largely taken the form of retrenchment. Those of tân nhạc have moved in the opposite direction, taking the form of controlled proliferation. Its repertory has grown in individual numbers, but at least one of its segments has yielded to a control of musical materials by extra-musical principles.

Cải Lương

Although considered a popular form (see Manuel 1988:198–204), cải lương struggles for its survival as live theater in Orange County, partly because of the form itself. Like opera, it requires a large number of especially trained singing actors and musicians as well as facilities for a large number of rehearsals.

Viet Hung, an eminent cải lương performer who lives in the area, feels the difficulties keenly. The shortage of dedicated and qualified personnel and of financial resources means that actors have to play multiple roles. This puts a tremendous burden on the actors and actresses, who have to make quick changes in character and in complicated costume and make-up. Often, amateur singers must be cast who require long hours of coaching. But since all but a tiny number of people involved in the production must work at full-time jobs during the day and sometimes at a second job afterwards, the heavy demands of mounting a cải lương production in Orange County have to give way to the short rehearsal time that participants can afford.

With little financial support for live cải lương, whoever undertakes its presentation must make do with school auditorium types of stage facilities. According to Viet Hung, this often means having access to the stage only two hours before performance time—barely enough to hang the scenery and get the light cues straightened out—a difficult adjustment for those who, like Viet Hung, were used to generous rehearsal time in Vietnam in facilities meant specifically for cải lương.

The use of cải lương for propaganda purposes also cast its shadow over the music's image in Orange County. Thomas Bird, artistic director of the Vietnam Veterans Theatre Company in New York, who served in the U.S. Army in Vietnam in 1965 and revisited Vietnam in 1990, reported that the chèo in Hanoi and cải lương in Ho Chi Minh City were "solidly didactic," with messages that had "the unmistakable scent of propaganda" (1990:9–10). (Chèo, a popular form of theater, is the northern counterpart of cải lương.) And Viet Hung, while qualifying this view, confirms government control: "Sometimes [the creators and performers] try not to change these cải lương too much, but they can offend the Viet Cong because of the history. But it is also a culture thing, so [the authorities] have to put up with it. Sometimes it is like: 'O.k., I'll change a little bit for you but you have to listen to the rest'" (translated by Viet Hung's son as his father spoke, June 25, 1990).

But cải lương's weakness in Orange County springs mainly from transplantation and re- or decontextualization. Everyone I spoke to, cải lương lover or not, contended that cải lương can only be properly appreciated where a sense of Vietnamese history and communal life—the wellsprings of cải lương inspiration—is part of daily existence. For many in Orange County, particularly the young, transplantation and the trauma of forced migration, created a rupture between what is continuous with their past and what securely belongs to their present.

Thus, Viet Hung thinks there is no market for live cải lương in the United States, and videotaped cải lương is decontextualized cải lương, vulnerable to distortions of cultural meaning: "The young are not into this kind of music. . . . The young do not understand because even if cải lương uses the same language [i.e., Vietnamese], it has different meaning. It is like a poem. The meaning changes and it is hard for the younger generation to keep up with the changes in meaning" (interview, June 25, 1990).

Tam Tri, one of the most versatile musicians in Orange County, recounts that when he asks his children or grandchildren what they are seeing on the screen while watching a cải lương on videocassette, "they say it 'has to do with boyfriends or girlfriends.' They give cải lương an American meaning."

Yet the involvement in cải lương or in segments of it by Vietnamese laypeople and professional musicians alike suggests that the form is too embedded in the culture to fade away.

I felt privileged when I was invited to cải lương rehearsals in a private home. In different parts of the house, different sections of the piece were being worked on. The composer, recently arrived from Vietnam, was still working with the librettist. There were two professional cải lương singers, one a refugee recently arrived who had been trained at the Saigon Conservatory, the other a longtime resident coaxed out of retirement in San Diego, a two-hour drive away. Each was working in a separate corner of the house, occasionally checking with the composer. An instrumentalist, highly proficient in a number of Vietnamese instruments and conversant with a repertory that straddles a number of genres, was playing a scalloped electric guitar until way past midnight, coaching a number of the singers mostly by rote. The performers, who had by then been rehearsing many nights a week but were not yet "off book," were confident that they would pull it off. Posters all over Little Saigon had already announced the performance, six weeks away.

Decontextualization itself may have effects that are not wholly negative. Cải lương's context is not just the history, legends, and everyday life from which it draws its subject matter but also the social stratum within which it thrives and with which it is associated. A pre-1975 arrival recounts that he had seen cải lương only once in Vietnam; his parents discouraged viewing it as socially inappropriate.[10] Recently, however, he had caught sight of a videotape and his curiosity was aroused. Now, he watches videotapes of cải lương and sees the form from the perspective of his previous formal training in Western European art music. He describes it in terms of musical motifs and Western formal structures, with a certain analytic detachment that matches his detachment from the social constraints that prevented his exposure to cải lương in Vietnam and that now allows him to indulge his intellectual curiosity.

Similarly, a six-year-old daughter of a cải lương singer, innocent of cải lương's social position in Vietnam, took great delight in watching her mother's videotaped performances in the comfort of their new and well-appointed suburban home, imitating her mother's gestures and learning the songs so well that she won second prize when, on the spur of the moment, she joined a song contest she was watching in 1992. Here again, the decontextualization of the vọng cổ that she sang and its relocation to a more socially acceptable venue—the song contest—exposed the form to an audience it might not have had in Vietnam.

Finally, Rick Murphy's performances of vọng cổ in clubs and festival settings have always attracted the attention of Vietnamese of all backgrounds, partly as a matter of curiosity or amusement, and partly out of appreciation for one non-Vietnamese American's effort to learn and perform a distinctively Vietnamese form without regard to its social location.

These instances raise the interesting possibility that the re- or decontextualization responsible for cải lương's decline or the alteration of its meaning in Orange County may turn out to be the catalyst for cải lương's revival and broader social acceptability.

Tân Nhạc

As a genre, tân nhạc now shelters a number of disparate forms and styles. In Orange County, it has become an unwieldy label for an amorphous body of music that can include Vietnamese popular, Westernized music, so-called New Wave or new music, and arrangements of folk music, all bound loosely by general features such as Vietnamese song text, the use of Western instruments, the Western tonal harmonic idiom (see, e.g., Phong Nguyen 1989), and a predilection for dance rhythms, particularly the Latin American.

I will preliminarily use the term, *tân nhạc* to refer to those parts of the repertoire that respond to the designation, Vietnamese popular music. Vietnameseness will be ascribed by the Vietnamese themselves, and it will be popular music in the commonsense usage of this term in the Western world. The principal components of this usage are broad-based appeal and the means—musical, technological, and socioeconomic—to facilitate distribution and adoption of the musical product (see Manuel 1988:1–23). These conditions make tân nhạc subject to limitation by local circumstances—the particular social contexts that shape its meaning and its use.

The question that immediately comes to mind when the non-Vietnamese ear hears tân nhạc has to do with its Vietnamese identity. On what grounds can this body of music claim to be Vietnamese even as individual items are being identified as tango, bolero, cha-cha-cha, and so forth? Almost invariably, the reply is that this music is part of the legacy from the French, incorporated into Vietnamese culture the way Chinese elements had been incorporated earlier.

Phong T. Nguyen (1989) traces the origin of tân nhạc to around 1938, when the French governor encouraged the growing popularity of Vietnamese songs, sung in Vietnamese, that drew from Latin American and French romantic songs as well as from some folk and traditional Vietnamese tunes, and that adopted Western harmony and instrumentation (see also Gibbs 1997 and Jamieson 1993: chap. 2). French officialdom and commerce had infused Vietnamese social life with Western music, particularly in urban areas. Vietnamese sent abroad to study brought back a taste for European music and contributed to its dissemination in Vietnam. Instruction, even in Vietnamese music, appropriated European pedagogical tools, including Western notation. But the process was selective. Not all Western elements were adopted. The process was situational and historically grounded. Not all Latin American dances, for example, are claimed as part of the legacy, even when they are admitted into contemporary social life. The lambada's popularity peaked and ebbed in Orange County in the early 1990s, while attachment to the tango, cha-cha-cha, bolero, and paso doble persisted.

The reinterpretation of these dances as Vietnamese rather than Western is further legitimized by their acceptability even in Hanoi. In 1993, Barbara Cohen, an American who served with the military during the war and returned to Vietnam to write the first guidebook to the country in English, recounted that she goes regularly to "tango bars"—clubs where dancing the tango is a central activity (personal communication: January 29, 1993). Susan Brownmiller reports a conversation with Cohen, who reassured her that the club in Hanoi where they had watched the tango dancing is "very authentic. No Westerners come here" (1993:100).

The composer and producer Hoang Thi Tho deemphasizes the role Latin American elements play in Vietnamese music (though not the ubiquity), insisting that they are no more than trappings. The substance of what makes the music Vietnamese, he said, "that essence, is in the scale, the melody" (interview, November 29, 1992). Other Vietnamese have articulated an idea that is complementary and more specific: no matter how "Americanized" the arrangement, one knows a piece to be Vietnamese when one recognizes the Vietnamese tune embedded in it.

These statements suggest not just a system that functions the way a phonemic system does for native speakers of a language—they can distinguish lexical meanings even when they cannot bring the formal rules to mind—but an actual body of tunes or melodies known by a wide Vietnamese public.

A thorough demonstration of this possibility is beyond the scope of this work, but the evidence that justifies entertaining it—the recurrence of the statements attesting to it and the credibility of the sources—cannot be ignored.

I had wondered about the accuracy and the significance of claims made by Vietnamese that very few new Vietnamese compositions were coming into existence. A famous Vietnamese composer residing in Orange County once told me: "Musical activity . . . is very poor. . . . They play the same things. They never renew the repertory." An educator, a nonmusician from a distinguished musical family, told me, "If you are interested in music, you will probably be able to learn the names of the songs that we have in Vietnam because we don't have many. Since we came here [to Orange County] there were few new songs." Suzanne Long, who with her Vietnamese husband owns and runs the club Caravelle, said that the music "is the same everything [as in Vietnam]—the words, the music—except for the musical arrangements," which she described as more modern and more upbeat because "it is necessary to make the old new so that it can appeal to the young" (interview, July 3, 1990).

Nam Tran, who produces audio- and videocassettes in addition to her television work, expressed a similar view: "Here, the music changes a bit but they are still the same—mixing traditional music and Western instruments just like we did in Vietnam." Putting that sameness in the context of a lifetime of war, she added: "The Vietnamese I have met all over [the world], they're all the same. They like their old songs. . . . The men like to feel as they did in the service. . . . At eighteen, they were drafted. Until 1975, that was their life. If you can show them what they were before and if you can show them that you appreciate what they did for the country, the men like it. For women, most were military wives, waiting for the soldiers to come home" (interview, July 17, 1990).[11]

Do Ngoc Yen, editor of the largest Vietnamese-language newspaper in the United States, *Người Viet,* published in Orange County (Westminster) was quoted in the *New York Times* as saying, "There are many new singers all the time but not many new songs. . . . It is as if they were singing all the time 'Smoke Gets in Your Eyes.'" In the same article, the author comments that Vietnamese popular songs have kept to key themes over the last thirty or forty years: loss—of homes and loved ones—and tragic hope (Mydans 1993:10).

A pre-1975 arrival assessed the situation somewhat differently but spoke to the same point: "There has been very little growth in Vietnamese music since 1975 . . . they sing the same songs." And John Tomlinson, a sound engineer who has worked with every major Vietnamese artist in his recording studio, alluded to the purposive nature of maintaining the "sameness": "They're using the same songs over and over again. . . . They never come up with anything new because they are trying to keep the memory of home alive so they use the same songs" (interview, November 11, 1992). Composer-producer Hoang Thi Tho took a different tack: "It is not that there are no new songs being composed. . . . But the people prefer the old songs that remind them of Vietnam before 1975" (interview, November 29, 1992).

There are historical grounds for these claims. According to Tran-Minh-Cham and Nguyen-Ngoc-Linh, "[T]his static concept [which] stems from the fact that the traditional repertoire contains only a limited number of tunes consecrated and adapted for use in specified circumstances" has its roots in Confucian ethics and the role it assigns to music in the maintenance of social harmony and the preservation of the social order (1969:99). And Tran Van Khe notes "the meagerness of the traditional repertory," an observation intended to underscore the importance of melodic variation in Vietnamese music (1975:45). Although these statements refer particularly to the traditional repertory, the "static concept" is worth keeping in mind.

It was not only the old songs that enjoyed the Vietnamese community's loyalty; it was also the artists who came to public attention before 1975. Thai Thanh and Duy Khanh, both past retirement age by 1990, were not merely respected as musicians; in 1990 and 1992, their performances—live and on cassettes and CDs—commanded higher prices than most other artists. Among Thai Thanh's children who are musicians and performers, one, Y Lan, is particularly talented and widely known through her many appearances and recordings. Many of my Vietnamese friends have raved about how well she "gets inside the words" and captures the poetry of the songs. But when asked who is the better artist, Y Lan or her mother, the answer is invariably Thai Thanh.

One Vietnamese woman, in her thirties when I interviewed her in 1990, gave voice to what many others had tried to say: Thai Thanh is superior because she "reminds you very strongly of Vietnam before 1975 and of the things that are human. . . . She can express those things that are valued in Vietnam before 1975." The sound engineer John Tomlinson countered: "That's a cultural thing . . . they look at older people with more respect."

Yet one wonders if respect for age alone explains those artists' staying power or if respect for age accounts for the dearth of remaindered audiocassettes by Pham Duy, Thai Thanh, Duy Khanh, Khanh Ly, and Hoang Oanh. Was it mere coincidence that these artists' names have become virtually inextricable from accounts of musical life in the Vietnamese diaspora? Trinh Cong Son, a composer who enjoyed great popularity before 1975, whose songs brought Khanh Ly to the attention of the Vietnamese public, but who remained in Vietnam and continued to compose there, arousing suspicions about his politics, enjoys little of the regard accorded his contemporaries in Orange County.

If what Hoang Thi Tho suggested is right—that the melodic material is the essence of Vietnamese music—and if there is in fact a circumscribed body of melodies from which Vietnamese popular music continually draws to proclaim its linkage to Vietnam, then what at first glance seems anomalous begins to make sense. The apparent stasis, the reported shortage of new songs, the devotion to the old—performers and items of repertory alike—does not contradict the proliferation of Vietnamese popular music and the creative energy that has fueled Orange County's active musical life. One is the complement of the other, and both are parts of an adaptive strategy that restricts melodic materials the better to conserve ties to a Vietnamese culture constructed out of these refugees' particular experience. In this respect, it is also a strategy to meet the heavy demands that the past and the present make on Vietnamese.

As refugees, they had made a commitment to the conservation of Vietnamese culture as they had known it before the communist take-over.[12] As resettlers, they must define themselves both to their cohorts and to their host society. In that body of popular music that draws from melodies directly associated with Vietnam, they have both an acoustic and a social means toward these ends. That repertory's Western sounds speak to and accommodate the larger society, even as the exclusivity of the Vietnamese identity is maintained through the in-language of the Vietnamese texts, the devotion to the musicians and performers who are icons of the Vietnamese diaspora, and the body of melodies widely recognized within the Vietnamese musical community.

The creation of identity thus dovetails with the conservation of tradition, of things considered part of the Vietnamese legacy, and hence of the things that identify Vietnamese as Vietnamese to their cohorts as members of what Eastmond called a "community of fate," bound not only by a common nationality and culture but presumably by a common political faith and by "bonds forged among those who went through an ordeal together" (Eastmond, Ralphsson, and Alinder 1994:8). To their conationals in Vietnam, they are overseas Vietnamese, a differentiation mutually acknowledged and formalized in Vietnam by the term "Việt Kièu," revised from the derogatory "nguy," a label change made official shortly before the normalization of U.S.-Vietnam relations. In the process, a musical corpus that on the basis of physical characteristics might have been considered unitary seems to have undergone fission to serve different functions. Hence, the ad hoc labels—love songs, sad songs, "prewar music" or *nhạc tiền chiến*, and romantic songs, among others (see, e.g., Gibbs 1996)—which await formalization when "the physically given . . . [has passed] through the filter of the functionally or relatedly meaningful" (Sapir 1958:46).

Traditional Music

Having outgrown their overreliance on what Charles Seeger called "the signals" (i.e., the sounds) and their presumably faithful duplication of some primeval forms, studies of traditional music are now better able to attend to tradition's mutability and teleological nature (see, for example, Anderson 1983; Hobsbawm and Ranger 1983; Shapiro 1985; Shils 1981). Tran Van Khe's observation that Vietnamese traditional music "no longer corresponds to the needs of the Vietnamese people" (1980:744) becomes more understandable, and his view that the "attempts to restore the dying traditional music by the creation of a 'new music' in a Western idiom" (752) signals the release of Vietnamese traditional music from certifiably indigenous forms. The "implantation of Western music" (744) has not only become admissible but has opened the door to a new store of changes within the realm of the traditional. In light of these changes and in the context of Vietnamese musical life in Orange County, the question becomes, How is traditional music to be recognized?

Contradictory opinions are rife, and Chau Nguyen, director of the traditional music group Lạc Hồng and a major advocate for traditional music, captured the confusion: "When people say 'traditional music,' they don't know what that means. . . . They cannot imagine what style, what form, but they know the term" (interview, November 19, 1992). The composer Hoang Thi Tho, for example, sees himself as a composer of traditional music, although westerners might mistake his works for Western but for the texts (interview, November 29, 1992). And Chau Nguyen told me he himself "mix[es] traditional styles and new forms" (Nguyen interview). His statement is given particular significance by the mission of Lạc Hồng: "to preserve, develop and publish Vietnamese traditional music throughout the United States," according to an Orange Coast College concert program for September 19, 1992. He has conducted his group in performances of arrangements of Pham Duy's music (e.g., "Mẹ xinh đẹp" [The beautiful motherland] and Nụ tầm xuân [Nostalgia for lost love]) as well as his own compositions.

When the subject of traditional music came up in conversation in Orange County, what often vied for attention to the music as sound was its use by the communist government.[13] "Before, the communists used traditional music for propaganda. That is why some people do not like it" (Pham Duy interview, November 7, 1992). Thu Nguyen, a pre-1975 departee, states his position emphatically: "I am not against the form of art, of drama, of traditional music. I am against the message ingrained in the product." He adds that something the communists have done and continue to do very well is this embedding of subtle and not-so-subtle messages into traditional music. He elaborated on the conflicting sentiments that result:

> When I have fifteen minutes to practice—and I have a piano, a violin, a guitar, a đàn tranh, a sáo—somehow, I find myself on the piano bench first. That must be coming from the subconscious somewhere. Maybe because I never had a chance to have a good or knowledgeable teacher who could show me how wonderful [Vietnamese traditional music] is. Another way to say it is that they failed to spark an interest in me even with my mind—not my feelings—my mind telling me that I have to do something about learning traditional music. . . . I tried to address the problem with my children. I bring them to Lạc Hồng [the Orange County traditional music group] performances. I buy instruments, put them in the house ready to be played any time. . . . But they haven't really done it. (interview, November 24, 1992)

Reacting to a leading musician's statement that "traditional music is dead," Thu Nguyen said: "In a way, that is probably right. But I do not want to agree. . . . There is some effort to resurrect [traditional music]. . . . I see a tremendous job ahead."

The changed social and historical context in resettlement and the intrusion of political elements into the concept traditional music has thus made Vietnamese more circumspect about this segment of their cultural heritage, even as they feel committed to its preservation. The general ambivalence is over what the physical manifestations of traditional music represent: Vietnamese culture or Vietnamese government propaganda? the inclusive body of music that embraces items from the tân nhạc repertoire and items proscribed by the current government in Vietnam, or the exclusive corpus that the Vietnamese government labels "traditional"?[14]

Opposing paradigms emerge:[15]

Communist	Noncommunist
The current government	The people
Traditional music as propaganda	Traditional music as cultural heritage

The vast majority of Orange County Vietnamese repudiate the items on the left in actuality or in principle. Communism stands less for Marxist ideology than for the complex tangle of factors that drove them from Vietnam, made them suffer, and caused their losses. The government is both symbol and arbiter of communist dogma, and it uses traditional music or manipulates it to serve the government's purposes.

Orange County Vietnamese identify with the items on the right. Being non-communist is an important justification for leaving the homeland and staying away; it is what all of Vietnam was believed to be before the partition of the country in 1954 and what part of it continued to be before the fall of Saigon in 1975. The "people" are those in Vietnam with whom Orange County Vietnamese identify and those who, to their minds, are like them—non-communists, people who accept as traditional not only that part of the musical repertory that antedates its use as propaganda but also those kinds of music that the communist regime forbade or suppressed.

The bifurcation of what traditional music stands for thus follows from its definition in political as well as historical terms, in ideological as well as pragmatic terms. It is not a coincidence that the point at which the oppositions were created is the same point at which forced migration began, the point at which the political and cultural function of traditional music came into dispute, and the point at which these differences began to be manifested in different repertories for what each faction called traditional music.

The divergent views of what constitutes Vietnamese historical continuity and contemporary functions are made explicit in these oppositions. For the authorities in Vietnam who determine what should be labeled and presented as Vietnamese traditional music, historical continuity is verified by physical or acoustic properties: Vietnamese traditional music is marked by acoustic features that demonstrate lineage, a direct descent from the Vietnamese musical system. It is also legitimized by present purposes as formulated by government authorities.[16]

For the Vietnamese in Orange County, however, historical continuity and the validation of a cultural lineage was breached when the Hanoi government destroyed the real (i.e., non-communist) Vietnamese culture, replacing its substance with communist (i.e., non-Vietnamese) meanings. Whether this is objective reality or rationalization, what matters is the force of their conviction, and the reality of its effects.

With opposing interpretations of historical continuity and contemporary function, it was inevitable that traditional music would stand for different repertories. Criteria for inclusion and selection would rest on different grounds. The Orange County repertory *excludes* the musical forms from present-day Vietnam that are perceived as carriers of communist messages. (These perceptions may draw from song texts or from the fact that the performers or composers at some point had enjoyed government support.) It *embraces* what the Communist government banned; proscription and sanction, after all, themselves carry meaning. It includes music whose physical attributes are historically continuous with the Vietnamese musical system—sounds that may coincide with what the current government calls traditional (e.g., chèo and quan họ)—as long as it is dissociated from government purposes.[17] And it includes those melody-marked items from the tân nhạc repertory that fulfill the function of tradition by conserving the memory of what is seen as a genuinely Vietnamese musical way of life.

The Vietnamese traditional music repertory has thus become broader and more inclusive in Orange County. Through the innovative use of Vietnamese as well as Western musical materials, traditional music has shown itself true to its teleological nature both as concept and as heard phenomenon. Like other musics sensitive to their functions, it is, to borrow Richard E. Ross's words, "less a sound than a strategy, not so much a style of music as a state of mind" (1998:20).

Vietnamese Music and the Larger Society

Powerful though they may be, the internal social, cultural, and historical factors that impinge upon the musical life of Vietnamese in Orange County do not by themselves account for what Vietnamese musical life has come to be in resettlement. Pressures from outside the Vietnamese community play an essential role in stimulating and shaping Vietnamese music in arenas that vary only in the insights they afford into the process.

Roman Catholic churches, for example, offer more occasions for Vietnamese to interact with others than do either Buddhist temples or Protestant churches: few non-Vietnamese participate in the activities at pagodas, and there are far more Roman Catholics than Protestants among the Vietnamese in Orange County. In the secular sphere, more interaction occurs in the economic and political arenas than in the strictly social.

Within these arenas, patterns of exclusion or inclusion, of insularity and reciprocity, can appear inconsistent, underscoring the complexity of group and community relations. In music, for example, the strong preference for Vietnamese song texts, the nightclub listings in separate telephone directories, the virtual exclusion of Western instrumentalists at Vietnamese public performances even when the musical instruments and the musical idiom are Western, suggest insularity. But there is also ample evidence to the contrary: Western elements abound in music that Vietnamese identify as Vietnamese, Vietnamese are quick to adopt Western technology and media in the production and dissemination of music, and Western listeners are often at a loss to identify what in Vietnamese popular music besides the song text marks the music as distinctively Vietnamese.

Two specific cases, one from the religious, the other from the secular sphere, exemplify the interplay between Vietnamese music and the larger society.

The Religious Sphere

In Orange County, the exclusionary features of the Vietnamese Roman Catholic mass—the language of the service, the announcements of the mass as Vietnamese, the overwhelmingly Vietnamese participants—are ameliorated to some degree by inclusionary features. The ritual of the mass is comprehensible to all Catholics, enabling anyone to attend, albeit with little opportunity for active participation. A description of another event designed with the parish's multiethnic community in mind will put interaction within the Orange County Catholic community into clearer focus.

On November 7, 1992, St. Barbara's Church in Santa Ana celebrated its thirtieth anniversary. To accommodate the large gathering of parishioners and well-wishers, the commemorative mass was held outdoors on the grounds adjoining the church. In acknowledgment of three major groups that comprise the church's membership, the mass was said in English, Spanish, and Vietnamese. But while the English and Spanish speakers differed only in the languages they used, one being translated to or alternating with the other, the Vietnamese speakers differed not only in language but in their manner of delivery and self-presentation. The English and Spanish speakers joined forces during communion and sang hymns in which strophes were sung in Spanish and refrains in English; the Vietnamese choral contribution consisted of two choirs—one male and one female, one standing at the rear of the congregation and the other close to the front—singing Vietnamese songs alternately or antiphonally. The English- and Spanish-speaking choirs were accompanied by amplified Spanish guitar and electric bass; the Vietnamese choirs were accompanied by organ. In responsorial sections, English texts were spoken and translated directly into Spanish; the Vietnamese used their distinctive congregational chanting style. Many women wore áo dài, and a group of men were in full regalia, in gold and green áo dài, resplendent as they marched in procession to receive communion.

The musical components of the Vietnamese contributions commingled Vietnamese elements—Vietnamese song texts, a strong pentatonic flavor, minimal part singing and, moving toward the Western pole of an imaginary continuum where the opposite pole is Vietnamese, harmonic organ accompaniment and an antiphonal style that incorporated Vietnamese and Western elements. One thus sees Vietnamese participation within the larger framework of Orange County Catholic observance reiterating the together-but-separate theme noted in the social sphere (see Chapter 4).

The Secular Sphere

In the Bataan and Palawan refugee camps, I had been pleasantly surprised by how easily I had found live music making. Public and private performances of all kinds of music, from cải lương to church music to rock, by individuals and by small groups, took place spontaneously or with a bit of encouragement or prodding from cohorts or camp personnel. But with resettlement came serious obligations and the pressure to "make it" in the United States.[18] In Orange County, people for whom music making had been a daily activity in camp stopped playing or singing for pleasure. "No time for music making" became a recurrent theme in Orange County, a variation on the theme of "survival mode" encountered in New Jersey. Professional musicians took on other income-producing activities—jobs or business enterprises with little or no relation to music.

One well-known singer ran a sandwich bar; another had a store for glass (windshields, etc.). When I mentioned to a friend that I had just spoken to one of Vietnam's most famous singers, whom he had idolized since childhood, his first question was "How does she earn a living?" He assumed that the singer's musical activities alone could not constitute a livelihood. Pham Duy told me that his musician-children had to have other jobs to supplement income from performances. Clubs are open only during weekends, and gigs—performance engagements at birthday parties, weddings, and so on—are sporadic, making it impossible to earn a living from performance alone. But unlike the New Jersey Vietnamese, these musicians did not consider their musical activities a hobby. Rather, they considered their extramusical work a contingency measure to enable them to live their lives as musicians.

For most Vietnamese, the love of music had been deflected from performing to listening. As one Vietnamese put it, their musical life is now lived largely through audiocassettes, which (the advent of CDs notwithstanding) remained the dominant medium for music consumption until the early 1990s.[19]

It is thus not surprising that less than two decades after their arrival, the Vietnamese had made Orange County perhaps the most prolific center of Vietnamese cassette production in the world. Professional as well as home recording studios produced and marketed cassettes. The sheer number of cassettes produced and their dissemination throughout Vietnamese communities worldwide suggest a potentially large sphere of influence for the music that came from Orange County.

But Vietnamese CDs or audiocassettes are very seldom advertised in American newspapers because the larger society is not seen as a market for these products. Unlike many popular musics from different parts of the world and certainly unlike the popular music of the Americas from which Vietnamese popular music has borrowed heavily, Vietnamese music production in Orange County is inner-directed; it has shown little interest in expanding its market beyond its Vietnamese consumers. With rare exceptions, music is performed, at least in public, for Vietnamese by Vietnamese.[20]

This situation has been altered little by the growing number of cassettes of strictly instrumental Vietnamese popular music that began to appear in the early 1990s. Devoid of the strongest marker of Vietnamese identity—the Vietnamese song text—these cassettes sound more comprehensible to Western consumers.[21] But it is not yet clear whether the trend toward the purely instrumental in popular music will gather momentum and make music by Vietnamese more accessible to non-Vietnamese audiences.

Despite the apparent insularity of the Vietnamese music industry, however, a number of factors—the importance of cassettes in Vietnamese musical life, the commodification of music and the technology it involves, the strong musical influences from the Americas and other parts of the Western world, and the active Vietnamese participation in the larger U.S. world of business—strongly recommend it as the arena where Vietnamese/non-Vietnamese musical interaction in the secular sphere might most productively be observed. Stepping away from music as acoustic product and from public performance sites and looking instead at the process by which music is produced for the media, one discovers the active participation and contribution of non-Vietnamese in the making of music that will be labeled and marketed as Vietnamese.

The Recording Industry

The first intimation of what might be learned from the Vietnamese cassette industry came during a recording session to which a popular Vietnamese singer had invited me. Her sound engineer, she informed me, was one of the most reliable in the business. She was not referring to his competence alone. This man restricted himself to the production of the master tape, which he turned over to the artist or producer who engaged him. He did not get involved with duplicating, distribution, publicity, or marketing. He thus avoided the conflicts of interest that could arise when artists who wished to market their own products engaged one of the many sound engineers who, in addition to operating their own studios, also distributed and marketed the tapes they produced.

This session was to be the last step in the recording process; the singer had come to overdub a tape prepared by the sound engineer, a non-Vietnamese American who had hired the musicians, all of them non-Vietnamese American as well.

Equipped with headphones, the singer stood facing a microphone in a small glassed-in cubicle. Locked into the tempi of the prerecorded items on the tape, she could make no tempo changes unless she was willing to make the corresponding adjustments in pitch. A faster tempo could only be effected by running the tape faster, thus raising the overall pitch level; a slower tempo meant a lower overall pitch level. At one point, the singer noticed that there were not enought beats to sing all the syllables in her text. But the tape was unrelenting; it was she who had to adjust the text. There was no room for spontaneous rubato or ritardando. The sound engineer even tried to persuade the singer not to slide to given pitches or add ornamentation to certain parts of the melodic line—practices not just acceptable but expected in most Vietnamese singing styles. These injunctions, however, the singer quietly ignored; in contrast to matters such as tempo, options pertaining to ornamentation and manner of attack were hers to take.

In some ways, the negotiations between the Vietnamese recording artist and the non-Vietnamese American sound engineer mimicked features of the interaction between Vietnamese and non-Vietnamese Americans in other spheres. There were no overt conflicts. There was considerable but not total loss of control on the part of the recording artist. Much of what is considered desirable from the Vietnamese point of view remained: the relatively consistent slow tempo, the sliding approach to pitches when the singer so desired, the ornamentation of the melodic line.

What made this particular event striking was a subsequent performance of the same song by the same singer in a Vietnamese nightclub with live musicians who were Vietnamese. Freed from the tyranny of the tape, performing in a context where she could interact with live musicians and be energized by the dancers on the floor, she breathed new life into the song and made it sound almost like a different song.

In 1992, John Tomlinson, a leading sound engineer in Orange County, described the production process: when an artist approaches him with a recording project, the first concern is the arrangement of the songs—with rare exceptions his clients are all singers. If the songs have not yet been arranged, Tomlinson directs the singer to an arranger, most frequently Le Van Tien, Tram Thi Thien, or Hoang Thi Tho—all very well-known musicians among Vietnamese in Orange County and abroad. Occasionally he recommends one of two or three non-Vietnamese American arrangers. "Between 1982 and 1985, Manny Hines used to arrange a lot of stuff. . . . He used computers or would program drums and play along. . . . That all transpired in Vietnamese music as well and played a big influence on what you hear now. He would take traditional songs and turn them into New Wave or New Age." The arranger takes into account the singer's vocal range, "the style of the songs they want—rhumba, samba-habanera, cha-cha-cha, paso doble—you name it, they do it to their traditional folk styles" (interview, November 11, 1992).

"After the style is determined, the arranger will write the form and then we come in and make a recording of basic tracks: bass, drums, and piano. We layer everything on—dub percussion, guitar, saxophones, violins. The actual orchestration depends on whether [the recording artist] tells the arranger 'Do what you want' or 'Make it exactly like the tape,'" the basic tracks Tomlinson gave the artist (Tomlinson interview).

This indicates the wide latitude that Tomlinson has, because arrangements are often given to him in skeletal form—"a chord chart with maybe a couple of instruments in it . . . really little more than scribbled notes with chord changes"—which he is then expected to flesh out (see Figure 5). For this reason he uses a fairly fixed group of non-Vietnamese American musicians. "One does not hire musicians anew each time because you want people who are familiar with the styles . . . . Our drummer has been working with us for twelve years. He understands what the styles are. The arranger just has to put a couple of scribbles here and there and the drummer knows what needs to be done. Same with the bass and piano player. So it is like everybody knows the style" (Tomlinson interview).

This is the procedure when the singer, the arranger, and Tomlinson are working together. If the singer and the arranger have worked independently of Tomlinson, then Tomlinson deals with the arranger, who makes the decisions as to orchestration. Usually the arrangement is for sixteen tracks; although twenty-four tracks are occasionally used, the cost can be prohibitive. "When the instrumental part is finished, the singer comes in and overdubs. There are generally no more changes made because it is such a cookie-cutter type of thing and because of the budget involved. It happens rarely that a singer will come and say, 'I can't sing that, change it'. . . . After the . . . instruments have been recorded, we mix the tape and we give [the artist] the final product. This used to be in the form of a quarter-inch reel. Now we give them digital [DAT]" (Tomlinson interview).

It is up to the artist to decide in what form to market the recording— cassette or CD. CDs are a fairly recent development in Vietnamese music

FIGURE 5. Sample of an arranger's score: a skeletal score to be filled out by instrumentalists (Courtesy of John Tomlinson).

production. Pham Duy and his son were the first in the field, followed by Khanh Ly.

Singer Hoang Oanh's account coincides essentially with Tomlinson's. She adds to it only those steps that are specific to her as an artist. When she has finished planning a project—thought of a title and selected the songs (usually a mix that includes songs about motherland, love songs, folk songs, or sung poetry, and more recently, Catholic hymns)—she contacts a Vietnamese arranger. She then books a studio, whose sound engineer hires the non-Vietnamese American musicians. She confirms Tomlinson's assessment of the musicians' skills: "They are very good; they do not even have to look at the scores ahead of time, they play everything on the spot."

While the musicians are being recorded onto tracks, she makes it a point to be present to ensure that the tempo and the execution are to her liking. When the mixing is finished, she comes in to overdub.

Hoang Thi Tho describes a similar process, except that he is his own arranger. He writes out every detail of his arrangement, insists on the musicians (all non-Vietnamese American except the pianist, who is his son) playing every note he has written, conducts them himself, and does his own mixing.

Most recording artists are their own producers, marketers, and distributors. Once the recording and duplicating are finished, they contact the dealers to announce the availability of the new product. Some of the dealers are large audio stores, but many are small establishments—bookstores or specialty shops. Artists distribute and sell locally, nationally, and internationally. It is a tremendous amount of work, and Pham Duy considers himself lucky because he has family members who share the tasks: he "creates"; his son is the "fabricateur," running the publishing and recording enterprises; his daughters are singers; and his daughter-in-law travels abroad to manage distribution, which is worldwide.

The artists say they can handle all aspects of record production and marketing because their market is strictly Vietnamese, but the case can also be made that the artist is driven by factors specific to the community. Both Nam Tran, herself a producer of videocassettes, and John Tomlinson note that competition is fierce. But winning is geared less to producing the best-quality products than getting the largest possible market share by undercutting prices. The result is an inability to compete in a market outside the Vietnamese community and a loss in overall production of Vietnamese music recordings. In 1990, according to Tomlinson, there were some twenty Vietnamese studios, most of them home recording studios, in Orange County. In 1992, the number was down to around seven. Hoang Thi Tho, however, said that the actual number is difficult to estimate because there are so many home recording studios.

Although, as Wallis and Malm (1984) have observed, independents must often rely on larger companies for manufacturing and distribution, this has not happened in Orange County. Nam Tran has approached a number of non-Vietnamese American companies but "they are not interested. American and Vietnamese interests are entirely separate" (interview, July 17, 1990). Still, Vietnamese artist-producers survive or keep cropping up perhaps because, like some of the groups Wallis and Malm have studied, they "are not guided solely by economic constraints; cultural goals, beliefs in what constitutes good music that should be spread around provide an equally powerful motive force" (1984:86).

Copyright protection hardly exists in the Vietnamese musical world, and the royalty system is virtually unknown. John Tomlinson believes that many of the songs used are in the public domain. This, however, is the case for only a portion of the repertoire. When a Vietnamese friend and I went to visit Khanh Ly, my friend showed the singer a collection of handwritten scores by a famous Vietnamese composer. Khanh Ly was delighted and asked if she might duplicate the scores and call my friend after copying them. My friend left her the scores. It all seemed so natural. Later on, Khanh Ly noted: "Sometimes I hear a song. I talk to the composer and he sends me the music. . . . We don't pay the composer because that is the Vietnamese way" (interview, July 16, 1990).

These kinds of informal transactions are consensual, but the consensual boundaries are breached with rampant unauthorized duplication of cassettes. Thus, the size of the market, competition, lack of copyright protection, and pirating forge a chain in which cause and effect are difficult to sort out. A well-known and respected artist discourages illegal duplication by selling jackets for cassette shells at "a very good price," so that printing more jackets for illegal copies is not cost effective. By encouraging dealers to come back for additional jackets, she is better able to estimate how many copies are sold.

Pham Duy finds unauthorized duplication impossible to control, "so you just forget; you can go crazy [otherwise]" (interview, November 7, 1992). And for Hoang Thi Tho illegal duplication simply goes with the territory: "Higher-quality tapes mean higher costs, but higher costs mean more illegal duplication. Someone buys the more expensive tapes and duplicates them. People with video rental stores buy one legal tape and copy the rest for rental. But nothing can be done. The Vietnamese music market is still a relatively small market. Going after those who duplicate illegally and/or market illegally duplicated tapes means high legal or enforcement costs which the Vietnamese from either side of the market—producers and sellers—cannot afford" (interview, November 29, 1992).

Endemic duplication has also created a probably unintended effect: it has established and reinforced links between the musical spheres of Vietnamese in Vietnam and their overseas conationals. Despite the U.S. trade embargo, U.S.-made tapes reached Vietnamese listeners in large numbers not through export channels but through personal networks and further duplication when the tapes reached Vietnam. Similarly, Vietnam-made cassettes became available in Orange County despite social and ideological constraints that otherwise make Orange County Vietnamese wary of buying products made in Vietnam.[22]

The relatively circumscribed world of Vietnamese and host society in Orange County has therefore expanded to include not just the world of overseas Vietnamese who make up a large part of the Orange County Vietnamese cassette market but also Vietnamese in the homeland. With the lifting of the trade embargo, relations between the musical world of Orange County and the larger world that it inhabits are likely to become even more complex. Music in Orange County, especially that which Vietnamese accept as traditional, has moved in a direction different from that taken in Vietnam. Musical common ground will surely need to be rediscovered.

But for the present, Vietnamese dependence on U.S. or Western technology, the impact of U.S. society and economic pressures on Vietnamese musical life, and the difficulties inherent in accommodating to a culture distant from their own are central concerns. The old familiar, informal arrangements among musicians and between them and the various parts of this musical arena within which they must operate, the accommodations made to live outside the Western convention of copyright protection, and the acceptance of illegal duplication as a fact of life at least for the present represent the choices that Vietnamese have made or inevitabilities they have adapted to. The control that they cede to non-Vietnamese American musicians and to U.S. technology, the amount of control they retain, the degree to which and the forms in which they will admit U.S. influence, and the lines they will draw to distinguish themselves as Vietnamese are matters for the continual negotiation and compromise that mark the interaction of groups who share not only common territory but a particular slice of history.

Codetta: After Normalization . . .

In February 1994, when the United States lifted the trade embargo against Vietnam, Vietnamese everywhere saw the writing on the wall: the resumption of diplomatic relations between the two countries was just around the corner. It came in July 1995, with a declaration by President Clinton, followed a month later by a visit to Hanoi by Warren Christopher, the secretary of state, to proclaim an official end to what he called decades of estrangement. "Normalization" was the short-hand way of referring to these events and their anticipated effects—transnational, intranational, political, and psychological. But the wounds inflicted by the war are slow to heal. Some that have been denied reassert their presence. Some that have festered find new life.

When rumors of impending normalization reached refugee camps, the populations' identity as members of a "community of fate" (Eastmond, Ralphsson, and Alinder 1994:8) bound by a common plight burst into consciousness. Realizing that normalization meant, among other things, the closing of the camps and repatriation for many of them, the refugees reacted dramatically. In Hong Kong, refugees rioted and fled after setting fire to their barracks (Gargan 1996:4). In Bataan, refugees hung huge signs outside their billets with messages such as "We'd rather die." Some attempted suicide; one doused himself with gasoline and was stopped from setting himself afire just in time (Shenon 1995:1). In Palawan, 700 refugees escaped from camp, preferring to take their chances among the local population (*Refugee Reports* 1997:9).[1] Others, however, chose to abandon their membership in that community and voluntarily returned to Vietnam.

Among the Vietnamese in California's Little Saigon, differentiation again invoked its ideological name. After the lifting of the trade embargo, Seth Mydans observed: "[I]t remains politically difficult here in Little

Saigon to support the end of the embargo and to do business openly with the Communist Government in Hanoi. . . . [A]ngry demonstrations and threats greeted advocates of normalization. Local political leaders chose their words carefully so as not to offend former Vietnamese military men and political prisoners who are still fighting the long-ago war in their hearts." Mai Cong, head of the Vietnamese Community of Orange County, spoke for one faction: "There may be joy in Hanoi, but there will be no celebrations in Little Saigon"; Trang Nguyen, president of Little Saigon TV and Radio, spoke for another: "In the past . . . people were calling each other Communists. Now they can unite on real issues" (Mydans 1994).

These sentiments reverberated in Vietnamese musical and music-related activities, reflected by events in four different parts of the country—Massachusetts, New York, New Orleans, and St. Paul.

In the summer of 1995, the Perfume River Ensemble, a Vietnamese group from Hue, came to perform in the Lowell (Massachusetts) Summer Festival with the support of the Vietnamese government and U.S. private and government organizations. Named after the river that runs across Hue, the ancient royal capital, the ensemble performed three times during the festival—the first time privately for an invited audience, the second and third times for the general public.

All three performances were marked by some form of protest from the local Vietnamese, of whom approximately 11,000 reside in the Lowell area. The mildest form of protest was the distribution of leaflets during the performance. Printed on Vietnamese Community of Massachusetts letterhead, the leaflet sought to "brief the American people on the truth about the Communist Regime in Vietnam," to remind the audience of a variety of "social ills" in that country, and to urge everyone to write to representatives and senators so that they might address common concerns over human rights.

The protest at the largest of the three performances was the most dramatic. A procession of Vietnamese led by two flag bearers made its way toward the stage as the performance began. One of the flag bearers carried a large American flag; the other carried the flag of pre-communist Vietnam with its three red stripes on a yellow background. Members of the procession carried small replicas of that Vietnamese flag, and they all stood quietly, right in front of the stage, withholding applause in silent protest throughout the performance. Police stood close by; particularly

The procession of flags led by Vietnamese, one carrying the U.S. flag, the other, the flag of the Republic of Vietnam, in protest over the Lowell (Massachusetts) Summer Festival's featuring the Perfume River Ensemble from Vietnam, 1996

noticeable because up until then, only rangers had circulated among the crowds, and, were it not for their uniforms, they could have been mistaken for merrymakers, joining in the celebration by marching in the parades and dancing in the streets.

In sharp contrast to this event was the Sixth National Conference of the Forum on Viet Nam, Cambodia, and Laos, which took place in New York just a month earlier. Also sponsored by U.S. organizations with the full cooperation of the Vietnamese government, the conference was attended by delegations of government officials, educators, businessmen, artists, writers, and musicians from Vietnam, as well as members of the corresponding institutions among the U.S. participants, which included Vietnamese residing in the States. On this occasion, the flag displayed prominently onstage was the flag of the Socialist Republic of Vietnam—a yellow star on a red background. Vietnamese folk and traditional music—so designated by the sponsors—was performed for the conferees by musicians who had come from Vietnam for the occasion.

A third event took place in New Orleans three weeks before the New York conference, billed as a concert of "Traditional Vietnamese Music in America," sponsored by a local Vietnamese organization, and performed by a Vietnamese American ensemble for a Vietnamese American audience and a handful of invited non-Vietnamese (one ensemble member was a non-Vietnamese American who had lived and studied for two years in Hanoi). Onstage was the pre-communist Vietnamese flag.

The fourth event was a Vietnamese Music Festival sponsored by the Composers Forum based in St. Paul, Minnesota, the following year.[2] The local Vietnamese community called for a boycott of the performances by Phu Dong Percussion, a group from Vietnam. Vietnamese poets who had initially consented to participate withdrew when they found out that Phu Dong was to take part. One of the flyers distributed during the event expressed sentiments identical to those expressed in Lowell:

> To the Vietnamese Americans, [the participation of the Phu Dong Percussion] is a contribution to normalize the image of the Vietnamese Communist Regime abroad through various cultural shows and activities. . . . Although the entertainers and artists may not be Communist party members and they may not promote Communist ideology through their performance, we still do not welcome their presentation since it contributes to the normalization of the regime's image in the community. . . . Vietnamese American communities, consisting essentially of victims of Hanoi, have confirmed their stance of rejecting this oppressive regime through protests of different groups representing Hanoi.

As in Little Saigon, there were dissenting voices. One of the newspapers covering the event quoted a protester: "They are not just here to express their art, they are also here with a political purpose—to represent a communist government"; another said, "It shouldn't matter what their view is because they are expressing themselves and their culture" (Marlyka 1996).

Although the reactions of Vietnamese to these events were consistent with those they had manifested all the way back to Palawan, there was an important difference instigated by normalization.

Communism in its evolved sense—quite distant from its early associations with nationalism and Marxist doctrine and by now the cause in the minds of refugees of all their pain and losses—has always been a powerful organizational principle in social relations among Vietnamese, both in camps and in resettlement. But its use has largely been internal and specific to the community, manifested in such matters as which Vietnamese other Vietnamese did business with, what songs they sang or refused to sing to each other, what they included or excluded in what they saw to be Vietnamese traditional music, the way they treated their cohorts who traveled to Vietnam or invested there, and so forth. Little if any effort had been made to communicate to the larger society the continuing importance of this ideology because Vietnamese believed that non-Vietnamese Americans, even if only tacitly, took this to be the case as part of their understanding of the Vietnamese presence in this country and of their own decades-long fight against communism.

But normalization challenged this view of the situation. Many Vietnamese saw normalization as now threatening to devalue or ignore an important element in Vietnamese relations with their host society—an element that was, in turn, an essential part of Vietnamese self-identification in the United States: their difference from their communist conationals. Without this distinction, the legitimacy of their claim to represent the true Vietnam and to be the true guardians of its culture would be seriously undermined. Normalization had made these public issues to Vietnamese, who therefore felt that their case had to be made to the larger U.S. society.

The use of English as the language of protest in the Lowell and St. Paul events and the flyers that directly addressed the American audience and the American media made this evident. Less obvious in intent was the use of the U.S. flag in Lowell. Side by side with the Vietnamese flag, it was a reminder that Vietnamese, by turning their backs on Vietnam and becoming refugees, had entered into a partnership with non-Vietnamese Americans—one based on a common opposition to communism in general and communist Vietnam in particular. To many Vietnamese, therefore, normalization was a unilateral withdrawal from this longstanding and, for all concerned, costly partnership.

This message, however, was only partially communicated to those for whom it was intended. In Lowell, many in the audience did not recognize either the pre-communist Vietnamese flag or that of the current regime and mistook the procession of flags to be local Vietnamese support for the musicians on stage. Nor was the music an efficient medium. The program was appreciated not as the rarely heard court and ritual music that much of it was, but simply as Vietnamese music, its identity revealed not by special acoustic attributes, but by the nationality of the performers, their costumes, their presentation, their instruments, and the unmistakably non-Western character of their sound. None of these gave the Vietnamese American protesters the non-communist identity they sought.

In the New York and New Orleans events, the same categories of actors interacted—Vietnamese, Vietnamese Americans, and members of the larger society—but within a framework that minimized conflict and ensured maximal efficiency of communication. In New York, this was accomplished by limiting the audience to those who could afford a $150 registration fee and those "with current or planned programs in Indochina." The possibility of protest (which, one of the organizers noted, they had entertained on the basis of past experience) was forestalled by holding the conference in private venues—Teachers College of Columbia University and a chartered boat cruising on the Hudson River.

Here, then, was a gathering of like-minded people, predisposed to reconciling or ignoring differences with Vietnam and among Vietnamese. The latter acknowledged their differences in speeches and discussion sessions, but those differences were not made a divisive issue either among Vietnamese or between them and the larger American audience. The use of the current Vietnamese flag, the Vietnamese folk music and dances performed by artists from Vietnam, the participation of Vietnamese officialdom produced no discord. The fundamental message communicated throughout the event was a ringing endorsement of normalization and an acceptance of the consequences on their identity that the protesting Vietnamese in Lowell and St. Paul had feared, namely the loss of their distinctiveness as Vietnamese non-communists.

The New Orleans event was a mirror image of the New York event in its cultural homogeneity (Vietnamese American) and the like-mindedness of all who participated. The underlying message, however, was a ringing affirmation of a Vietnamese identity expressed through music that reflected both the U.S. experience and Vietnamese tradition as the participants defined it. The pre-communist Vietnamese flag onstage proclaimed their cultural affiliation, and the audience endorsed the traditionality of a program that ranged across genres, from vọng cổ to tân nhạc, from solo instrumental performance on the *đàn bầu* to group performances that incorporated audience participation. This was an inclusive Vietnamese traditional music, constructed in the diaspora but resting on a foundation that is conceptually pre-communist Vietnam. There were few non-Vietnamese Americans in the audience, but U.S. acceptance of the music presented as traditional Vietnamese was indicated by the support of the National Endowment for the Arts.

By making it possible to bring together dichotomized segments of Vietnamese society to interact in a U.S. context, normalization has thrown into sharp relief processes of identity construction among forced migrants. The counterpoint of themes generated—tradition, identity, and cultural expression, as these are shaped by the push and pull of national, political, ideological, and group allegiances—can be seen as they are actually woven into musical life. The three-way tension between the migrants-turned-resettlers, the country and the people they left behind, and the society of which they are now a part, is rendered more clearly. And the rupture in the Vietnamese social fabric that has been both cause and effect of forced migration can be examined not only in the United States but also in Vietnam.

The trickle of Vietnamese returning to Vietnam has grown into a wave (although few go back to stay), and, Mydans reports, they have raised consternation among local authorities, who worry about the U.S. influences that the visitors might exert upon Vietnamese society, and about former refugees who may still endorse the overthrow of the communist government. These receive special scrutiny, and the visitors are aware of it (Mydans 1996).

The flow of musical products and ideas into Vietnam as a result of normalization also reveals the signs of rupture and dichotomization from the Vietnam side of the picture. As Western popular music proliferates, Vietnamese popular music embraces Western influences virtually unchecked, even as Vietnamese in the United States guard against unbridled Americanization or Westernization. Excluded from what the authorities showcase and control as traditional music, popular music has been largely freed from government restrictions to become a commodity unambiguously responding to market forces. As traditional music has become institutionalized and responsive to official definition in Vietnam, it has, in the States, opened itself selectively and adaptively to popular music, U.S. and Vietnamese, responding only to "the people" as guardians of tradition.

One can argue that, in spirit and intent, the Vietnamese in Vietnam and those in the States hold the same views of traditional music. Centuries-old lineages must legitimize it. Whoever establishes rightful ownership of tradition can lay claim by history and musical genealogy to what the literature has often referred to as the Vietnamese soul. While some or all of popular music represents that part of Vietnam that it can share with others, traditional music is specific to Vietnam, a special piece of cultural property.

But the two groups of Vietnamese differ in the chain of interpretations that give tradition continuing validity by bringing past objects, practices, and ideas to the present. It is a different present that each group inhabits, and traditional music is not the same set of sounds for each.

Traditional music thus became contested ground because politics and ideology can manipulate history to their own ends. It became contested ground when it was co-opted by the current Vietnamese government to serve its purposes. Those who do not identify with that government have therefore had to dissociate themselves from government-sanctioned traditional music, which they see as incompatible with their identity as true Vietnamese. Edward Said is far from alone in taking the word *refugee* to be political, but he describes what refugees do with simple poignancy: they "reassemble . . . a broken history into a new whole" (1990:360).

Normalization has also illumined an important marker of the refugee experience. Having felt coerced to leave, forced migrants profess a deep longing for return to the homeland. For the Vietnamese, the longing was intensified by the fear that hostile relations between Vietnam and the United States would stand in the way of their ever seeing their Vietnam again. These sentiments have pervaded Vietnamese love songs and sad songs and have found perhaps their most sustained expression in Pham Duy's suite *Songs of the Refugee's Road.*

With official barriers to return now removed by normalization, reasons for forced migrants not returning must be reexamined. "Not as long as the government is communist" is the most common Vietnamese reply. And this may well be the case. But the experience of other former refugees and exiles suggests other possibilities. In his book *Cuba in the Heart of Havana,* David Rieff quotes a Cuban immigrant: "We Cubans are realists. . . . None of us are going back, you'll see, no one but a magnate here and retiree there will go back. But our dream [of return] gave us strength when we needed it, and if we can't quite let go, is that really so terrible?" (Talbot 1993:14).

Perhaps the Vietnam that former refugees dream of returning to has become a static, idealized image—one that they know they will no longer find. Crapanzano describes that predicament eloquently: "To return, after years of absence, to the land where one has grown up is to risk shattering one's past. At a distance, memories embellish, distort, go uncorrected. They are the stuff of personal mythology and . . . they are wedged in a seemingly timeless textual reality that strengthens their mythic status. The places one remembers may no longer be there" (1992:13).

The three-way tension thus becomes that between the *idea* of Vietnam as homeland, the physical presence of the United States, and the cultural forms that must be constantly shaped and reshaped to lend coherence to the label Vietnamese American—which, whether Vietnamese Americans ascribe it to themselves or not, is ascribed to them by others. The process is ongoing and complex. It involves social realities that may respond to what Nietzsche called fictive realities. And music, as their mirror or their embodiment, projects their image not through its capacity for exactitude of meaning but through its capacity for ambiguity, for harboring a multiplicity of possible meanings. These, in turn, are revealed to us not merely through the sounds that are their perceivable form but through people's enactment of the thoughts and sentiments that are their response to life's contingencies.

Epilogue

> The chronicle of diasporas . . . constitute[s] the ground swell of
> modernity . . . . Considering the violent dispersal of people, cul-
> tures and lives, we are inevitably confronted with mixed histories,
> cultural mingling, composite languages and creole arts that are
> also central to *our* history.
> —*Iain Chambers*, Migrancy, Culture, Identity

> The ambiguity of definitions and the struggle with identities over
> time reflect the essence of the refugee condition.
> —*Marita Eastmond, "National Conflict and Refugees"*

Returning from one of my field trips, I was confronted by a colleague's
question, "Well, what did you learn?" For a number of years now, I have
been trying to answer that question, and I shall try again.

In the beginning, there was a debilitating premise from which I sought
release. This book chronicles that effort and the insights into music and
forced migration that I gained along the way. But that release was not the
intended end of my pursuit; it was a way station, a means to an end.

Shortly after I began following the Vietnamese journey, I came face to
face with another impression (in Peirce's sense, the beginning of Pure Play
that can lead to scientific study): that migration, forced or otherwise, is the
necessary condition for most of the issues that power current ethnomusicological investigation. Displacement—being in a context where one is not
native, living a musical life where the dominant language may not be one's
first (musical) language—automatically raises important questions about
music and meaning (both as object and as act), musical identity, musical
and cultural boundaries, the nature of tradition (especially as historical validation of identity), and various other related matters. The indigenous, the
native, the "authentic" have loosened their grip on the ethnomusicological
imagination; the transplanted, and the border-crosser have steadily replaced them at center stage.[1] And migration, as the fundamental instru-
mentality by which these statuses are achieved, deserves closer examination.
If what stands in the way of a critical look is the conceptual lock of the taken
for granted, then forced migration as the anomaly that violates paradigm-

induced expectations may indeed turn out to be "a prelude to discovery" (Kuhn 1970:57), or at least a goad to refine the questions that we ask.

Lacking the advantage of common understandings and the wide range of shared knowledge among those engaged in paradigm-directed investigations, this study has tried to make explicit the procedures of its abductive methodology. From the complexity of the amorphous and disorderly details of close-to-the-ground observation, one can now move to the relative simplicity of abstraction, which yields the rudimentary scheme shown in Figure 6.

To a small degree, this classificatory scheme is already in use, but it is hardly part of ethnomusicology's theoretical and methodological armory (see, e.g., Hirshberg, Monson, and Zheng in Reyes Schramm 1990). The prevailing practice or habit is to conflate data on transplanted musics and locate them within an overarching paradigm that does not recognize the music of forced migrants as a distinct category, or, more accurately, does not recognize forced migration as a significant variable in the description and explanation of transplanted music. The diagram suggests that the habit is not always a good one, for reasons elaborated upon here but which now are again reduced to an abstraction that transcends the singularity of the Vietnamese case (see Table 2).[2]

Three crucial ethnomusicological components are embedded in the diagram in Table 2: the contextual setting, the (implicit musical) act, and the human agent—the last two conjoined in the act/actor orientation of

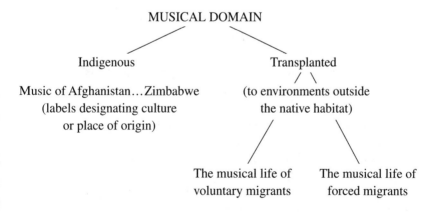

FIGURE 6.   The musical domain: a rudimentary classificatory scheme.

TABLE 2   Contrastive Features: Forced and Voluntary Migration

Forced Migration	Voluntary Migration
Public, mass movement, particularly at the start	Private, individual, familial move
Chaotic at the outset	Orderly
Lack of control, particularly on the migrants' part. Political and moral pressures on the receiving country tend to condition reception (from altruism to hostility)	Control on both migrants' and receiving country's part
Lack of predictability about destination, length of journey, transiency between home country and receiving country and hence, the possibility of a longer period of in-betweenness, legal and psychological.	Destination certain; direct route from home country to country of destination. No ambiguity of legal status.

TABLE 3   Contrastive Internal Relations: Forced and Voluntary Migrants

Forced Migrants	Voluntary Migrants
Rupture with government of home country	Relation with home country not publicly registered
Loyalty to status quo ante home	Loyalty to and relations with country not a matter of group sentiment
Sense of having been coerced to leave, accompanied by a professed longing to return home	Desire to return attenuated by having left on one's own volition and the perception that one can return at will
Loyalty divided between the remembered home country and the host society results in adaptive strategies that will accommodate to the latter while maintaining loyalty to the former against the possibility of return	Sense of having an option—to return or to remain—supplants conflict of loyalties
Relations with those who did not leave often problematic and marked by hostility, resulting in what Eastmond called double marginalization for those who return	Relations with those left behind vary from individual to individual

the description. Out of these emerge the relata—the population under study (those who left, foregrounded by those who stayed behind), the country of origin, and the country of resettlement—and, more important, the relations among them (see Table 3).

In Table 3, the psychological and emotional content of migration that outlasts the legal statuses assigned to migrants becomes clearer. Here, too, the choices that migrants make as they reconstruct life in resettlement— choices that determine the form and meaning of their music in the new environment—find their rationale. In these respects, Table 3 reinforces the teleological nature of choice by summarizing the human relations that motivate selection.

Like all classificatory schemes, particularly those that order human activity, these categories are not mutually exclusive. (Some voluntary migrants, for example, as individuals though not as a class, may also feel alienated from their country of origin.) What they disclose are bases for differentiation. But leakages and exceptions notwithstanding, the discontinuities and fissures that mark forced migration are difficult to miss.

Relations between forced migrants and their conationals who stayed behind, which have only recently attracted the attention of scholars, have become evident among the Vietnamese particularly since normalization opened the possibility of return. With the elimination of those political barriers that had forcibly kept conationals apart, the dichotomy noted in the Codetta (see also Chapter 4) gains in significance. Eastmond (1992) has noted the friction among the Chileans and their conationals who have returned from California. So has Zonke Majodina, who found that those who remained in South Africa held "very negative views of the [South African] returnees" (Harrell-Bond 1993:1). The emerging pattern has led Nicholas Van Hear of Oxford's Refugee Studies Programme to launch a systematic study of the phenomenon in various parts of the world. If the musical dichotomization observed for Vietnamese returnees holds true, then we should see more such cases in different refugee groups' home countries.

That tradition is selective is by now axiomatic.[3] But the *grounds* for selection differ among forced and voluntary migrants.

Fully conscious of their new environment, all migrants make choices that are adaptive, but the form or meaning or both of those choices differ according to the pool of materials from which they allow themselves to draw and according to perceptions of who and what they are adapting to and for how long. Conflicting loyalties impose constraints unknown to those who feel free to make either-or types of commitments. Hence, the Vietnamese in the United States place limits on their adoption of Western musical elements by putting them under the protection of the traditional.[4] That this step reflects the ambivalence of conflicted loyalties—that which Eastmond so poignantly captured in her phrase "the torment of remembering, the fear of forgetting" (1992:304)—is clarified by the contrastive step taken by the government in Vietnam when it allowed free rein to Westernized popular music, treated it as a commodity, banished it from the traditional, and thereby removed all ambiguity from its status within the context of Vietnamese musical culture.

The nature of the cleavage between the refugees and their home country—the political and ideological breadth and depth of it and the public and publicized nature of it—finds no equivalent among voluntary migrants (in contrast, see Bousquet 1991 and Dorais, Pilon-Le, and Nguyen Huy 1989). Added to the dichotomization among conationals, questions of musical identity and questions pertaining to the traditions from which identity draws for both materials and legitimacy therefore are more urgent and acute among refugees. Among Vietnamese forced migrants, the past is a discontinuous, truncated chronology. Their validated past bypasses the segment that begins in 1975 and goes farther back to the pre-communist past, while at the same time what they call tradition embraces the communist-rejected present. Among Eastmond's Chileans, the past is a pre-Hispanic past that "revitalize[s] indigenous musical forms and instruments" (1992:299). In both the Vietnamese and the Chilean case, the choices constitute a double-edged strategy. They express resistance to the politics and ideology of the government they repudiate as well as to the society where they have resettled—a society to which they cannot allow themselves to fully belong if they are to safeguard their culture until that dreamed-of day when it can finally be reinstalled in the home country. "Choosing to see themselves as part of a triumphant ideology or a restored people" (Said 1990:360), while a coping mechanism for those who felt coerced to leave, makes them susceptible to double marginalization, first in the new environment and, second in their home country, should they choose to return.

The centrality of the political element in contemporary refugee phenomena cannot be underestimated. It is at the root of the relations in the

"Forced Migrants" column of Table 3. In contrast, its presence in the column marked "Voluntary Migrants" is diffuse if it is there at all. It is no wonder then that the virtually apolitical model used to account for the general migrant experience, particularly in the United States—the seamless historical continuity it suggests and the gradual evolution of social relationships implicit in it—has in light of the refugee experience been called naïve (Eastmond 1992:297). The choices of myths, legends, sounds, and other forms of what Conquergood called "performative behavior" (1988:180) inevitably reflect a political function that addresses radical discontinuities, social and ideological cleavages, and the deep ambivalences that are the result of conflicted loyalties between past and present. Those choices convey a political meaning, particularly in the early stages of reconstructing and redefining a collective identity when conflicts tear at refugee-resettlers most strongly. Hence, the importance in the Vietnamese case of what was perceived to be communist as criterion for acceptance or rejection for the musical repertoire. Similarly, the resistance to what the government labeled traditional on the basis of what was perceived to be a political function to which it was assigned.

The translation of nonmusical criteria into musical sound is, of course, problematic. But it is part of meaning making, which, in turn, is part of what it is to be human. It is part of the ongoing search for plausibility, intelligibility, and credibility, which is well-served by distinguishing between expression and meaning systems—a step to which forced migration phenomena alert us with a sense of urgency. For the removal of refugees from the primary source of cultural nourishment on the one hand and their reduction—temporary but traumatic—to a state of dependence on those who take on their care and reception on the other, exert great pressure on the refugees to use non-native elements in their expression system in order to convey meaning—not only to members of their own group but to others in the larger, more diverse society of which they have become a part.

Thus, on the basis of musical features alone, many if not most of the items in the Western-sounding repertory of Vietnamese in Vietnam and abroad can be placed within a Western classificatory scheme. They can be assigned to genres or types such as pop, rock, New Wave, and so on. But to settle for such labeling is akin to judging a book by its cover. The Western elements so unmistakable in the expression system may render the meaning system inaccessible, if one stops at the analysis of acoustic features. And the seeming sufficiency of attaching Western labels to Western-sounding forms could lead to missing important markers on the road to a more comprehensive explanation of the music as a system whose status as such depends upon the integrity of the bond that ties expression or form to meaning.

For these reasons, I preferred to err in the direction of giving full value to labels such as "sad songs" and "love songs" rather than in the direction of conventionally labeled genres. In so doing, I was left free to explore the meanings of these songs in contexts that tend to severely test relations between expression system and meaning system. Perhaps eventually they will happily reside in conventional niches. But I suspect that when they do, they will be distinguished not just by their forms but by their meaning and function.

Music, like language, consists of stable parts and parts in flux. At any given point in its history, music, like language, may be a "mottled picture characterized by variation, discontinuities and numerous anomalies. . . . As far as theory of grammar is concerned . . . there is nothing obligatory, necessary, or inevitable about the coherence of language data *in the short term*" (Shapiro 1983:92–93). Determining the degree of codedness is an abductive process that is hard on our desire for more or less absolute order, but there are times when nothing else will do.

If we need an occasional reminder that musical systems do not come in neat packages, that even if they did, humans, being creative, will see to their departure from neatness, and if we wish to see at close range the persistence and power of musical expression under the most trying conditions, forced migrants, tragically, give us occasion to do so. In many respects, as the epigraphs of this Epilogue suggest, the world of forced migrants and the issues it raises are fast being reflected in the rest of contemporary life. And while it would be infinitely better were Smyser wrong in his view that "refugee movements will continue to be an element of international affairs," that would be wishful thinking, for he is undoubtedly right when he concludes: "One can therefore sadly predict that refugees will keep appearing even if we cannot predict when or where" (1987:111). The least we can do is learn from them.

APPENDIX

Program for June 15, 1990

Song	Composer	Performer(s)
Hạ Trắng*	Trịnh Công Sơn	Ngọc Minh
Không bao giờ ngăn cách*	Trần Thiện Thanh	" "
Gặp nhau làm ngơ*	Trần Thiện Thanh	" "
Trả lại em yêu*	Phạm Duy	" "
Hoa biển*	Anh Thụy	Minh Hiếu
Qua cầo gío bay	(Folk song)	Rick Murphy
Túp lều lý tưởng*	Hoàng Thi Thơ	" "
Cờ bay	Nguyễn Ánh 9	" "
(?)	Nguyễn Đức Quang	" "
Việt Nam, Việt Nam	Phạm Duy	" "
Tạ từ*	Tô Vũ	Nguyễn Kim Long
Em đến thăm anh một chiều mưa*	To Vu	" "
Hoa trinh nữ*	Trần Thiện Thanh	" "
Aline	Christophe	" "
Tiếng còi trong sương đêm	(?)	Thu Hồng
Buồn vương màu áo*†	Ngọc Chánh	Ý Lan
Bao giơ biết tương tư*	Ngọc Trong/Pham Duy	" "
Mong manh*†	(originally a French song)	" "
It's a Kind of Hush*	(?)	" "
Thúy thú và biển cả*	(?)	Lyn and Công Thành
Em đi*	(?)	" " "

177

Song	Composer	Performer(s)
Lối về xóm nhỏ*	(?)	Lyn and Công Thành
Trúc đào*†	(?)	" " "

___

*Love song
†Composed after 1975

Program for July 6, 1990 (Independence Day Celebration)

Song	Composer	Performer(s)
La Bamba	(?)	Ngọc Huệ
Main dans la main*	Christophe	" "
Bao giờ biết tương tư*	Phạm Duy/Ngọc Chánh	" "
You're My Heart, You're My Soul*†	(?)	" "
Đòi yêu em*	Trần Thiện Thanh	Anh Chương
Từ nửa vòng trái đất*	Trần Thiện Thanh	" "
Tình thư của lính*	(?)	" "
Tuyết trắng	Trần Thiện Thanh	" "
Tiếng ca đó về đâu	(?)	Minh Hiếu
Sầu lẻ bóng*	Lê Anh Bằng	" "
Đừng trách gì nhau*	(?)	" "
Không bao giờ ngăn cách*	Trần Thiện Thanh	" "
Lối về xóm nhỏ*	(?)	Lyn and Công Thành
Trúc đào*†	(?)	" " "
Em đi*†	Đức Huy	" "
Tình yêu thủy thủ	(?)	" "
Chiều tây đô	Lam Phương	Giao Linh
Hạnh phúc lang thang*†	Trần Ngọc Sơn	Giao Linh
Chuyện tình người đan áo*	Trần Sa	" "
Nhật ký đời tôi*	Thanh Sơn	" "
Paris có gì lạ không em*	Ngô Thụy Miên/ Nguyen Sa	Nguyễn Kim Long
Aline*	Christophe	" "
Máu nhuộn bãi thượng hải	("A Chinese song")††	Tuấn Đạt

Song	Composer	Performer(s)
Tạ từ trong đêm*	Trần Thiện Thanh or	Tuấn Đạt
	To Vu	" "
Rừng lá thấp	Trần Thiện Thanh	" "
Người ở lại Charlie	Trần Thiện Thanh	Tuấn Đạt
		and Kim Chi
Anh hùng xa điêu	("A Chinese song")††	" "
I Can't Stop Loving You*	(?)	Kim Chi
Ngày vui còn đâu*	(?)	" "
Tình cho mây khói*	(?)	" "
Vọng cổ (title unknown)		Thu Tâm
Tiếng còi trong sương đêm	(?)	Thu Hồng
Hàn mặc tử*	Trần Thiện Thanh	Duy Thanh
Còn nhớ hay không*		" "
Có bao ky niệm nhỏ*	Phạm Duy	Ý Lan
Bài hát cho người kỷ nữ	(?)	Ý Lan
Mùa thu chết*	Phạm Duy	Ý Lan
Túp lều lý tưởng*	Hoang Thi Tho	Rick Murphy
Hôi sợ vợ	A. V. T.	Rick Murphy
Xuân này con khong về	(?)	Rick Murphy

*Love song
†Composed after 1975
††In Vietnamese traditional theater, Chinese influence continues to be evident in "songs called 'foreign' or 'Chinese' (*hat khach*)" that are sung to Sino-Vietnamese texts (Tran Van Khe 1990:36).

Đ Ê M   Đ Ô N G   P H Ư Ơ N G   Program for July 3–4, 1990

Song	Dance Designation
American song (Isle of Capri)	New Wave
Cơn mưa phùn	Slow
Mai	Valse
Khuê tango đi vắng	Tango
Bài ca sao	Rhumba
American song	Cha-cha-cha
Tuổi đá buồn	Slow

Song	Dance Designation
American song	New Wave
Bài không tên số lo	Boston
Sao đành xa em	?
Dòng sông xanh	Valse
("Blue River"/Johann Strauss's	
"By the Beautiful Blue Danube")	
Buồn vương màu áo	Tango
?	Lambada
Nắng xuân	Rhumba
?	Cha-cha-cha
Unchained Melody	Slow
American song	New Wave
Trên đỉnh mùa đông	Boston
Hạ hồng	Valse
L'amour c'est pour rien	Tango
Ô mê ly	Paso doble
Ơn em	Rhumba
O sole mio	Cha-cha-cha
Hello	Slow
Black Is Black	New Wave
American song	New Wave
American song	Slow
Domino	Valse

Note: Song and dance designations were provided by Vietnamese research assistants who accompanied me on these occasions. Tape recording was not permitted.

NOTES

Preface

1 As is now common practice in the literature, the term *migrant* will be used in the most general sense to include immigrants and emigrants.

2 The International Rescue Committee defines an asylum seeker as "a person already within the United States who is seeking U.S. protection because of an inability or unwillingness to return home due to a well-founded fear of persecution" (International Rescue Committee Field Reports 1991:3).

3 Israel Zangwill's play of 1909, which popularized the term *melting pot*, includes the following lines from act 1: "America is God's crucible, the great Melting Pot where *all the races of Europe* are melting and reforming. . . . God is making the American" (emphasis added). What the monumental blinders hid from view was a population movement that David Brion Davis, Sterling Professor of History at Yale University and an authority on slavery, called "the greatest forced migration in human history" (1998:53): the slave trade that displaced millions from Africa to the New World. To the best of my knowledge, only Monson (1990) has looked into the ethnomusicological implications of African-American music making in the context of forced migration.

4 The Displaced Persons Act of 1948, which was the first refugee legislation in the United States, and a variety of subsequent legislation pertaining to refugees were aimed largely at Europeans displaced by the Second World War. In 1957, the Refugee-Escapee Act broadened the admission standards to include "persons fleeing persecution in Communist countries or countries in the Middle East" (Leibowitz 1983:15). While this enabled non-Caucasians like Chinese and Koreans to qualify for entry under the act, not until the immigration reforms of 1965 and the Refugee Act of 1980 were refugee admissions freed from the restrictions of the national quota and preference systems.

5 This difficulty was attenuated by the many hours of English instruction given the Vietnamese in camps in preparation for resettlement, the eagerness that

many of them displayed for practicing their English, the English proficiency that many of them brought from Vietnam, and the proficiency that most of them had achieved by the time they were resettled in the United States.

Introduction

1 The most widely recognized global definition of *refugee* and the one that is "prevailing in international law" (Zolberg et al 1989:4) was established by the United Nations in the 1951 Convention Relating to the Status of Refugees: a person who "as a result of events occurring before 1 January 1951 and owing to well-founded fear of being persecuted for reasons of race, religion, nationality, membership of a particular social group or political opinion, is outside the country of his nationality and is unable or, owing to such fear, unwilling to avail himself of the protection of that country; or who, not having a nationality and being outside the country of his former habitual residence as a result of such events, is unable or owing to such fear, is unwilling to return to it" (quoted in Smyser 1987:11). The Protocol of 1967 removed the "events occurring before 1 January 1951" delimitation. The applicability of the UN definition, however, is severely constrained because not all nation-states are signatories to the Convention or the Protocol, different countries have legislated their own modifications to it, and others have created their own definitions.

2 The figure for refugees comes from the *World Refugee Survey of 1997*, and for IDPs from *Forced Migration Review* (1998:4).

3 This is part of the subtitle of Bettleheim's book *The Informed Heart* (1986).

4 Ian Buruma echoes Bettelheim in his book *The Wages of Guilt* (1994). Taking a close look at the way Germans and Japanese have dealt with their role in the Second World War and the way Americans have dealt with their role in the Vietnam War, Buruma finds that traumas and memories endure to a remarkable degree.

5 At the Bellevue/ New York University Program for Survivors of Torture, an asylum seeker named Aziz reportedly said, "I wanted to tell [the doctor] as little as possible . . . . I thought, 'I don't know who you are, I'm escaping my country and don't want anyone to see me'" (Rosenberg 1997:34).

6 Quoted by Howard Gardner in "'The Prehistory of the Mind': An Exchange" in *The New York Review*, March 14, 1998:61.

7 In her important book on Ugandan refugees in the Sudan, *Imposing Aid*, Barbara Harrell-Bond includes drawings by children that "speak" volumes on their experience of flight and its attendant fears.

8 The label *evacuee* is often self-ascribed. Evacuees were considered asylum seekers or refugees by the U.S. government (see, e.g., Kelly 1977).

9 Bousquet justifies excluding the Chinese-Vietnamese on the ground that "they

are not accepted as 'Vietnamese' by the ethnic Vietnamese [in Paris]" (1991:9). Dorais, Pilon-Le, and Huy approach the issue from the Sino-Vietnamese side. Most of the Sino-Vietnamese, they observe, "are not really concerned about what is happening—or could happen in Vietnam." Many of them identify more with the Chinese than with the Vietnamese in Quebec City and prefer to join the Chinese Association rather than its Vietnamese counterpart (1987:49).

10 The songs were "Mười năm tái ngộ" and "Tôi Xa Hà Nội." The first was in A B A form with the B part in minor mode and the A parts in major. The second was in A B A B A form, the whole piece in major mode. Both had a codetta of two lines that used melodic material from the main sections.

11 Inspired by Wilhelm Dilthey, Bruner sees lived experience as the "primary reality" that becomes manifest in expressions such as narratives, theatre, music. For him, the advantage of experience over the more commonly collected data of behavior is that it includes feelings and "reflections about those actions and feelings," thereby having the potential to bring us closer to "indigenous meaning"(1986:5).

12 Zemtsovsky's *homo musicans* as "a bridge spanning culture and text" (1997:190) makes what I think is a parallel case to that of people constituting the link between expression and content systems. He does so in greater detail and with more eloquence.

13 This citation form follows the convention used in citing from the works of Charles Sanders Peirce, most of which were published posthumously. The number to the left of the decimal point refers to the volume of the *Collected Papers;* numbers to the right are paragraph numbers.

14 I use "scientific" here not in Wilhelm Dilthey's sense of the nature of explanation (*Erkären*) in the natural sciences but in the sense of explanation for the purpose of understanding (*Versetehen*) as the aim of the science of man or *Geisteswissenschaft* (Dilthey 1989: book 2, sec. 4).

15 See, e.g., Adelman 1992:8–9, Fallers 1974:1, Herder 1969:324, and Smyser 1987:4. Common beliefs and common ways of understanding ensure that the laws needed to maintain the state's sovereignty are intelligible and enforceable. The tensions between the sovereignty of refugee-receiving countries, the refugees' human rights, and the United Nations' and international communities' policies involving both raise some of the most difficult problems pertaining to forced migration.

16 Chambers sees the drive to find "the 'mythical uncontaminated space' of an authentic 'native' culture" particularly Western (1995:72).

Part I: Prologue

1 See, for example, Adato 1994, which documents in texts and photographs the meeting of a Vietnamese mother and daughter after eighteen years apart, or, for a fuller account, Nguyen Qui Duc 1994.

2 This echoes the words of Barry Stein: "The heart of the refugee experience is trauma and loss. . . . From this suffering comes the likelihood of certain changes in the refugees' behavior that will persist throughout the resettlement process" (1983:4–127).

3 Gradually, the importance of camp experiences in reconstructing life in resettlement, particularly when camp stay extends over a number of years and offers its share of traumatic events, is being acknowledged and studied. Notable examples of studies of Southeast Asian camps are Hitchcox 1990 and Knudsen 1983, 1988.

Chapter 1

1 In 1995, as the United States moved toward normalization of relations with Vietnam, the Vietnamese Refugee Camp in Palawan, along with others in Southeast Asia, closed down. In 1997, it was reinaugurated as a "Vietnamese Village" to accommodate Vietnamese who had refused to return to Vietnam when ordered to do so under the Comprehensive Plan of Action intended to end the Indochinese refugee situation in Southeast Asia.

2 The term *asylee* may also be applied to those in a first-asylum country, a "country that has granted temporary safe haven for individuals escaping oppression" (*International Rescue Committee Field Report,* Fall 1991:3; also see the Introduction). In Palawan, in daily speech as well as in formal reports, *refugee* and *asylee* were used interchangeably; the camp was named "Vietnamese Refugee Camp," despite the fact that most of its population had not yet attained legal refugee status.

3 These figures from a UNHCR report (see Reyes 1983:1) differ somewhat from information provided by WESCOM, the Philippine Western Command, which places the Palawan camp area at approximately 7 hectares (17.29 acres or .02 square mile).

4 The numbers seem to vary. In 1983, a flow chart at the VRC office showed seven zones and sixteen committee members. Hitchcox reports nine zones and fourteen sections (1990:155); Knudsen shows sixteen sections (1983:47).

5 Knudsen describes the VR Council as a "partly autonomous unit" whose main objective is to make in the Palawan camp a "Vietnam in miniature" (1983:50). In a statement drafted by the Executive Committee, the VR Council noted their efforts to "recreate a 'small Vietnam' within the Filipino setting" (Reyes 1983). See the description of the flag ceremony in Hitchcox 1990 (156–57). As Hitchcox has noted, former military officers were well suited and willing to assume council leadership positions. They represented an ideological bond shared by all—opposition to communism—and were as a general rule well ed-

ucated. In addition, while many disliked the label *refugee* as an ascribed group identity, "the ex-military is one group whose sense of self-worth incorporates the fact that they are refugees. The tremendous loss of pride that was suffered at the time of surrender . . . is partially restored within the camp where it is possible for them to construe the label of 'refugee' as a badge of defiance" (231).

6 Regional differences between northerners and southerners had been exacerbated by the division of the country at the Seventeenth Parallel in 1954.

7 Knudsen (1990) described these reversals in detail. Positions of leadership or power were "usurped" or surrendered to leaders of boat teams in the process of escape by sea. The grounds for the customary (Confucian) deference and high status accorded to scholars and professionals were weakened or ceased to apply. The egalitarian relations encouraged by some camp personnel were disorienting, and the hierarchical relations familiar in Vietnam gave way to other power relations.

8 Minerva Reyes, UNHCR Social Services Coordinator in Palawan in 1983, gave me a list of seven festivals that, according to her, Vietnamese celebrated campwide or in groups, depending on resources and initiatives taken by people who happened to be in camp at the time of the festivals. Again, the changing composition of the camp population, especially the arrival and departure of Vietnamese who had assumed leadership positions, affected what festivals were actually celebrated in any given year. The festivals (in addition to Tet, the mid-autumn festival, and Buddha's birthday, which are the most constant) are the Trung Trac Sisters Day (in honor of two important Vietnamese heroines), sixth day of the second month of the lunar calendar; Ancestor's Day, tenth day of the third month of the lunar calendar; Mourning Day (to commemorate the fall of Saigon), April 30; and Vietnamese National Day, November 1.

9 Asylees could establish refugee status in the Palawan camp. Many then went on to resettle in Australia, Canada, Germany, Norway, Finland, and other countries. The emphasis of the camp, however, remained on first asylum—providing temporary safe haven to all who were "escaping oppression" (*International Rescue Committee Field Reports* 1991:3).

10 In rare instances, asylees became long-stayers because they rejected offers of resettlement in the hope of being resettled in a country of their own choice. In other camps, notably in Hongkong and Thailand, repatriation had been increasingly pressed upon long-stayers to underscore the temporary nature of a camp stay.

11 Hitchcox, (1990:262) reports that at the time of her fieldwork in 1986, "30 % of the camp population have been living there for more than two years. One hundred and four people [approximately 3% of the population] have been there for more than four and up to seven years." Minerva Reyes (1983),

UNHCR Social Services Coordinator, reported 98 of 2427 asylees (4 percent) in 1983 as long-stayers, but in the same report, she stated that two-thirds of that number were on their way to being long-stayers. Part of the discrepancy is perhaps explained by the rates of rejection, which were often predictive of chances for future resettlement. Hitchcox notes that of her Palawan sample population of 608, 76 or 12.5 percent had been rejected at least once and 22 or 3.61 percent had been accepted (the rest of the cases, presumably, still awaited resolution). This yields a rejection rate of approximately 71 percent.

12 For more detailed descriptions of the Palawan camp, see Knudsen 1983 and Hitchcox 1990.

13 This community receptiveness has been confirmed by a number of observers. William Applegate, director of the Joint Voluntary Agency in 1983, who has had extensive experience in Southeast Asian camps, contrasted the positive attitudes of the local population in Puerto Princesa with, for example, the "traditional animosity" between the Thai and the Vietnamese and the growing resentment of the Hong Kong Chinese over what Vietnamese refugees got as entitlements while relatives who fled mainland China to come to Hong Kong were repatriated (interview, November 7, 1983). Lieut. Martin Pagaduan, officer-in-charge of VRC in 1983, cited a number of instances when Vietnamese participated in town affairs to demonstrate his point that the townspeople accepted the Vietnamese and that there was good rapport between the two groups (interview, November 8, 1983).

14 This "doctoring" involves carving the fingerboard deeper between the frets, making the fingerboard look scalloped. This gives the strings more play so that the guitarist can press, push down the string, or manipulate it to produce the pitches, the modal nuances, and the ornamentation that the Vietnamese musical idiom requires. Also called *lục-huyền cầm* (literally, guitar; see Jones-Bamman 1991:73–75) or Vietnamese guitar, the instrument has six strings.

15 Cải lương is also called Southern Reformed Theater (Nguyen and Campbell 1990:28; Pham Duy 1975:112). It is designated *southern* because of its strong association with South Vietnam, and *reformed* or *modernized theater* because its evolution to its present form goes back only to 1918 (Tran Van Khe 1980:751). Cải lương draws its themes from Vietnamese or Chinese history and mythology or from contemporary daily life. Its music is primarily in the *bac* or *nam* modes of the Vietnamese modal system.

16 The tango, particularly when sung with Vietnamese text, is considered by Vietnamese to be Vietnamese on the grounds that it is part of their cultural heritage—learned from the French and incorporated into Vietnamese cultural life. Even in Hanoi, where the definition of what is Vietnamese tends to be narrower than in Ho Chi Minh or among overseas Vietnamese, the tango is

played and danced regularly in Vietnamese night clubs and tango bars (Barbara Cohen, personal communication).

17 Reyes (1983) in her report, "Mental Health Needs and Programmes in VRC" attributes a great deal of asylee anxiety to resettlement concerns, such as: Will some country accept them for resettlement? Will resettlement separate family members? Will they be able to adapt?

18 The analysis that follows in the text first appeared in abridged form in Reyes 1999.

19 *Vọng cổ* ("longing for the past" or "nostalgia for the past") was originally an individual composition by Cao Van Lau (Sau Lau). It became part of cải lương, evolved within that context, and there achieved such a preeminent position that "[t]o many Vietnamese 'Vọng Cổ' is cải lương—and vice versa" (Nguyen and Campbell 1990:37; see also Pham Duy 1975:142–49, and Tran Van Khe 1980:750). "Lan và Điệp" is a cải lương with a Romeo and Juliet type of plot.

20 The public-private aspects of the cải lương presentation for the midautumn festival were also evident in Hitchcox's description of the Tết celebration she observed in Palawan (1990:242–44). The family- and home-centered aspects of the traditional Vietnamese celebration—the preparation of special foods, the customs governing sweeping the house, the visits (here to friends, since most family members were absent in Palawan)—were adhered to as parts of the private domain. Honoring the kitchen god, Ong Tao, and participating or watching the dragon dance, however, were held in the center of camp as public events.

Chapter 2

1 This restaurant was run by Vietnamese-Filipinos, Vietnamese, Pilipino, and English speakers born of Vietnamese mothers and Filipino fathers. A number of these couples had met during Operation Brotherhood, a Philippine aid program initiated by former President Ramon Magsaysay in the 1950s to provide medical and other service personnel to Vietnam.

2 The Homecoming Act allowed the children of Vietnamese mothers and U.S. servicemen born between the mid-sixties and the mid-seventies to enter the United States without undergoing the screening procedures that asylum seekers must undergo. It allowed close relatives—mothers and guardians, for example—to accompany Amerasians to the States. The Comprehensive Plan of Action was an agreement between the UNHCR and seventy-four countries—all the first-asylum countries, the resettlement countries, and Vietnam—that was intended to end and resolve the problems attendant to the refugee exodus from Indochina. It stipulated that asylum seekers would be screened by Southeast Asian countries

of first asylum according to UNHCR criteria, and that resettlement countries would accept all those who qualified for the status of refugee. Those who were screened out—found ineligible for refugee status—were to be repatriated.

3 This program, part of a 1979 Memorandum of Understanding between Vietnam and the UNHCR, allowed family members in Vietnam to join overseas kin in forty receiving countries.

4 In the early 1980s, refugees bound for Germany and Norway were also prepared for resettlement in the PRPC and given language instruction.

5 Such problems were called "cases"—cases of postponement or cancellation of resettlement because of ill health, the discovery of irregularities in one's papers or background, the surfacing of a criminal record, or, as in an instance with which I became familiar because the man involved was my Vietnamese language tutor, a false accusation. Despite the active intervention of a respected NGO, this man and his wife were held back when a criminal record was said to have been discovered. The wife was showing signs of cracking under the pressure of her neighbors' and billet mates' suspicion that they were communists or criminals. As far as the NGO could ascertain, the refugee was the victim of his cohorts' envy. He had been given refugee status way ahead of his companions in the escape boat; his cohorts wanted him to experience the anguish they had felt at being held back.

6 I am grateful to Phong Tuyet Nguyen for identifying these song categories when he heard the samples from field tapes.

7 Hitchcox (1990) and Knudsen (1983, 1988) use the term *passivization*, a state induced by the routines which they saw as largely meaningless and numbing to the refugees. At the same time, Hitchcox notes, in this process the assent of the subordinate group—the refugees in this case—is a necessary ingredient. In many conversations, resettled former refugees often expressed the view that many of the programs had little positive impact on their lives. However, the Bataan refugees were not only going along but actively participating in the projects planned for them; they saw such participation as a nice break from routine if not as helping to hasten their departure.

8 These highly complex interactions have been described in detail by Linda Hitchcox (1990) and James Tollefson (1989).

9 The Vietnamese created labels to signal the differentiation: *Ô Đi Bo* for the ODP's (O for the pronoun *ông*, meaning "you"; *đi*, a form of the verb "to depart"; *bô*, a form of the verb "to walk"—thus, to depart by walking), and *Ô Đi Ghe* (*ghe* meaning "boat") for the boat people.

10 Major Ed Lopez, the head of security at the PRPC in 1988, told me that there had been no crime among the refugees—"at most, drunkenness and moving without permission to another billet," which were punishable by deten-

tion in the "monkey house." This pattern held until 1995, when refugees in Bataan collectively staged protests and actively resisted authority in response to the threat of forced repatriation as CPA came into effect and rumors began to circulate that normalization of relations between the United States and Vietnam would mean shutting down the Philippine camps. (See Shenon 1995a.)

11 For a full description of Amerasians, see De Bonis 1995, an account based almost entirely on interviews conducted at the PRPC.

12 "Love Story" is by Francis Albert Lai and Carl Sigman (Famous Publisher); "Yesterday Once More," by John Bettis and Richard Carpenter (Almo Music Court, and Hammer and Nail); and "The Great Pretender," by Buck Ram (Panther Music Court).

13 At the beginning of the mass, for example, the officiating priest lit a josh stick, raised it above his head, bowed, and stuck the josh stick into an oversized urn in front of the altar. The procedure was repeated by two young girls who came forward before the offertory.

14 Tape recording was also severely inhibited in both my 1988 and 1991 visits by field conditions. Torrential rains, locally called "siyam-siyam" (literally, nine-nine) for the nine continuous days of heavy downpour, made such a racket on the tin roofs that it was impossible to record.

15 Strictly instrumental music was rare. In 1991, a Vietnamese organist played Beethoven's "Turkish March" and "Für Elise" during breaks in choir rehearsal. On another occasion, a young Vietnamese composer was trying out his work with an ensemble of electric keyboard, đàn tranh, and violin. I did not get to hear the finished work.

16 Discussions about music were carried on in English, with some participants either translating their own comments from Vietnamese into English after checking with the others, or having themselves translated by others. (Three of the discussants had studied at the Saigon Conservatory; the others had no formal training in music but were music lovers and amateur performers whose skill ranged from elementary to near professional levels. Most could read Western or Vietnamese notation. Most were informally trained or self-taught.) Translation blurred the refinements necessary for an accurate culture-specific classificatory scheme. But ambiguity was functional in this case—an insight I would have missed had I insisted on pinning down distinctions. More important, the results of such insistence might not have reflected the thinking of the people who were making the music at that place and at that time. Of particular interest to me was the kind of translation that Geertz describes: "not a simple recasting of others' ways of putting things in terms of our own ways of putting (that is the kind in which things get lost), but

displaying the logic of their ways of putting them in the locutions of ours. . . . [a] catching of 'their' views in 'our' vocabularies" (1983:10).

17 *Popular music* has been variously defined (see, e.g., Manuel 1988, chapter 1). I use it here in the vernacular sense to refer to music intended for the broadest possible audience to which the largest number of people have, as a consequence, had the widest exposure, such that the music has become readily recognizable or familiar. In the PRPC discussions, the familiar features were those of Western popular music—its harmonic practice, particularly in instrumentation, the strophic form in songs, and the striking frequency of Latin American rhythms such as cha-cha-cha, tango, and bolero. Chapter 5 offers an extended discussion.

18 The Vietnamese constitution ratified in 1979 by a government the legitimacy of which was never accepted by South Vietnam "unequivocally stated . . . the hegemony of the party over everybody and everything in Vietnam" (Jamieson 1993:361). "Literature and art in the broadest sense were again didactic rather than expressive, public rather than personal, social rather than individualistic" (369).

19 This young man was ethnic Chinese. The significance of this datum lay in: (1) the attitudes of ethnic Vietnamese toward ethnic Chinese, which tended to be exclusionary; and (2) the relatively apolitical attitudes of the ethnic Chinese (see Bousquet 1991 and Dorais, Pilon-Le, and Nguyen Huy, 1987). Hence, what seemed insensitive on the part of the young man may have stemmed from naiveté and ingrained premigration attitudes.

20 I could not help but wonder about how accurately dates of composition, particularly of popular songs, could be remembered. But dates seemed to be important data and, as Jamieson noted, "to a degree that would be astonishing in the United States, Vietnamese in all walks of life could recite long passages from poems . . . and discuss novels thirty years old as if the characters lived next door" (1993:Preface). Writers, poets, and musicians had played an important political role in the history of Vietnam, and many are remembered in that context.

21 Zolberg applies the term *classic refugees* to those "whose life or well-being was directly threatened by the state or its agents." ODPs and Amerasians, he notes, are refugees only for administrative purposes (Zolberg, Suhrke, and Aguayo 1989:167)

22 Hardly anyone writing on Vietnam, whether in favor of the current government or not, fails to impressed by the importance of nationalism in Vietnamese life. See, e.g., Bousquet 1991, Hitchcox 1990, Jamieson 1993, and Karnow 1983.

Part II: Prologue

1 The Vietnamese evacuee quoted in the epigraph was interviewed by Gail Kelly at Fort Indiantown Gap, Pennsylvania, September 25, 1975 (Kelly 1977:85).

2 Quoted in Eastmond, Ralphsson, and Alinder 1994:9 from a refugee in Sweden, which also had a dispersal policy.

3 This term is Rumbaut's: "the very essence of the refugee existence [is] . . . the coerced nature of their homelessness" (1989:167).

4 From a manuscript kindly provided by the composer. This portion of text is from the first song, "Ta Chống Cộng Hay Ta Trốn Cộng?" (Did we Fight or Did We Flee?).

5 After the cold war and the normalization of relations between the United States and Vietnam, when communism had lost much of its sting and its importance to the United States, it continued to play an important role in Vietnamese community relations in the States. A suspected violation of the anti-communist bond can still create ruptures among the Vietnamese overseas population.

Chapter 3

1 Vietnamese evacuees distinguish themselves from refugees by citing the literal meaning of *evacuee:* someone who has been removed from a danger zone. Strongly implied is the value of the evacuees for the people or the agency instrumental in their relocation.

2 See Knudsen 1988 for descriptions of "boat teams"—the composition of refugees in a number of single boats.

3 The controversy revolved primarily around issues of mental health, refugee adaptation, and the costs to both the host community and the individual refugees. Opposition to scattered resettlement cited the psychological and emotional support that refugees are deprived of when they are not allowed to seek out and live with kith and kin. The argument was that the cost of coping with mental health problems and a longer period of adjustment outweighed the advantages attributed to scattered resettlement. Scattered resettlement as a policy was subsequently abandoned.

4 Interviews with Minh Tran of the Adult Learning Center (October 17, 1983) and Scott Wasmuth of the International Institute (October 24, 1983).

5 The Mutual Assistance Associations (MAAs) are nonprofit organizations developed by Indochinese refugees in the United States. By 1992 there were more than 1,200 MAAs throughout the country, still in the early stages of organization. Their effectiveness, actual and potential, came from the Indochinese expectation that they become surrogates for the extended family that many of the refugees missed and that in their homeland was a "practical form of governance" (Abhay 1992:9).

6 The parallels between the New Jersey Vietnamese and those from Quebec City (among the earliest arrivals in North America) at this stage of community development are striking. Dorais, Pilon-Le, and Nguyen Huy (1987) describe the political differences between groups of Vietnamese, the use of Tết

as the principal event for bringing the Vietnamese together, and the avowed objectives of the groups, which revolved around mutual assistance, conserving Vietnamese culture, and, explicitly or implicitly, developing good relations between the Vietnamese and the host society.

7　I use the term *groups* in a generic sense. Dr. Can Ngoc Hoang distinguished between *association* and *group*. The associations were: Vietnamese Catholic Association, Vietnamese Buddhist Association, Association for Vietnamese Community Development, Association of Free Vietnamese, Dien Hong Foundation, Vietnamese Socio-Cultural and Youth Association, Cambodian Association, and Laotian Association. The groups were: Cao-Thang Group, Thao Viet Group, ViNa Group, and V.I.P. Group.

8　The term *overseas Vietnamese* has become the preferred label for Vietnamese living abroad. It replaces the term *refugee* ascribed by non-Vietnamese, a reminder of painful events that are part of its definition. It also replaces *nguy*, a pejorative term ascribed by Vietnamese in Vietnam and translated as "reactionary." (The dictionary translation is "dangerous" or, depending on the linguistic tone used, "deceitful.") With the normalization of relations between Vietnam and the United States in 1996, *nguy* has been replaced in Vietnam by Việt Kiều, which translates as "Vietnamese citizens residing abroad," or "overseas Vietnamese."

9　Pham Duy is Vietnam's best-known composer. Originally a northerner, he moved to the south after the Geneva Accord divided the country, joining the exodus to the United States when Saigon fell in 1975. *Con Đường Cái Quan* was conceived in 1954 and completed in 1960.

10　Vu's experience with theater goes back to Vietnam when, during his high school days, he became a member of a marionette troupe headed by his father. Considered a musical group as well as a youth organization that did social work in refugee camps, the troupe also aimed "to preserve the Vietnamese tradition of music." In the United States he put programs together for student organizations at Ohio University and Virginia Tech where he had been a student. In New Jersey, he produced his first program for Tết in 1980 at Brookdale College. Two years later, he was invited by the Association of Free Vietnamese to do the Tết program for them. He did so again in 1984 and 1986, using mostly friends and family relations as performers. All these programs "try to convey a message. . . . [W]e try to have a theme" drawing upon historical events or figures. At Bell Labs, where Vu worked, he and a group of other employees performed choral works at noon concerts. Music for him, however, is strictly a hobby (interview, February 11, 1984).

11　The published score from which Vu Thanh Vinh worked for the production and which contained only the melodic lines was a 1979 version. A 1989 version, also published in California by PDC Productions and Pham Duy, is a multi-part vocal score with "additional voices by Nghiem Phu Phi [and] Chords by Pham Duy Cuong." Inevitably, therefore, the chordal treatment, while utilizing Western harmony in both the Woodbridge performance and the 1989 score, do not always coincide.

12 The Broadway influence was most evident in the lighting, the use of technology, and the apron that jutted from the proscenium and went around the orchestra pit, enabling continuity of action during scene changes. The manipulation of various aspects of staging, meticulously charted by Vu, was particularly admirable given the limitations of a school auditorium and the very small amount of time it was made available for technical set-up.

13 The informal, almost impromptu atmosphere was heightened by the absence of a program, so I was unable to obtain the title of the piece and the name of the composer.

14 Usually, the midautumn festival is celebrated and there is a summer get-together, but no occasion has the across-the-board drawing power of Têt. Other public celebrations attract segments of the population. As Dr. Can noted, "We have the Catholic Association, which takes care of Noël; the Buddhist Association organizes other religious events" (interview, February 25, 1984).

15 Minh Tran puts it categorically: "The Vietnamese community is right now in the process of taking form. They are not formed yet. So if they were, for example, like the Chinese in Chinatown, they can have a Vietnamese school which can teach the Vietnamese language to Vietnamese children. And then . . . the Vietnamese heterogenes [i.e., the diverse segments of the population] and the Vietnamese traditionals can come together. . . . [T]hat will help the generations to maintain the generations" (interview, October 17, 1983).

16 This hobby concept recurred in people's descriptions of their musical activity. The Lang Du Band members mentioned it frequently, citing engagements in which they played for free and received only reimbursement for the cost of transporting instruments and equipment. All of them, they explained, had jobs. Loan had infant twins at the time and went to school at night after work. Phung, the singer, had a toddler.

17 The period covered by this statement seems to be bounded by 1954 and 1975, that is, between the departure of the French and the fall of Saigon, since love songs were proscribed by the Socialist government of Vietnam until the late 1980s.

18 Shils's concept of "pastness" is based on his belief that tradition derives not from a single chronological chain that is called the past but from parts of a past or from different pasts that serve a function in the present (1981; see also Reyes Schramm 1986).

19 For an analysis of the apparent discrepancy between Westernized forms and traditional content, see Reyes Schramm 1986.

20 The *Concise Oxford Dictionary* defines preoccupation as "a mental distraction," implying the presence of a more central concern from which preoccupation deviates.

Chapter 4

1 Pham Duy left North Vietnam in 1954 to move to the south when the north came under Communist control. He left Vietnam and came to the States in 1975 when Saigon fell.

2 The first four are terms that Orange County Vietnamese used to refer to "style."

3 In general, few Vietnamese in Orange County refer to themselves as Vietnamese Americans. For the majority, at least until my last visit in 1995, the most unselfconscious way Vietnamese referred to themselves was still as Vietnamese.

4 Some estimates (such as that from Golden West College, which has a large Vietnamese student population, and that from the Vietnamese Community Center of Orange County) go as high as 100,000. Other groups are put into collective categories by the U.S. Bureau of Census, e.g., Asian and Pacific Islander.

5 Before the impact of ODP arrivals became palpable, Strand and Jones (1985), in their study of Indochinese refugees, reported that one out of twelve residents in Santa Ana was a refugee and 85 percent of the refugee population were Vietnamese.

6 Pre-1975 arrivals are more accurately designated pre-1975 departees from Vietnam. Some may have been caught by the fall of Saigon in countries like Japan or France, and, unable to return to Vietnam, subsequently came to the United States. Their voluntary departure from Vietnam before 1975 and their reasons for leaving are an important point of contrast. Now that return to Vietnam has become possible, they may choose to go back, in which case they are classic immigrants: having resided in a country of their choice, they retain their citizenship or permanent residence in the adopted country and return to the country of origin as visitor. Or they may choose not to return. Those I interviewed cited their objection to the present Vietnamese government. In these cases, their absence from the homeland corresponds more closely to what Rumbaut identifies as an attribute of forced migrants—"the coerced nature of their homelessness" (1989:167). The refugee status of pre-1975 arrivals, therefore, is at best an ambiguous one; some are not refugees at all, and they are a small group. A pre-1975 arrival calculated their number in Orange County to be around 150, but he added that this is a very rough estimate since they do not consider themselves a group and may see each other only on important occasions such as Têt. The

far more numerous post-1975 arrivals are mostly refugees as defined by both the United Nations and the United States.

7 It was not easy nor was it perhaps desirable to interview a pre- and post-1975 arrival together. In the case of a married couple, one of whom came before 1975 and the other after, the wife popped in and out of the room, made laconic comments, and stayed out of the conversation until it switched to banter and small talk.

8 The designation remains, although its significance as diacritic has become residual. In November 1992 a benefit "Walk for Boat People" was announced through large banners in Little Saigon and other locations in Orange County.

9 Downward mobility, particularly among the elite and professionals whose skills are not easily transferable from Vietnam to the United States (e.g., lawyers, doctors, government officials), is well documented. See, for instance, Gordon 1989:32; Haines 1985:38–44; Kelly 1977:163–64; Kim 1989:96; Montero 1979:54–55; Stein 1983:4–128; Strand and Jones 1985: chap. 8; Wright 1980:513.

10 After World War II, the U.S. government for the first time acknowledged the difference between refugees—then called Displaced Persons—and voluntary migrants or immigrants. The Vietnamese influx that began in 1975, however, was the first of that magnitude involving a non-Western population. The government effort to deal with refugees as a legal category and not as culture- or nation-specific groups gave rise to the Refugee Act of 1980 and the massive institutionalization of aid to refugees. For a summary history of U.S. policy governing refugees, see Glazer 1985, Gordenker 1987, the preface to Haines 1985; Smyser 1987; and Teitelbaum 1983; especially useful is Leibowitz 1983.

The benefits and constraints of aid institutionalized by government legislation and aid given by private individuals or institutions, such as that which helped resettle forced migrants prior to the enactment of U.S. laws governing refugees, are probably comparable. Public and private agencies have helped forced migrants adapt, begin new lives, and reunite with family. But privately administered aid varies widely in scope, resources, quality, motivations, and effects. Government-legislated aid is nationwide in scope, varies little in intent, and is more standardized in its administration. Hence its impact—good and bad—tends to be more general across the whole group toward which the aid is directed.

11 The present Socialist Republic of Vietnam's flag is red with a yellow star in the middle, the flag of Ho Chi Minh's Democratic Republic of Vietnam. The flag of the Saigon regime is yellow with three horizontal red stripes that stand for Vietnam's three traditional regions: north, central, and south. In Orange County, until the time of my fieldwork, the Socialist Republic of Vietnam's flag was never flown. That of the former South Vietnam flew daily over a pagoda on First Street in Santa Ana, a few blocks from Little Saigon.

12 By the end of 1993, friends from Orange County reported the operation of a

Vietnamese radio station that broadcasts nine hours a day, from 6:30 A.M. to 3:30 P.M. One Vietnamese comments that it is especially appreciated by those who do not speak English, and that it serves as "glue that binds the community." TV broadcasts from Little Saigon have increased operating hours to one hour a day, and Saturday finds some eight Vietnamese programs on TV (personal communication).

13   This achievement parallels that which Freeman claims for the Vietnamese in Santa Clara County, California: they have "revitalized a deteriorating downtown core" (1989:15).

14   *Good Morning, Vietnam* is a movie set in 1965 Saigon starring Robin Williams in the role of a soldier/disc jockey. Based on a real-life character, the film raises issues concerning, among other things, the problematic relations between U.S. personnel in Vietnam and local Vietnamese.

15   Published in Santa Ana, this daily devotes a great deal of space to regional coverage. Its Sunday edition can have as many as fourteen sections and 180 pages. Periodically, sections like "Community News" appear, covering Westminster, Garden Grove, Cypress, and Midway City, where Vietnamese are a substantial part of the population.

Chapter 5

1   A visit to this club in Ho Chi Minh showed that it had become a dancing club. A listening club, the Đai Đong, had something of what Khanh Ly had described. One of the club's entrances was for the performers who came on their motorbikes, which they parked right by the stage. After singing two or three songs, each drove off to the next engagement.

2   Permanent singers appear regularly and act as MC for the duration of the performance. Other singers prefer to "hop" from club to club, singing a set of songs at each and keeping themselves free to accept better-paying engagements out of town.

3   One vọng cổ and one love song could not be dated, but the subject matter of the latter—a soldier who says goodbye to his lover as he goes off to fight against the French—suggests a pre-1975 composition date.

4   On the basis of aural evidence *New Wave* was virtually indistinguishable from what would be called *rock* in the American mainstream. The fuzziness of the two terms, however, and the problem of matching the terms to the music must be acknowledged. As the *New York Times* critic Jon Pareles noted, the rock of the 1990s is becoming a "polymorphous mess . . . encompass[ing] hip-hop, dance music and the rest of the mess" (1993). The problem extends beyond the United States. On October 17, 1990, the British House of Lords debated the

definitions of *pop* and *rock* in connection with a ruling that governs radio programming, according to which one station must be given to pop programs. According to the 8:50 radio report on Radio 4 of the British Broadcasting Company (93.5 FM), the House of Lords concluded that "pop includes rock."

5 Dancing clubs have been, and apparently continue to be, a very real part of urban life in Vietnam. Nguyen Qui Duc, returning to Vietnam after having left as an evacuee recalls, "I wandered about looking for the Ha Noi of fifty or sixty years ago . . . I wanted to see elegant people dancing the tango" (1994:253). Justin Wintle describes such a scene: Dancing the samba, or the tango, "the adults come into their own. They rehearse the steps meticulously, expertly, as though judges were present" (1991:158). It is probably this rehearsed, choreographed aspect that led Susan Brownmiller (1993), referring to Hanoi clubs, to compare the style of dancing to that of Vernon and Irene Castle.

6 This Strauss composition seems to have found a place in the Vietnamese repertoire of popular music. Its penetration into Vietnamese musical life is indicated by Nguyen Qui Duc's account of an incident during his father's incarceration in a remote Vietcong prison: "The rest of Tết passed in dullness, though he could hear other prisoners practicing for a performance he was not allowed to see. Their singing entertained him, while a violinist rehearsing the 'Blue Danube Waltz' brought him moments of unexpected happiness" (1994:129). The piece was also part of the dance band repertory I heard in New Jersey.

7 See Tran Van Khe's description of the Vietnamese pitch system. In brief, he notes that it is "pentatonic with or without two auxiliary degrees" (1980:747). The use of Western instruments with fixed pitches such as the piano or the organ, however, compels the use of equal temperament.

8 This may be why, of the collections I have seen, none were in the form of a printed hymnal; rather, they were handwritten and mimeographed. Lately, in Orange County, many had been recopied by hand or by computer and photocopied for the sake of better legibility and wider dissemination.

9 A *clave* is both a percussion instrument consisting of two hard wood sticks struck against each other and the rhythmic time line that it plays.

10 The low social status of cải lương may also be a vestige of the legal code established by Le Thanh Ton in the fifteenth century, which made outcasts of actors and slaves. "Male actors could not become mandarins, nor could actresses marry aristocrats" (Karnow 1983:105).

11 How central military service has been in the lives of Vietnamese is indicated by the following statistic: until the 1980s, Vietnam's army was the fourth largest in the world (Wintle 1991:177).

12 The search for freedom, which is the reason most commonly given by Vietnamese for fleeing, "covers a wide variety of motives . . . but the common

underlying feature is the wish to preserve a way of life that vanished with communism" (Hitchcox 1990:64–65).

13 See Le Tuan Hung 1997. For policies governing the use of music, literature, and poetry in Communist Vietnam, see also Jamieson 1993.

14 Wintle (1991) describes the extent to which the government, local and national, controls matters pertaining to music. In early 1993, a research group of which I was a member was not allowed to travel from Hanoi to a village a few miles away to listen to a musical form for which it was famous (*quan họ*, a responsorial form) because we did not have permission. Later that same year, Miller and Nguyen (1993) noted difficulties of the same nature.

15 The usefulness of these dichotomies lies neither in objectifying each term nor in establishing strict mutual exclusivity. Subjectivity is at the heart of each when used by individuals; this is evident from the statements quoted earlier. The dichotomies are intended to clarify by contrast and to point up the importance of the dynamics set up between opposing categories, which do have a basis in fact. Truong Nhu Tang (1985), for example, offers substantial evidence of the first two dichotomies (communist/non-communist, government/people) in post-1975 Vietnam. And Nguyen (in Miller and Nguyen 1993) documents government control of what is admissible or presentable as traditional music.

16 Changes, however, are ongoing. In his description of the events immediately following the communist take-over, Nguyen Qui Duc noted that: "colorful clothing and the áo dài disappeared, along with sentimental songs and rock-and-roll . . . anything hinting of bourgeois hedonism closed down" (1994:99). In the late 1980s the government lifted sanctions on love songs and on most pre-1975 songs, although in early 1993, friends in Ho Chi Minh City told me that the ban on Pham Duy's and Hoang Thi Tho's music as well as Kim Tuyen's recordings had not yet been lifted. Nguyen Qui Duc himself remarks on the predominance of love songs and the appearance of pre-1975 songs in present-day urban Vietnam. And Trinh Cong Son, a well-known composer who chose to remain in Vietnam, acknowledged that yes, there are still "'forbidden zones' but life today is better than it was in the early days of reunification" (Kamm 1993:7).

17 The following chapter offers an example of music taken to be Vietnamese traditional music on the basis of physical attributes but protested against because the performing group was sponsored by the Vietnamese government. A similar example of a form rejected owing to its changed meanings in the context of the former Yugoslavia's ethnic conflicts is offered by Petrovic. Her studies of the vocal genre *ganga* before and during these conflicts led her to conclude: "What is significant about ganga today is not its form or sound but its new message and a new construction of its meaning" (1995:70).

18 While the regimen that gave refugees time to make music in refugee camps was also seen as discouraging initiative and encouraging dependency (see, e.g.,

Hitchcox 1990:15 and Knudsen 1983), Orange County's former refugees looked back nostalgically at those days, even as they admitted that the nostalgia was akin to one for lost—and romanticized—youth, with its relatively few responsibilities and assured food and shelter.

19 There is, however, a phenomenon that bears watching. In 1992, I noticed a growing number of karaoke studios in Little Saigon where individuals were expressing themselves musically. Hardly in evidence in 1990, these had increased dramatically in two years (see Wong 1995).

20 In addition to Rick Murphy, a non-Vietnamese American, and Lyn Thanh, an Australian, mentioned earlier in this chapter, a notable exception was Dalena, described as a "mystery lady" because she is phenotypically Caucasian but her Vietnamese diction, it is said, is better than that of most Vietnamese singers. Rumor within the Vietnamese community, where she had a large following, was that she might be Amerasian. The "mystery" was solved when a *New York Times* article identified her as a non-Vietnamese American (surnamed Morton) with "a stunning ability to mimic the sounds and rhythms of a number of languages" (Mydans 1993:10). By the time the article appeared, Dalena had released five albums of Vietnamese songs, had sung for Vietnamese audiences abroad, and was awaiting an opportunity to sing in Vietnam, where she has become well-known through bootleg tapes.

21 An important example is the newest version of Pham Duy's best-known song cycle, *Con Đường Cái Quan* (1960), variously titled in English "The National Road," "Mandarin Road," and "Route of Union." This 1992 release, which is strictly instrumental, adds synthesizers to the orchestration. The effect is best appreciated when compared with a pre-1975 recording of the original, essentially vocal, version with Thai Thanh, Duy Khanh, and Nghiem Phu Phi (pianist)—all now in Orange County—in the cast. With its Vietnamese text, the singing style of the recorded artists, and the strategic use of Vietnamese musical instruments along with Western ones (all acoustic), the older version, taken in its entirety, cannot be mistaken for Western.

22 Sometimes Vietnamese origin is acknowledged in very small print in inconspicuous locations on the tape jacket. Sometimes one can only infer the tapes' origin. For example, a Vietnamese friend pointed out to me a number of cassettes featuring artists who are resident in Vietnam and have never been in the States.

Codetta

1 Under the leadership of a Vietnamese Catholic nun, Sr. Pascale Le thi Triu, the Center for Assistance to Displaced Persons (CADP), an NGO with a long history of service to asylum seekers in Palawan and other camps, succeeded in gaining the support of the Philippine government and the Bishops' Conference

to prevent forcible repatriation of Vietnamese and to allow those who had grounds to fear persecution to remain in the Philippines. With the help of overseas Vietnamese and the participation of Vietnamese in the Philippines, a Vietnamese Village was inaugurated in Palawan in March 1997. Vietnamese living there are given access to education and can work and obtain small loans to start income-producing activities (*Refugee Reports* 1997:8–9).

2 I was not present at this event. My information comes from Minnesota newspapers, flyers, and a videotape of the events kindly provided by Miranda Arana.

Epilogue

1 The term *transplanted* is applied to music marked by a past from a culture of origin, and a present in another culture to which it must adapt or remake itself. The usage borrows from the practice that informed such works as Oscar Handlin's classic, *The Uprooted* (Boston: Little, and Brown, 1952), and John Bodnar's *The Transplanted* (Bloomington: Indiana University Press, 1985).

2 Edward Said provides some historical justification for the forced-voluntary migrant distinction. Forced migrants, according to him, are descended from different ancestors or have different antecedents. Refugees and exiles are the products of the age-old practice of banishment, a forcible uprooting that is punitive and carries with it the stigma of unbelonging. Voluntary migrants share more with adventurers and expatriates, whose absence from "home" is a matter of choice and, at least in principle, is reversible at will (1990:363).

3 Edward Shils (1981) demonstrates persuasively that tradition derives not from a single undifferentiated past but from parts of a past or from different pasts that can serve a function in the present. See also Hobsbawm and Ranger 1983; Anderson 1983.

4 In Orange County in 1990, many Vietnamese were critical of what they saw as an indiscriminate adoption of Western musical influences in Vietnam. A famous composer told me that in Vietnam, "popular music is more American than the music of those who are here [in the States]. They even imitate Michael Jackson and Madonna!"

REFERENCES

Abhay, Krisna. 1992. "Leadership and Management: A Comparative Study of MAAs." *Refugee Participation Network*, June, pp. 9–11.

Adato, Allison. 1994. "I Must See My Daughter Again." *Life*, June, pp. 36–44.

Adelman, Howard. 1992. "Ethnicity and Refugees." In *World Refugee Survey 1992*. Washington, D. C.: American Council for Nationalities Service.

Anderson, Benedict. 1983. *Imagined Communities: Reflections on the Origin and Spread of Nationalism*. London: Verso.

Barth, Fredrik. 1969. Introduction to *Ethnic Groups and Boundaries: The Social Organization of Difference*. Edited by F. Barth. Boston: Little, Brown.

Bettelheim, Bruno. 1979. *Surviving and Other Essays*. New York: Knopf.

————. 1986. *The Informed Heart: A Study of the Psychological Consequences of Living under Extreme Fear and Terror*. New York: Penguin.

Bird, Thomas. 1990. "Theatrical Glasnost, Vietnam-Style, Is Still Waiting in the Wings." *International Herald Tribune*, December 21.

Bonfantini, Massimo A., and Giampaolo Proni. 1988. "To Guess or Not To Guess?" In *The Sign of Three: Dupin, Holmes, and Peirce*. Edited by Umberto Eco and Thomas A. Sebeok. Bloomington: Indiana University Press.

Bousquet, Gisele L. 1991. *Behind the Bamboo Hedge: The Impact of Homeland Politics in the Parisian Vietnamese Community*. Ann Arbor: University of Michigan Press.

Brownmiller, Susan. 1993. "Curtain up on Vietnam." *Travel and Leisure*, April, pp. 98–160.

Bruner, Edward M. 1986. "Ethnography as Narrative." In *Anthropology of Experience*. Edited by Victor W. Turner and Edward M. Bruner. Urbana: University of Illinois Press.

Buruma, Ian. 1994. *The Wages of Guilt: Memories of War in Germany and Japan*. New York: Farrar, Straus and Giroux.

Caplan, Nathan; John K. Whitmore; and Marcella H. Choy. 1989. *The Boat People and Achievement in America: A Study of Family Life, Hard Work, and Cultural Values*. Ann Arbor: University of Michigan Press.

Carettini, Gian Paolo. 1988. "Peirce, Holmes, Popper." In *The Sign of Three:*

Dupin, Holmes, and Peirce. Edited by Umberto Eco and Thomas A. Sebeok. Bloomington: Indiana University Press.

Cassirer, Ernst. 1944. *An Essay on Man: An Introduction to a Philosophy of Human Culture.* New Haven: Yale University Press.

Census of Population and Housing 1990: Summary Tape File #1. County of Orange. 1991. Machine readable data file. State of California, State Census Data Center.

Chambers, Iain. 1995. *Migrancy, Culture, Identity.* London and New York: Routledge.

Conover, Ted. 1993. "The United States of Asylum." *New York Times Magazine,* September 19.

Conquergood, Dwight. 1988. "Health Theatre in a Hmong Refugee Camp: Performance, Communication, and Culture." *Journal of Performance Studies* 32(3):174–206.

Crapanzano, Vincent. 1992. "This Home Can Never Be Home." *New York Times Book Review,* October 18, p.13.

Daniel, Valentine. 1984. *Fluid Signs: Being a Person the Tamil Way.* Berkeley: University of California Press.

Davis, David Brion. 1998. "A Big Business." *New York Review,* June 11, pp. 50–53.

De Bonis, Steven. 1995. *Children of the Enemy: Oral Histories of Vietnamese Amerasians and their Mothers.* Jefferson, N.C., and London: MacFarland.

Dilthey, Wilhelm. 1989. *Selected Works: Introduction to the Human Sciences.* Vol. 1. Edited by Rudolf A. Makkreel and Frithjof Rodi. Princeton, N.J.: Princeton University Press.

Dorais, Louis-Jacques; Lise Pilon-Le; and Nguyen Huy. 1989. *Exile in a Cold Land: A Vietnamese Community in Canada.* New Haven, Conn.: Yale Center for International and Area Studies.

Dunning, Bruce B. 1989. "Vietnamese in America: The Adaptation of the 1975–1979 Arrivals." In *Refugees as Immigrants: Cambodians, Laotians, and Vietnamese in America.* Edited by David W. Haines. Totowa, N.J.: Rowman and Littlefield.

Eastmond, Marita. 1992. "National Conflict and Refugees: Re-creating Chilean Identity in Exile." In *Ethnicity and Nationalism.* Edited by Anthony D. Smith. International Studies in Sociology and Social Anthropology, vol. 60. London and New York: Brill.

Eastmond, Marita; Lilian Ralphsson; and Birgitta Alinder. 1994. "The Psychosocial Impact of Violence and War: Bosnian Refugee Families and Coping Strategies." *Refugee Participation Network,* March, pp. 7–9.

Eco, Umberto, and Thomas A. Sebeok, eds. 1988. *The Sign of Three: Dupin, Holmes, and Peirce.* Bloomington: Indiana University Press.

Eitinger, L., and David Schwarz, eds. 1981. *Strangers in the World.* Bern, Switz.: Hans Huber. Quoted in Linda Hitchcox, *Vietnamese Refugees in Southeast Asian Camps* (Oxford: St. Antony's/Macmillan, 1990).

Erlanger, Steven. 1990. "For Vietnamese in U.S., Uneasy Ties to Home." *New York Times*, August 26.

Erlmann, Veit. 1990. "Migration and Performance: Zulu Migrant Workers' (*Isicathamiya*) Performance in South Africa, 1890–1950." *Ethnomusicology* 34(2): 199–220.

"Fact Sheet." 1991. Unpublished paper for limited internal circulation. Bataan: Philippine Refugee Processing Center. July.

Fallers, Lloyd A. 1974. *The Social Anthropology of the Nation-State*. Chicago: Aldine.

Felsman, J. Kirk, and Irene C. Felsman. 1986. "Vietnamese Amerasians: Identification and Identity." *Cultural Survival* 10(4):57–58.

Focus: Orange County. 1991. Balboa, Calif.: Metro Lifestyles and Design.

Forced Migration Review [formerly *Refugee Participation Network*]. 1998. Oxford: Refugee Studies Programme.

Freeman, James M. 1989. *Hearts of Sorrow: Vietnamese-American Lives*. Stanford, Calif.: Stanford University Press.

Frelick, Bill. 1992. "Call Them What They are—Refugees." In *World Refugee Survey 1992*. Washington, D. C.: American Council for Nationalities Service.

Friedrich, Paul. 1979. "The Symbol and Its Relative Non-Arbitrariness." In *Language, Context, and the Imagination*. Edited by Anwar S. Dil. New Brunswick, N.J.: Transaction Books.

Furnham, A., and S. Bochner. 1986. *Culture Shock: Psychological Reactions to Unfamiliar Environments*. London and New York: Methuen. Quoted in Linda Hitchcox, *Vietnamese Refugees in Southeast Asian Camps* (Oxford: St. Antony's/Macmillan, 1990).

Gargan, Edward A. 1996. "200 Vietnamese Refugees Flee Detention Camp in Hong Kong." *New York Times*, May 11.

Geertz, Clifford. 1973. *The Interpretation of Cultures*. New York: Basic Books.

———. 1983. *Local Knowledge: Further Essays in Interpretive Anthropology*. New York: Basic Books.

Gibbs, Jason. 1996. "*Nhạc Tiền Chiến*: The Origins of Vietnamese Popular Song." Paper delivered at the Northern California regional meeting of the Society for Ethnomusicology.

———. 1997. "Reform and Tradition in Early Vietnamese Popular Song." *Nhac Viet* 6:5–33.

Glazer, Nathan. 1985. *Clamor at the Gates: The New American Immigration*. San Francisco: Institute for Contemporary Studies.

Glazer, Nathan, and Daniel P. Moynihan, eds. 1975. *Ethnicity: Theory and Experience*. Cambridge: Harvard University Press.

Gordenker, Leon. 1987. *Refugees in International Politics*. New York: Columbia University Press.

Gordon, Linda W. 1989. "National Surveys of Southeast Asian Refugees: Methods, Findings, Issues." In *Refugees as Immigrants: Cambodians, Laotians, and*

Vietnamese in America. Edited by David W. Haines. Totowa, N.J.: Rowman and Littlefield.

Gould, Stephen J. 1989. *Wonderful Life.* New York: Norton.

Greenfeld, Liah. 1992. *Nationalism: Five Roads to Modernity.* Cambridge: Harvard University Press.

Haines, David W., ed. 1985. *Refugees in the United States. A Reference Handbook.* Westport, Conn., and London: Greenwood.

————. 1989. *Refugees as Immigrants: Cambodians, Laotians, and Vietnamese in America.* Totowa, N. J.: Rowman and Littlefield.

Harrell-Bond, Barbara E. 1986. *Imposing Aid: Emergency Assistance to Refugees.* Oxford: Oxford University Press.

————. 1993. "Editorial." *Refugee Studies Programme Annual Report.*

Harrowitz, Nancy. 1988. "The Body of the Detective Model: Charles S. Peirce and Edgar Allan Poe." In *The Sign of Three: Dupin, Holmes, Peirce.* Edited by Umberto Eco and Thomas A. Sebeok. Bloomington: Indiana University Press.

Herder, Gottfried v. 1969. *J.G. Herder on Social and Political Culture.* Edited and translated by F.M. Barnard. Cambridge: Cambridge University Press.

Hitchcox, Linda. 1990. *Vietnamese Refugees in Southeast Asian Camps.* Oxford: St. Antony's/Macmillan.

Hobsbawm, Eric, and T. Ranger, eds. 1983. *The Invention of Tradition.* Cambridge: Cambridge University Press.

The ICMC Refugee Training Program, Bataan, Philippines. Preparing Refugees for Resettlement. 1989. Manila: International Catholic Migration Commission.

International Rescue Committee Field Reports. 1991. New York: International Rescue Committee.

Isaacs, Arnold. 1997. *Vietnam Shadows.* Baltimore: Johns Hopkins University Press.

Jakobson, Roman. 1978. *Six Lectures on Sound and Meaning.* Translated by John Mepham. Cambridge: MIT Press.

Jamieson, Neil. 1993. *Understanding Vietnam.* Los Angeles: University of California Press.

Jones-Bamman, Richard. 1991. "The Đan Trành and the Lục Huyền Cầm: A Question of Compatibility and Change." In *New Perspectives on Vietnamese Music.* Edited by Phong T. Nguyen. New Haven: Yale Center for Southeast Asia Studies.

Kamm, Henry. 1993. "Vietnam Poet Sings a Song of Endurance." *New York Times,* April 4.

Karnow, Stanley. 1983. *Vietnam: A History.* New York: Penguin.

Keller, S. L. 1975. *Uprooting and Social Change: The Role of Refugees in Development.* Delhi: Manohar Book Services. Quoted in Linda Hitchcox, *Vietnamese Refugees in Southeast Asian Camps* (Oxford: St. Antony's/Macmillan, 1990).

Kelly, Gail. 1977. *From Vietnam to America: A Chronicle of Vietnamese Immigration in the United States.* Boulder, Colo.: Westview.

Kessner, Thomas, and Betty Boyd Caroli. 1981. *Today's Immigrants, Their Stories: A New Look at the Newest Americans.* New York: Oxford University Press.

Kim, Young Yum. 1989. "Personal, Social, and Economic Adaptation: 1975–1979 Arrivals in Illinois." In *Refugees as Immigrants: Cambodians, Laotians, and Vietnamese in America,* ed. David W. Haines. Totowa, N.J.: Rowman and Littlefield.

Knudsen, John Christian. 1983. *Boat People in Transit: Vietnamese in Refugee Camps in the Philippines, Hongkong, and Japan.* Bergen, Norway: Department of Social Anthropology, University of Bergen.

————. 1988. *Vietnamese Survivors: Processes Involved in Refugee Coping and Adaptation.* Bergen, Norway: Migration Project, Department of Social Anthropology, University of Bergen.

Kuhn, Thomas. 1970. *The Structure of Scientific Revolutions.* 2d ed., enlarged. Chicago: University of Chicago Press.

Kunz, Egon F. 1973. "The Refugee in Flight: Kinetic Models and Forms of Displacement." *The International Migration Review* 7(1):125–46.

————. 1981. "Exile and Resettlement: Refugee Theory." *International Migration Review* 15(1):42–51.

Le Tuan Hung. 1997. "Traditional and Modern National Music in North Vietnam between 1954 and 1975." *Nhac Viet* 6(Fall) :35–70.

Leibowitz, Arnold. 1983. *Immigration Law and Refugee Policy.* New York: Matthew Bender.

Manuel, Peter. 1988. *Popular Musics of the Non-Western World: An Introductory Survey.* New York: Oxford University Press.

Marlyka, Jim. 1996 "Vietnamese Performers Draw Protest." *Minnesota Daily,* April 1.

Miller, Terry, and Phong T. Nguyen. 1993. "Searching for Roots and Facts. A Report from Vietnam." Special issue. *Nhac Viet* 2(2).

Monson, Ingrid. 1990. "Forced Migration, Assymetrical Power Relations, and African-American Music: Reformulation of Cultural Meaning and Musical Form." *World of Music,* 32(3):22–43.

Montero, Darrel. 1979. *Vietnamese Americans: Patterns of Resettlement and Socioeconomic Adaptation in the United States.* Boulder, Colo.: Westview.

Mydans, Seth. 1993. "Miss Saigon, U.S.A." *New York Times,* September 19.

————. 1994. "To Vietnamese in America, the Homeland Beckons." *New York Times,* February 12.

————. 1996. "Returnees Ante up Venture Capital: Their Ideas." *New York Times,* August 3.

Nguyen, Manh Hung. 1985. "Vietnamese." In *Refugees as Immigrants: Cambodians, Laotians, and Vietnamese in America.* Edited by David Haines. Totowa, N.J.: Rowman and Littlefield.

Nguyen, Phong Thuyet. 1989. "Music in Exile: Vietnamese Immigrants in the United States." In *New American Music.* New York: World Music Institute.

───── 1991. "Introduction and Ethno-Historical Perspectives on the Traditional Genres of Music." In *New Perspectives on Vietnamese Music*, Lac-Viet Series No. 14. New Haven: Yale Center for International and Area Studies, co-published with Association for Research in Vietnamese Music.

Nguyen, Phong Thuyet, and Patricia Shehan Campbell. 1990. *From Rice Paddies and Temple Yards: Traditional Music of Vietnam*. Danbury, Conn.: World Music Press.

Nguyen Qui Duc. 1994. *Where the Ashes Are: The Odyssey of a Vietnamese Family*. New York: Addison-Wesley.

Office of Refugee Resettlement. 1992. "Refugee Resettlement Program Annual Report FY 1991." Report to the Congress, January 31. Washington, D. C.: U. S. Department of Health and Human Services.

Pareles, Jon. 1993. "It's Noisy! It's New! It's 90's!" *New York Times*, Arts and Leisure section, January 3.

Peirce, Charles Sanders. 1935–66. *Collected Papers of Charles Sanders Peirce*. Edited by Charles Hartshorne, Paul Weiss, and Arthur W. Burks. 8 vols. Cambridge: Harvard University Press.

"The Persistence of Dreams." 1992. Noted with Pleasure section. *New York Times Book Review*, June 7, p. 35.

Petrovic, Ankica. 1995. "Perceptions of Ganga." *World of Music* 37(2):60–71.

Pham Duy. 1975. *Musics of Vietnam*. Edited by Dale R. Whiteside. Carbondale and Edwardsville: Southern Illinois University Press.

───── . 1990. "Songs of the Refugee's Road." Manuscript.

Portes, Alejandro, and Ruben Rumbaut. 1990. *Immigrant America: A Portrait*. Berkeley: University of California Press.

Refugee Reports. 1997. "CPA Footnote: Nun's Effort Leads to Local Integration Option for Vietnamese in the Philippines." July. (U.S. Committee for Refugees newsletter)

Reyes, Adelaida. 1999. "From Urban Area to Refugee Camps: How One Thing Leads to Another." *Ethnomusicology* 42(2):201–220.

Reyes, Minerva. 1983. "Mental Health Needs and Programmes in VRC [Vietnamese Refugee Camp in Puerto Princesa, Palawan, Philippines]." Report to the United Nations High Commissioner for Refugees Office in the Philippines, July 5.

Reyes Schramm, Adelaida. 1986. "Tradition in the Guise of Innovation: Music among a Refugee Population." *Yearbook for Traditional Music* 18: 91–101.

───── . 1989. "Music and Tradition: From Native to Adopted Land through the Refugee Experience." *Yearbook for Traditional Music*, 21:25–35.

───── . 1995. "Vietnamese Traditional Music: Variations on a Theme." *Nhac Viet* 4(1):7–24.

───── , ed. 1990. "Music and Forced Migration." Special Issue. *World of Music* 32(3).

Rose, Peter I. 1985. "Asian Americans: From Pariahs to Paragons." In *Clamor at the Gates: The New American Immigration*. Edited by Nathan Glazer. San Francisco: Institute for Contemporary Studies.

Rosenberg, Tina. 1997. "To Hell and Back." *New York Times Magazine*, December 28.

Ross, Richard E. 1998. Review of *Night Beat: A Shadow History of Rock and Roll*, by Mikal Gilmore. *New York Times Book Review*, March 1, p. 20.

Rubin, Barbara. 1980. "Iranian Women: An Anatomy of a 'Failed' Ethnography." In *Let's Meet Our Neighbors: Studies in Ethnicity*. Edited by Adelaida Reyes Schramm. Jersey City, N.J.: Jersey City State College.

Rumbaut, Ruben. 1989. "Portraits, Patterns, and Predictors of the Refugee Adaptation Process: Results and Reflections from the IHARP Panel Study." In *Refugees as Immigrants: Cambodians, Laotians, and Vietnamese in America*. Edited by David W. Haines. Totowa, N. J.: Rowman and Littlefield.

———. 1991. "The Agony of Exile: A Study of the Migration and Adaptation of Indochinese Refugee Adults and Children." In *Refugee Children: Theory, Research, and Services*. Edited by Frederick L. Ahearn and Jean Garrison. Baltimore: Johns Hopkins University Press.

Rutledge, Paul James. 1992. *The Vietnamese Experience in America*. Bloomington: Indiana University Press.

Said, Edward. 1990. "Reflections on Exile." In *Out There: Marginalization and Contemporary Cultures*. Edited by Russell Ferguson, Martha Gever, Trinh T. Minh-ha, and Cornel West. New York: New Museum of Contemporary Art, and Cambridge: MIT Press.

Sanger, David E. 1995. "In a War-Haunted Hanoi, U.S. Opens Formal Ties." *New York Times*, August 6.

Sapir, Edward. 1958. "The Psychological Reality of Phonemes." In *Selected Writings of Edward Sapir*. Edited by David G. Mandelbaum. Berkeley and Los Angeles: University of California Press.

Sebeok, Thomas A. 1991. *A Sign Is Just a Sign*. Bloomington: Indiana University Press.

Sebeok, Thomas A., and Jean Umiker Sebeok. 1988. "You Know My Method: A Juxtaposition of Charles S. Peirce and Sherlock Holmes." In *The Sign of Three: Dupin, Holmes, and Peirce*. Edited by Umberto Eco and Thomas A. Sebeok. Bloomington: Indiana University Press.

Seeger, Charles. 1994. "Singing Style." In *Studies in Musicology II: 1929–1979*. Berkeley and Los Angeles: University of California Press.

Shapiro, Michael. 1983. *The Sense of Grammar*. Bloomington: Indiana University Press.

———. 1985. "Teleology, Semeiosis, and Linguistic Change." *Diachronica*, 2(1):1–34.

———. 1991. *The Sense of Change*. Bloomington: Indiana University Press.

Shenon, Philip. 1995a. "'Boat People' Prefer Death to Homeland." *New York Times*, March 16.

————. 1995b. "Vietnamese in the Philippines Fight Returning." *New York Times,* International Edition, March 17.

Shils, Edward. 1981. *Tradition.* Chicago: University of Chicago Press.

Smyser, W. R. 1987. *Refugees: Extended Exile.* Washington Papers/129. New York: Praeger, with the Center for Strategic and International Studies, Washington, D.C.

Stein, Barry. 1983. "Refugee Resettlement Programs and Techniques." In *Immigration Law and Refugee Policy* by Arnold Leibowitz. New York: Matthew Bender. First published in *The Select Commission on Immigration and Refugee Policy Staff Report,* Appendix C, 1980.

Strand, Paul J., and Woodrow Jones Jr. 1985. *Indochinese Refugees in America: Problems of Adaptation and Assimilation.* Durham, N. C.: Duke University Press.

Sword, Keith. 1992. "Responses to Geopolitical Change: Refugee Flows in the Post-Communist Era. A Report on the Third Annual Meeting of the International Research and Advisory Panel January 1992." *Journal of Refugee Studies* 5(2):87–105.

Takaki, Ronald. 1989. *Strangers from a Different Shore: A History of Asian Americans.* Boston: Little, Brown.

Talbot, Toby. 1993. "The Dream Is No Longer Havana." *New York Times Book Review,* September 12, p.14.

Teitelbaum, Michael S. 1983. "Right versus Right: Immigration and Refugee Policy in the United States." In *Immigration Law and Refugee Policy.* Edited by Arnold Leibowitz. New York: Matthew Bender.

————. 1985. "Forced Migration: The Tragedy of Mass Expulsions." In *Clamor at the Gates: The New American Immigration.* Edited by Nathan Glazer. San Francisco: Institute for Contemporary Studies.

Thernstrom, Stephan; Ann Orlov; and Oscar Handlin, eds. 1980. Introduction to *Harvard Encyclopedia of American Ethnic Groups.* Cambridge: Harvard University Press.

Tollefson, James. 1989. *Alien Winds: The Re-Education of America's Indochinese Refugees.* New York: Praeger.

Tran-Minh-Cham, M. M., and Nguyen-Ngoc-Linh. 1969. *Vietnamese Realities,* 3d ed. Saigon: N.P.

Tran Van Khe. 1975. "Vietnamese Music." In David Morton, ed. *Selected Reports in Ethnomusicolgy.* Vol. 2(2):35–47.

————. 1980. "Vietnam." In *New Groves Dictionary of Music and Musicians.* Vol. 16. London: Macmillan.

Truong Nhu Tang (with David Chanoff and Doan Van Toai). 1985. *A Vietcong Memoir: An Inside Account of the Vietnam War and Its Aftermath.* New York: Vintage.

Truzzi, Marcello. 1988. "Sherlock Holmes: Applied Social Psychologist." In *The Sign of Three: Dupin, Holmes, Peirce.* Edited by Umberto Eco and Thomas A. Sebeok. Bloomington: Indiana University Press.

Turner, Victor, and Edward Bruner, eds. 1986. *The Anthropology of Experience.* Urbana: University of Illinois Press.

Wallis, Roger, and Krister Malm. 1984. *Big Sounds from Small Peoples.* New York: Pendragon.

"Who's Who at ICMC?" 1990. Paper prepared for internal circulation. Bataan: Philippine Refugee Processing Center.

Wintle, Justin. 1991. *Romancing Vietnam: Inside the Boat Country.* New York: Pantheon.

Wong, Deborah. 1994. "'I Want the Microphone': Mass Mediation and Agency in Asian-American Popular Music." *Drama Review,* 38(3):153–67.

World Refugee Survey 1996. 1997. Washington, D.C.: U.S. Committee for Refugees.

Wright, Mary Bowen. 1980. "Indochinese." In *Harvard Encyclopedia of American Ethnic Groups.* Edited by Stephan Thernstrom. Cambridge: Harvard University Press.

"Young Adult Refugees at Bataan." 1991. Unpublished paper for limited internal circulation. Bataan: Philippine Refugee Processing Center. July.

Zemtsovsky, Izaly. 1997. "An Attempt at a Synthetic Paradigm." *Ethnomusicology* 41(2):185–205.

Zetter, Roger. 1991. "Labelling Refugees: Forming and Transforming a Bureaucratic Identity." *Journal of Refugee Studies,* 4(1):39–62.

Zolberg, Aristide; Astri Suhrke; and Sergio Aguayo. 1989. *Escape from Violence: Conflict and the Refugee Crisis in the Developing World.* New York: Oxford University Press.

INDEX